The distortion of a text is not unlike a murder.
The difficulty lies not in the execution of the
deed but in the doing away with the traces.

(S. Freud, *Moses and Monotheism*,1939)

T0344530

Filippo Annunziata

Contracts, wills, marriages and rings
Opera and private law

SilvanaEditoriale

Contents

Presentation

There is not one centimetre, not a single millimetre, not an atom of the creation, which is not governed by rules, regulations and laws. The laws of physics, chemistry, of the sciences, govern the universe billions of light years after the Big Bang. And we too, in the words of Lucretius, are ruled by those eternal laws that ruled the stars. Humanity itself is stardust. But, unlike mountains or flowers, we carry on our shoulders an additional weight, a further cumbersome burden of principles, precepts, laws, customs, rules of courtesy, and good manners. They are peculiar and intrinsic to human nature, because they enable us to survive and live in harmony. They are moral laws, ethical standards, and social values. Some of these values have been embodied in mandatory rules, expressed as laws, possessing the particular characteristics of universality, abstraction and enforceability, laws that generate obligations and rights, divide our actions into licit and illicit, right and wrong, legal and illegal.

Some of us might be tempted to believe there exist spaces or moments off duty, freedom from rules, or at least a pause or suspension, however momentary or limited, of this dense network of rules, this prison of laws. Perhaps in poetry? In painting? In literature? Perhaps in music? No, not even the world of Art is rule-free, devoid of rules. It is far from being heedless or careless of the rules of prosody and syntax, the geometry of space, and the measurement of time. The extent to which laws pervade the arts beggars belief, even extending to the sphere that seems closest to the Pythagorean harmony of the stars, the supreme freedom of thought: music. It is the undoubted merit of Filippo Annunziata, both a magnificent professor of the Law of financial markets at the Università Bocconi in Milan and a refined musicologist, to have undertaken this intelligent and skilful foray into significant aspects of private law in opera. The viewpoint Annunziata adopts is not the most conspicuous, popular or striking, so to speak, of the criminal law: think of the fatal duel fought by the womaniser and compulsive libertine at the start of Mozart's *Don Giovanni*, or Turiddu's dagger in Mascagni's *Cavalleria rusticana*, the commission to kill in Verdi's *Rigoletto*, or the fiendish bargain ('give me the fiddle') in Stravinsky's *Histoire du soldat*. Annunziata surveys the legal points raised by some famous expressions of musical theatre from the technically more complex and subtle, and certainly less common, observatory of private law. But *which* private law? Annunziata deals with the legal issues present in his chosen operas in accordance with the law in force at the time and place when the events occurred; but he adds, and not just for completeness' sake, some useful comparisons with existing law. The rules in force in eighteenth- or nineteenth-century France or Germany or Vienna, or in the territories of the Habsburg empire, like Milan or Venice, were not always the same as those in force today under the current system of Italian private law. Annunziata's pages are a continuous, bracing plunge into past and present, with rapid flash-forwards from yesterday to today. The pages range across the rules and customs of remote periods, which sometimes appear to us somewhat quaint and distant from a modern sensibility, as expressed in the most recent tendencies of doctrine and jurisprudence.

The issues he deals with are numerous, spanning family law and contract law, legal transactions for a consideration and those performed free of charge, contractual liability and the law of torts. The books amounts to a quick refresher course, an elegant anthology of important measures of private law.

A few examples, starting with *La sonnambula* by Vincenzo Bellini are worth offering to understand the original approach adopted to the opera in question. Elvino and Amina are in love and both rightly want to get married. So Elvino gives Amina, as a token of his love, a precious family ring that belonged to his mother and perhaps even his grandmother: hence a valuable gift, by both its economic and affective value. When this masterpiece (1831) had its premiere, the Concordat had not yet been signed, so two weddings were necessary: first the civil marriage contract and then the final consecration with the religious ceremony. Elvino, after bestowing the precious ring in the official context of the *contrat de mariage*, has some misgivings about Amina's fidelity. When he discovers her in Count Rodolfo's bedroom, he is enraged and demands the dissolution of the marriage contract and restitution of the ring. At last he discovers that Amina was innocent: she was in the Count's room only because she was sleepwalking, and at the end of the story, in short, all's well that ends well. But on what basis could Elvino demand the return of a gift? Was it under § 1247 of the Austrian Civil Code (*ABGB*) of 1811, which considered gifts between marriage partners as an exception to the general rules governing gifts under art. 1246, or would it have given effect to the latter law? And what would be the rule for gifts with a view to marriage under the Napoleonic Code of 1804, hence under French law? Of the two Codes, Austrian law should apply, given that opera was performed for the first time at the Teatro Carcano in Milan, at that time under Habsburg rule. And what rule would apply to nuptial gifts under the Italian Civil Code of 1942? And is the right to restitution of the object given subject to prescription? And if so, what term is fixed for its return? As Annunziata notes, the case, in short, is intricate, and the solutions variable. Fortunately, we are assured of a happy ending to the opera: Elvino marries Amina, amid joy and general rejoicing. And the engagement ring, in the best tradition, remains with the bride, and the couple lives happily ever after.

Another case dealt with masterfully by the author is *Das Rheingold*, Richard Wagner's masterpiece. Wotan, the supreme deity of the German pantheon, the guardian of order and balance in the world, enters into a contract with the giants by which they undertake to build the grand castle of Valhalla for a price. In exchange, the gods will hand over the divine Freia, the sister of Fricka, Wotan's wife. Freia is an important goddess in the economy of the Nibelung paradise, because she had the essential task of cultivating the sacred apples that nourish the gods. This contract, however, is flawed from the start, with an *arrière pensée* by both parties. Wotan expects the immense dwelling place of Valhalla to be built to the highest standards, but has no intention of ever handing Freia over to the other party. The giants, for their part, want Freia as payment for the work done, because their real purpose is to starve the gods by depriving them of their divine cook, and once the gods are starving, it will be an easy task for the giants to capture Valhalla.

Having completed their task and consigned the dwelling place to their client, the contractors (the giants) rightly demand payment of the agreed fee, insisting on fulfilment of the terms of the contract: 'Verträgen halte Treu'! Wotan takes good care not to carry out his part of the bargain. The giants then admonish him that his credibility, his very power, the whole balance of the world, rests on keeping one's given word: 'Was du bist, bist du nur zur Verträge.' Wotan is torn: on the one side he is well aware of all this, but on the other he realises that fulfilling the terms of the contract and giving up Freia, would be suicide for himself and all Olympus, opening the doors of Valhalla to the final victory of the giants and the downfall of the gods, to *Götterdämmerung*. Hence Wotan openly refuses to comply, but says he is willing to offer the giants a *datio in solutum* (acceptance in lieu), hence to offer something else instead of the payment stipulated. Instead of Freia, he will give them gold. Wotan has a plan: to filch the Rhine gold from the dwarf Alberich, who stole it in his turn from the graceful Rhine maidens, and give this immense treasure to the giants, so silencing their claim. Wotan means to give the giants all the gold of the Rhine, but to withhold the magic ring, forged by Alberich, with its extraordinary magic powers, capable of conferring on its owner *Macht und Schätze*, 'power and treasures'. Now in the Germany of Wagner and Wotan (and Kant, Hegel, Fichte, Schelling, Goethe, Schopenhauer, Marx, Nietzsche and Brahms), the Roman law current in the German nation held sway, the *System des heutigen römischen Rechts*. The *BGB*, the German Civil Code, would come into force later, in January 1900. According to Roman law, Wagner's story is a tangled skein of private law, which is not easy to unravel. Annunziata tries: the agreement between Wotan and the giants is a contract, because the giants (the contractor) give an undertaking to the client (Wotan) to perform a work (Valhalla). But this is an atypical contract, because the payment is not in cash but in kind. Both parties had negotiated in bad faith, so both should be held responsible for *culpa in contrahendo*. In fact, here we have a case of bilateral fraud, determining fraud, meaning the contract is annullable. But there is still more to it: the payment in kind agreed (surrender of a person instead of money) is illegal, contrary to public order, which actually makes the contract null. The proposed *datio in solutum*, delivery of gold instead of the goddess, sounds like 'conversion of the null agreement', i.e. a means to enable the flawed contract to still produce its effects. But, alas, even the payment in lieu of fulfilment is unlawful, because the purchaser (Wotan) is not the owner of the gold that is the object of his proposal. The precious metal is to be stolen from the dwarf Alberich, who in turn (as we know) has stolen it from the Rhine maidens! The story, then, with its wheels within wheels, twists and turns, continues through *Die Walküre*, *Siegfried* and *Götterdämmerung*.

Annunziata is also drawn to operas that revolve around the grey, bespectacled, fussy figure of the public notary (Puccini's *Gianni Schicchi*, Donizetti's *Don Pasquale*), and especially operas with a plot centred on the typical intricacies of family law in force at the time when the librettos were devised. Besides dealing with *La sonnambula*, as we have already seen, the author devotes pages to Mozart's *Marriage of Figaro* (betrothal) and *Così fan tutte* (the Josephine reforms of civil marriage), and Cimarosa's *Il matrimonio segreto*. In the eighteenth century, and even the nineteenth, marriages kept hidden were rare but not unknown, and the possible economic repercussions in the family circle were always feared. What for the Germans was the *Ehe zur linken Hand* (the groom held the bride's hand in his left hand), for the French was *Il matrimonio segreto*. According to the Lombard tradition, the due of the secret wife was the gift of the morning, *ad morganaticam*, the *morgengab*, and the marriage was termed morganatic. Two young people would marry in secret because their love was opposed by their parents, who had very different matches in mind for their children, or else because a difference in class (the Count and the beautiful servant girl) prevented the union from being made public, and so forth. Even Louis XIV made a morganatic marriage with Madame de Maintenon, *zur linken Hand*, as did Victor Emmanuel II with the beautiful Rosin!

But we must say that, despite the author's stated intentions, private law, family law and contract law are little more than a pretext that intrigues and attracts. They provide a technically elegant opportunity to guide the reader through the fabulous universe of musical theatre, which is both theatre (stage, script, set design, acting, directing, lighting, colour, spectacle and magic) and music (singing, solos, duets, choruses, polyphony, recitatives, overtures and orchestral interludes). A mix which all (or almost all) the greatest composers have measured themselves against, creating unparalleled masterpieces. Annunziata, in addition to the delicate legal aspects of the plot, entertains the reader with literary precedents, the origins of the texts (librettos), and the cultural and musical references in each work selected. The libretto (*La Traviata*) that Francesco Maria Piave gave to Verdi's genius was based on *La dame aux camellias*, a poignant, short, intense, novel by Alexandre Dumas *fils*. For Rigoletto, Francesco Maria Piave was inspired by Victor Hugo's *Le roi s'amuse*: the archetype of Rigoletto is Triboulet, and of Sparafucile, Saltabadil! For *Le Nozze di Figaro*, Lorenzo Da Ponte was inspired by *La Folle journée* by Beaumarchais.

In the pages of this delightful work, Annunziata unites in marriage (a marriage not secret, not morganatic, not *zur linken Hand*) law, music and culture. It seems lawful to believe and hope that the three spouses, amid general joy and jubilation, in keeping with the best tradition, will live happily ever after.

Giovanni Iudica
Emeritus professor of Private Law
Università Luigi Bocconi, Milan

Introduction
Opera as neuter plural

That the boom in cultural studies has reshaped opera studies and re-launched them globally is a very remarkable development, whose consequences, not yet wholly clear to those involved, need to be more fully discussed by us musicologists. The recent development of new approaches to opera, understood as a cultural fact, has transformed our idea of opera as above all a musical and theatrical fact. The now firmly established appeal of the anthropological perspective, the increase in performance studies (especially those dealing with mediatized performances), the great favour accorded to psychoanalytic interpretations (above all post-Lacanian: e.g. those by Michel Poizat and Slavoj Žižek), 'archaeological' methodologies (in Foucault's sense) that focus on the 'discourses', more or less institutionalized, through which opera has in turn renegotiated its cultural space, etc.: all of these new approaches are accustoming us to consider opera as a phenomenon in continuous metamorphosis, to be unceasingly reinterpreted in different keys: as a neuter plural, in fact. Now, this multiplicity of approaches (in some ways perturbing) should, I believe, be seen as an enrichment and a great opportunity for musicology. The score is also a performance project and the opera (from whatever angle we look at it) can certainly not do without the dimensions of music and sound, which interact with the various contexts, dramatic and discursive, dealt with by historians, sociologists, anthropologists, economists, librettologists, mediologists, semioticians, scholars of psychoanalysis and comparative acoustics (and much else).

So we should welcome new approaches and new keys to interpretation, including the one presented by Filippo Annunziata in this refined book rich in promise. Why not read operas *also* as court cases?

This seems the principal assumption on which the author takes his stand, drawing on studies of the legal imagination (James Boyd White) and their recent developments, but applying them for the first time in a consistent, structured way to the field of opera. The interest in the legal perspective in music has been growing rapidly in recent years. I am thinking, for example, of such a libretto as Peter Szendy's *Écoute. Une histoire de nos oreilles* (2001), which shows clearly how the cultural construction of the conception of 'opera' (in the sense of *opus, Werk*) goes hand in hand with the development of the formidable modern legal institution of copyright. The legal approach proposed by Annunziata no longer addresses the more striking facts of criminal law, but the less obvious and almost latent aspects governed by private law. This implies first and foremost deciding which regulatory context the cases examined should be referred to. If Annina has to go to Paris to sell all Violetta's assets, if Alfredo wants to make a gift of his possessions to Violetta, well then all this skein – if one wants to unravel it in legal terms – has to be dealt with by taking into account first and foremost the Austrian Civil Code in force at the time and place when the opera was first performed: in Venice, at the Teatro La Fenice, on 6 March 1853. This is all the easier in the case of a work that, though it was set in an earlier age, as form of prior censorship (it is well known that *La Traviata* continued through much of the nineteenth century to be set in the eighteenth century), yet the story and the social context were patently contemporary. Naturally we have to bear in mind the literary and theatrical sources from which the librettos were taken, with the various legal provisions related to them (in this case the Paris of the period when Dumas *fils* published and staged his *Dame aux camélias* both in the form of a novel and a *pièce mêlée de chant*, respectively in 1848 and 1852).

But what about those works that are set in a time remote from the opera premiere, hence from the public they were addressed to? In these cases an interesting tension may grow up between the past of the *fabula* and the present work. That the contract Wotan has executed (and intends to disregard) is a somewhat bourgeois agreement to build his grand Valhalla is not without consequences, naturally, in the interpretation of the Tetralogy as an allegorical construct that speaks to us, among much else, of the modern capitalist world. Dealing with the problem of the failure to pay the agreed consideration to the giants Fasolt and Fafner in the light of German law in force at Wagner's time is therefore as inevitable as it is stimulating hermeneutically. Elsewhere, one needs to be more willing to problematize the coexistence of the different time frames in opera. Especially since in a 'museum' setting like one of our theatres, the opera is now also at some distance in time from its premiere, hence the time of the *fabula* is no longer superimposed just on the time of the first performance, but also on that of present-day audiences. In this respect, the comparative references Annunziata offers are timely and relevant to the private law in force today. These overlapping time frames are one aspect of opera that the legal approach can bring out significantly.

Returning to the thematization of the time of the fable, I would like to offer an example taken from an opera which Annunziata does not examine. He devotes a chapter to *La sonnambula* and the ring that Elvino gives Amina, which has very strong symbolic connotations (as well as legal implications: it seals the civil marriage contract, pending the final consecration with the religious ceremony). The theme of the ring as a symbol of a twofold bond is almost always controversial in many works, and could be approached from many angles. An extraordinary opera by Verdi, which is also legally significant is *Stiffelio*. But the example that I would like to look at comes from Donizetti's *Lucia di Lammermoor*. As we know, Edgardo and Lucia have exchanged a ring as a love token and in a (para)matrimonial rite in all respects (musically confirmed by the parallel movement of the voices). Apart from questions concerning the cultural and legal status of a secret marriage in force at the time the opera was performed, we should also bear in mind the stage direction published at this point of the scene in Cammarano's libretto. It reads: 'At the time to which this event took place in Scotland, it was a common belief that the violator of an oath performed with certain ceremonies was subjected on this earth to an exemplary heavenly punishment, almost simultaneous with the act of oath-breaking. Hence the oaths of lovers, far from being regarded as a matter of little weight, had at least the importance of a marriage contract.'

What relation is there between the ancient Scottish traditions (embodied in the opera through a sort of legal local colour) and modern reforms concerning civil marriage? It is clear that when Raimondo dismisses the oath between the two lovers, speaking of it as a superstitious or even blasphemous act ('Tu pur vaneggi! I nuzïali voti / che il ministro di Dio non benedice / né il ciel, né il mondo riconosce.'), he seems to speak the language of an established order with which we cannot sympathize. But even when Edgardo demands the return of the ring ('giving vent to his repressed anger, he throws the ring to the ground and treads on it'), railing against poor Lucia, we remain puzzled and dismayed. Every system of rules of past and present seems designed to victimize the poor woman, who is left with no way out but madness. Significantly, in her famous mad scene, Lucia utters her terrified exclamation: 'il fantasma! il fantasma!', echoing Edgardo's traumatic entry during the wedding feast, when the chorus sings 'Edgardo! Oh, terror!', again on a descending semitone and with a harmony that passes in the same way from the diminished seventh to the dominant seventh by chromatic slippage of the bass. As can be seen, apart from their legal contexts, operas refer to a legal mentality/sensibility (and its space-time coordinates) that music undertakes to express and orient dramatically. Annunziata's book opens a door leading into a new dimension, capable of enriching the already dense and multifaceted panorama of the operatic tradition. For the contribution he has made, we musicologists are grateful and (if I may conclude with a wish) *look forward to seeing him again.*

Emilio Sala

Contracts, wills, marriages and rings

Opera and private law

I
Opera at the crossroads of private law

1. The writings that make up this book propose to look at some of the masterpieces of European musical theatre from a legal perspective, and in particular one that starts from the rules of private law.

The universe of opera, ever since its inception in the early seventeenth century, has recounted great stories, now immortalized in the collective imagination and handed down through generations of listeners. These stories have helped shape our collective consciousness. Opera characters often embody great passions, deep conflicts and existential dramas: history and passions sweep them away inexorably and they frequently meet violent, tragic ends. Sometimes their stories unfold in imaginary worlds, or belong to the myths of classical antiquity, inhabited by heroes, deities, and fantastic creatures: much of the *opera seria* tradition, until the late eighteenth century, responds to these canons. In the genre of *opera buffa*, as consolidated in the eighteenth century, the characters embody the great archetypes of comic theatre, as well as the social customs of the period: the elderly tutor, the young women of marriageable age, the affianced couple, the penniless young man, the impoverished nobleman, the rich old widow, and the witty maidservant. Musical theatre, like all forms of entertainment, speaks and interacts with an audience that is, first of all, that of the time and place for which the theatrical work, with its multiple components (libretto, music, set design, performance) was originally conceived. In this, like every art form, it reflects the schemes, structures, and logic of its own day.

Works belonging to the genre of musical theatre, because of their intrinsic search for spectacular elements, are well suited to a transversal interpretation, hence they lend themselves to being read also in a legal key, especially in the perspective of the criminal law. The stories that the tradition of musical theatre gives us commonly represent events with a criminal significance. Murders, kidnappings, extortion, abductions, massacres, and other events are frequent, and if carefully examined can be found even in operas where such matters are less conspicuous.[1]

Even in the more recent examples of musical theatre, which continues to develop in significant ways, the legal theme, together with the social and political, emerges with considerable prominence, as shown by certain operas produced in the second half of the twentieth century down to our own times.[2]

The stories told by the librettos of musical theatre also address issues that touch on the sphere of private law; they often deal with contracts, donations, wills, promises of marriage, family relationships, securities, and much else. The plots of some librettos are interwoven with matters of this kind. In Gaetano Donizetti's *L'elisir d'amore*, poor Nemorino, in love with the beautiful but aloof Adina, is the victim of contractual fraud perpetrated by Dr. Dulcamara, and much of the plot turns on this scam. In Vincenzo Bellini's *La sonnambula*, Elvino takes back the engagement ring he has just given Amina, believing her unfaithful. In this way he revokes a gift made with a view to marriage, and perhaps infringes a legal rule. In Richard Wagner's *Das Rheingold* we witness a sensational case of breach of contract (a story that, today, would be splashed over the front pages of the newspapers!), and in this way we see the emergence in the nineteenth century of a new sensibility to the market economy and the increasingly central value of contracts, i.e. economic transactions in social relationships. In Mozart's *Le nozze di Figaro* we discover a strange wedding vow, which becomes enforceable in the event of non-payment of a debt. In the stories of the great

---

1 For example, in comic opera, where one would expect these elements to be less present. In Rossini's *Il barbiere di Siviglia*, the paradigmatic opera buffa of the nineteenth century Italian tradition, a panoply of crimes are committed, from housebreaking, to falsification, to quasi-kidnapping.
2 See, to give only a few examples, the opera *Claude* (2013), composed by Thierry Escaich, based on Victor Hugo's novel *Claude Gueux* (1834), which deals with the theme of prison conditions (the libretto is by Robert Badinter, several times French Minister of Justice and a promotor of the campaign that led to the abolition of the death penalty in France in 1981). Luigi Dallapiccola's *Il prigioniero*, represented for the first time in Florence in 1950, deals with the subject of prison and justice, and is set in Spain, in the time of Philip II and the Spanish Inquisition; *Giordano Bruno* (2015) was composed by Francesco Filidei to a libretto by Stephen Busellato.

OPERA AT THE CROSSROADS OF PRIVATE LAW

operas, there pass before the eyes of the public issues and problems that the law deals with by the instruments of private law. But *what* are these instruments?

To answer this question I propose to analyse ten works belonging to the mainstream operatic repertoire, which manifestly contain an event, an issue, that can be analysed from the perspective of private law. The analysis focuses on operas that clearly express this profile, in which the issues bound up with private law are crucial on the dramaturgical plane, and not merely 'accidents'. Hence these are not texts in which the themes of contract, family law, and testaments are merely alluded to, but texts in which these issues prove decisive in the development of the action and the story that the opera unfolds.

For the majority of the works analysed – with the exception of Richard Wagner's *Das Rheingold* and Puccini's *Gianni Schicchi* – the analysis is conducted in the light, firstly, of the legislation applicable in the place of the first performance. This seeks to investigate the possible impact on the public of that particular narrative, in a perspective that underlines a fact that, in reality, is never irrelevant: namely that a play is conceived first and foremost with a view to a form of representation and in relation to a given audience. The importance of the moment of reception (understood as the simultaneous presence of strictly textual elements, music, scenery and, in general, the performance) by the public for which it is intended or presented should not, in fact, be overlooked, especially in the case of works belonging to the genre of musical theatre. For some time now, both musicological, historical and aesthetic studies have brought out the fact that the relationship with the audience determines the theatrical product from its genetic phase, hence from its initial conception by librettist and composer. The audience influences stylistic choices, the construction of the story, the very structure of the drama, even before the reception of the text; and it conditions the work's circulation after its first performance, exposing it to constant changes, revisions, adaptations in relation to its *public* use. It changes the perception of the work and the keys to its interpretation as a function of the time and the place of performance. The final product, inherently unstable, is therefore almost never the result of a choice made in isolation by the composer and even less by the librettist, but stands in a dialectical relation to the audience for which it is intended and addresses,[3] a relation that, especially in the dynamics of nineteenth-century opera, also involves the fundamental role of the impresario.[4] Works in the operatic tradition were created in this way, almost always in the eighteenth and nineteenth centuries, in relation to a specific audience and, when the audience changed, they were altered, transformed and adapted.[5] In Italy, in the early decades of the nineteenth century (at least down to the outbreak of the 1848 risings), relations with the public were also coloured in very specific ways, because of the ties – though perhaps less clear than some traditions suggest – with the popular and Risorgimento cultures.[6]

The rereading, in a legal key, of some of these texts, in the light of the laws applicable in the place where they were first performed, is therefore meant as a first, obligatory verification of the results of the transversal analysis that these pages seek to carry out. Many of the issues addressed by the operas that are the subject of analysis constituted at the time, or at least offered, schemes deeply felt in the social consciousness and thus in the legal substrate of the society of their day. Notable, in this respect, is the case of Domenico Cimarosa's *Il matrimonio segreto*, which deals with a theme in many ways crucial, being deeply rooted in the social experience of the seventeenth and eighteenth century, namely that of clandestine marriages. It is equally interesting to observe the emergence of the

3   See, for example, the work by Ph. GOSSETT, *Divas and Scholars: Performing Italian Opera*, Chicago: University of Chicago Press, 2006.
4   On Alessandro Lanari – one of the most important entrepreneurs in the first half of the nineteenth century, involved in the production of various leading works in the repertoire of the time, including *La sonnambula*, studied in this volume – see M. DE ANGELIS, *Le carte dell'impresario. Melodramma e costume teatrale nell'Ottocento*, Florence: Sansoni, 1982.
5   For a particularly good example, related to France after the outbreak of the Revolution, D.Z. DAVIDSON, *France after Revolution. Urban Life, Gender, and the New Social Order*, Cambridge: Harvard University Press, 2007.
6   On these issues the literature is copious. Here a few essential references will be given, without any pretence to completeness, including C. SORBA, *Teatri. L'Italia del melodramma nell'età del Risorgimento*, Bologna: Il Mulino, 2001; IDEM, *Il melodramma della nazione. Politica e sentimenti nell'età del Risorgimento*, Bari: Laterza, 2015, and the important studies by J. ROSSELLI, which in varying degrees anticipated many strands subsequently developed by both historians and musicologists. Specifically, see (in their Italian translation) *L'impresario d'opera. Arte e affari nel teatro musicale italiano dell'Ottocento*, Turin: EDT, 1985: *Sull'ali dorate. Il mondo musicale italiano dell'Ottocento*, Bologna: Il Mulino 1992; 'Il sistema produttivo 1780-1880', in L. BIANCONI, G. PESTELLI (edited by), *Storia dell'opera italiana*, vol. 4, Torino: EDT, 1987, pp. 79-165.

theme of the contract and money in nineteenth-century texts. In Verdi's *La Traviata*, money plays a major part; in Wagner's *Das Rheingold*, the economic transaction represented by the contract is taken as a basic element of the social order. Some of the works analysed are set, I believe not coincidentally, in crucial moments of transformation of socio-cultural structures; they reflect the circulation of models and values, as shown and confirmed by their relations with the literary sources from which the stories are taken.[7]

2. The analyses conducted here lie at the cross-roads between various strands of research, which – given their articulation and depth – I certainly do not claim to sum up or retrace completely. In other words, I limit myself to pointing out some possible connections and points of contact. In the first place, in many ways the writings collected here can be related to the broad spectrum of *Law and Literature* studies, which have now flourished for many years, first in the United States and then in Europe: a strand of research which, as noted, proposes in particular to analyse texts that are 'literary' in the broad sense from a legal perspective. On closer inspection, it can be seen to be a current, or rather several currents, with different methods, criteria and purposes, depending on the authors and schools, although united by the intention of undertaking the analysis of a 'literary' work (hence theatre, film, poetry, and other forms) from the perspective of law. The birth of the school that deals with the relations between law and literature is generally seen as going back to the seventies-eighties, although there are antecedents. The approach to the interrelations between law and literature follows, primarily, two strands: the study of the representation of legal issues in literary texts (including the theatre); the analysis

---

7   As will be shown, in the adaptation of the story from various sources (for example, a play) to the opera libretto, the legal issues are often addressed and recounted differently. This is one of the many aspects of the circulation of models, and which reflects the mutual influences between different systems and traditions: an issue that concerns not only the law (especially in a comparative-historical perspective) but also the history of the theatre, and music. In particular, with regard to relations between the musical theatre in Italy and France, see D. COLAS, A. PROFIO, *D'une scène à l'autre. L'Opéra en anglais Europe*, 2 vols., Wavre: Mardaga 2009. On the more general issue of the relations between literary sources and libretti, M. TATTI (edited by), *Dal libro al libretto. La letteratura per musica dal '700 al '900*, Rome: Bulzoni, 2005.

of legal texts (rules, legal documents and opinions, treatises), as 'literary' products (this is the meaning of *Law and Literature*, on the one hand, and *Law as Literature*, on the other[8]). The method is used for different purposes, which have given rise to various undercurrents, depending upon the objectives that the interpreters pursue at different times, their sensibility and their cultural background: from the most general, with the analysis of literary texts treated as offering the opportunity to better understand fundamental human needs and, therefore, also the legal values that characterize society, all the way down to the most specific ones that explore more precise approaches or points of view: ethics, the status of women, political and social inequalities, the ethical value of justice, the role of the trial, the function of judges and Courts, and many other profiles.

Although there are significant precedents in Italy,[9] the homeland of the school is identified the United States, and the generally recognized founder was James Boyd White who, with *The Legal Imagination* (1973) is widely considered one the most important authors historically in the development of the study of law as literature.[10] White's attention was devoted mainly to the figure of the jurist (judge, lawyer, legislator) as an actor in a creative process. In the United States, before White, two other authors who should be mentioned are John Wigmore and Benjamin Cardozo, who at times endorsed the role of writers or poets as disseminators of legal culture in the twentieth century. In any case, since the early eighties the movement has gained in strength and become recognizable, creating different schools and approaches, and finding expression in conferences, publications and university courses of various kinds in the United States and elsewhere.[11]

---

8   The distinction already appears, for example, in the anthology edited by E. LONDON, entitled *The World of Law*, 2 vols., New York: Simon & Schuster, 1960.

9   For a full reconstruction of the origins of the movement, and the antecedents with respect to the seventies and eighties, which marked the real emergence of the School of Law and Literature, see A. SANSONE, *Diritto e letteratura*, Milan: Giuffrè, 2001.

10   According to A. POSNER, 'Law and Literature: A Relation Reargued', in *Virginia Law Review*, no. 72, 1986 pp. 1351 ff., 'Only since the publication in 1973 of James Boyd White's *The Legal Imagination* has a distinct, self-conscious field of law and literature emerged.' His opinion is shared almost unanimously: see for further references A. SANSONE, *Diritto*, cit., pp. 34 ff.

11   For a detailed survey, though no longer very recent, see A. SANSONE,*Diritto*, cit., pp. 83 ff. For recent developments, some of considerable interest, even beyond the perspective of *Law and Literature*, see R. CESERANI, *Convergenze. Gli strumenti letterari e le altre discipline*, Milan: Bruno

The method and the schools have today taken different forms, so that there is no general consensus about the methods or objectives of this approach. The principal strands – as reconstructed in a no longer recent essay in 2001 – are bound up with profiles such as legal anthropology and the history of law, the sociological-juridical perspective, the philosophical-political approach and the philosophy of law.[12] As the work proceeds, however, the strands tend to become more fragmented, as shown recently by Posner in a massive study of the subject,[13] and also to return critically to their own approaches and methodologies. Posner – one of the most representative exponents of this line of study – has himself said that law and literature have different functions, though there are aspects that make their comparison useful and fruitful: in doing so, he has placed himself in a position that in certain respects is critical of the approaches into which the analysis of *Law and Literature* is divided. In the debate that followed Posner's stand, Stanley Fish accepted his general thesis (law and literature are different activities), while stating that it is not the differences between the legal texts and literary ones that determines the different activities, but their different 'interpretive strategies'.[14] Martha Nussbaum stated that the *Law and Literature* approach can be useful, as it can help fulfil justice: the literary work stimulates the imagination and enhances one's ability to empathize with other people's actions.[15] This approach can help strengthen the capacity to formulate ethical judgments, although it cannot replace rules and the legal system.

Mondadori, 2010. Recently, note the creation of a course, available online, by The Great Courses, a North American institution that for years has produced and marketed video courses held by academics on many different subjects: the course is S. SAGE HEINZELMAN, *Representing Justice: Stories of Law and Literature*, available at the following address: http://www.thegreatcourses.com/courses/representing-justice-storiesof-law-and-literature.html.

12　See SANSONE, *Diritto*, cit., pp. 111 ff. Information on the situation of studies on the subject are obtainable from the web pages of the Associazione Italiana di *Law and Literature*, founded in 2008 (http://www.lawandliterature.org), to which should be added more recently G. TUZET, 'Diritto e letteratura. Finzioni a confronto', in Ann. Univ. Ferrara-Sc. Giur., Nuova Serie, XIX (2005), available online at the following address: http://www.lawandliterature.org/area/documenti/Tuzet%20-%20Diritto%20e%20letteratura.%20Finzioni%20a%20confronto.pdf.

13　See R. A. POSNER, *Law and Literature*, Cambridge: Harvard University Press, 2009.

14　S.E. FISH, 'Doing What Comes Naturally. Change, Rhetoric, and the Practice of Theory', in *Literary and Legal Studies*, Durham: Duke University Press, 1989.

15　M.C. NUSSBAUM, *Poetic Justice: The Literary Imagination and Public Life*, New York: Beacon, 1996.

The analysis of the relations between texts that are literary in the broad sense and the law has also long been studied by scholars who do not expressly draw on the various strands of the rich vein of *Law and Literature*. This relationship has long been explored by scholars of the theatre and theatrical history. In this case, attention is directed not only to more or less significant texts for the theatre, but also to the issue of representation and, more broadly, to dramaturgy, even far beyond the dimension peculiar to theatrical texts. To this field belong the analyses of different objects of study, such as the dramaturgy of public festivities, the representation of processions or official celebrations,[16] the ritual of public torture or public executions.[17]

In the various lines of inquiry, and schools evoked above, little attention, at least to date, has been devoted to a reading, in the perspective we are concerned with here, of works for musical theatre; a reading that, moreover, inevitably starts from the libretto but which should not neglect music and broadly performative factors.[18] So far, opera seems to have escaped the main currents of the studies in question, although it is a product that, in its phase of greatest expansion (in the eighteenth and nineteenth centuries), had a dominant role in the context of European cultural history.[19] In this respect, the studies collected here therefore seek to suggest possible new avenues of research aimed at investigating the broader relations between music and law, in their possible configurations: a strand, in short, of *Law and Music*.[20]

---

16   See, for example, C. BERNARDI, *La drammaturgia della Settimana Santa in Italia*, Milan: Vita e Pensiero, 1991.

17   The literature on the subject is extensive, beginning in the nineties: A. CASCETTA (edited by), 'Aspetti della teatralità a Milano nell'età barocca', in *Comunicazioni sociali*, 16/1-2 (1994), with studies that seek specifically to reconstruct the spectacle of guilt and expiation in the rituals of tortures; A. CASCETTA, R. CARPANI (edited by), *La scena della gloria. Drammaturgia e spettacolo a Milano in età spagnola*, Milan: Vita e Pensiero, 1995. For a specific and particularly interesting case, see the volume by P. FRIEDLAND, *Political Actors. Representative Bodies & Theatricality in the Age of the French Revolution*, Ithaca: Cornell University Press, 2002.

18   As is well known, discussion of the literary value of the opera libretto is highly articulated, and now goes back some time: see the contributions collected in F. DECROISETTE, *Le livret d'opéra, oeuvre littéraire*, Paris: PUF, 2010.

19   See, however, the volume edited by M. TOUSEIL-DIVINA, *Droit et Opéra*, Paris: LGDJ, 2008; E. ŁĘTOWSKA, K. PAWŁOSKI, *O operze: i o prawie*, Warsaw: Wolters Kluvers, 2014.

20   G. RESTA, *Variazioni comparatistiche sul tema: "diritto e musica"*, available on the website www.comparazionedirittocivile.it.

3. The analysis conducted here also belongs to the course of what, in general, can be described as new critical-methodological approaches to the study of opera. For many years now the analysis of works of musical theatre has followed articulated and multidisciplinary logics, which transcend the purely musical component, and range from comparative literature to cultural history, philosophy, feminist criticism, the relations between opera and cinema, psychology, and medicine. The very structure of opera, in which numerous heterogeneous elements coexist and are combined, lends itself particularly well to this type of analysis, as shown by the numerous and important contributions that have appeared.[21] If some of them seem to go too far in pursuing the transversal methodological approach, the liveliness of the observations in this area, leading to results far removed from traditional musicological analysis, is in itself a phenomenon worthy of attention, especially where the studies examine aspects concerning more generally cultural history in its various branches and interdisciplinary outcroppings.[22]

---

21   See, among the many, the essays collected in R. MONTEMORRA MARVIN, D.A. THOMAS (edited by), *Operatic Migrations. Transforming Works and Crossing Boundaries*, Aldershot: Ashgate, 2006, and the following texts: P. CONRAD, *Romantic Opera and Literary Form*, Berkeley: University of California Press, 1977; IDEM, *A Song of Love and Death: The Meaning of Opera*, New York: Poseidon, 1987; G. SCHMIDGALL, *Literature as Opera*, Oxford: Oxford University Press, 1977; H. LINDENBERGER, *Opera: The Extravagant Art*, Ithaca: Cornell University Press, 1984; IDEM, *Opera in History: From Monteverdi to Cage*, Stanford: Stanford University Press, 1998; P. ROBINSON, *Opera and Ideas: From Mozart to Strauss*, New York: Harper & Row, 1985; J. TAMBLING, *Opera, Ideology and Film*, Manchester: Manchester University Press, 1987; A. GROOS, R. PARKER (edited by), *Reading Opera*, Princeton: Princeton University Press, 1988; A. ARBLASTER, *Viva la libertà! Politics in Opera*, London: Verso, 1992; L. HUTCHEON, M. HUTCHEON, *Opera: Disease, Desire, Death*, Lincoln: University of Nebraska Press, 1996; IIDEM, *Bodily Charm: Living Opera*, Lincoln: University of Nebraska Press, 2000; C. ABBATE, *Unsung Voices: Opera and Musical Narrative in the Nineteenth Century*, Princeton: Princeton University Press, 1996; J. BOKINA, *Opera and Politics From Monteverdi to Henze*, New Haven: Yale University Press, 1997; P. KIVY, *Osmin's Rage: Philosophical Reflections on Opera, Drama, and Text*, Princeton: Princeton University Press, 1998; M.K. HUNTER, J. WEBSTER (edited by) *Opera Buffa in Mozart's Vienna*, Cambridge: Cambridge University Press, 1997; S. McCLARY, *Feminine Endings: Music, Gender and Sexuality*, Minneapolis: University of Minnesota Press, 2002; M.A. SMART (edited by), *Siren Songs: Representations of Gender and Sexuality in Opera*, Princeton: Princeton University Press, 2000; IDEM, *Mimomania: Music and Gesture in Nineteenth-Century Opera*, Berkeley: University of California Press, 2004.
22   The topic is extensive, and impossible to deal with here. For a first approach to cultural history, as a specific method of research that emerged in the nineteenth and twentieth centuries, see, *ex multis*, P. BURKE, *Varieties of Cultural Histories*, Ithaca: Cornell University Press, 2007; A. ARCANGELI, *Cultural History: A Concise Introduction*, London: Routledge, 2012.

4. The prospect that concerns us here – the attempt to grasp the legal aspects of opera, from the standpoint of private law – is therefore one of the many possible manifestations of the methods of inquiry that seek to offer enthusiasts and scholars of opera food for reflection that goes beyond the purely musical and theatrical element. In this respect, the analysis of the works that I proposed to carry out, clearly shows how, in musical theatre as elsewhere, the passing of history shifts the focus of interest in issues concerning the law. While, in the late eighteenth century, the themes that emerge are those most relevant to the profiles – in general – of family law (weddings, betrothals, marriage settlements, etc.), in the nineteenth the themes that emerge reflect the progressive transformation of the social fabric, the secularization of relationships, the emergence of the element of negotiation, and money. Hence it is no accident that this evolution was accompanied, in about the mid-nineteenth century – the period that follows perhaps the moment of greatest splendour of the Italian operatic tradition – by the spread of a new legal culture accessible to all, though not exactly 'popular', since it was directed at least to those sections of the population who were not only literate but also sensitive to issues of legal knowledge. Some recent studies have reconstructed the phenomenon that led, in the mid-nineteenth century, to the publication in many European countries of books intended to raise people's awareness of law. Again in this period, we observe the emergence of various techniques for popularizing legal texts through the medium of art, literature and other media. In particular, in around 1850-1860, the first editions of manuals with a practical approach appeared in Italy and France. They explained, in simple language, and with numerous examples, the commonest aspects of Law for the lives of citizens: these topics, unsurprisingly, are similar to those also explored in this study (marriage, donations, wills, contracts).[23]

Now, though it is true that the earliest examples of these publications are later than most of the operas analysed here, it should be considered that their emergence was not a sudden development, but reflects a lon-

---

23   A. MONTI, 'La legge alla portata di tutti: come fare a meno dell'avvocato', in A. PADOA-SCHIOPPA (edited by), *Avvocati e avvocatura nell'Italia dell'Ottocento*, Bologna: Il Mulino, 2009, pp. 383–424.

ger-term movement that began before the issue of the publications in question.

The most significant work in Italy, marking the start of a true literary current, was *L'avvocato di sé stesso*. The first edition was issued in Milan in 1857 by Manini and it was long much in demand.[24] It has been observed that this volume – which in its various editions grew to a considerable size, with over 700 pages – presented 'very banally, whatever might affect the lives, relationships or possessions of people at that time, presented in such a way as to deal with their problems, hence without raising issues of a doctrinal character, which lent depth to the writings of jurists'.[25] Of particular interest are the very full sections that present schemes and forms for drafting deeds, contracts and appeals. Similar phenomena characterized France, Austria and Baden. Although treatises or 'practical' guides to law or legal handbooks are also found under the *Ancien Régime*, in the nineteenth century the scope of the phenomenon was greatly enlarged, even growing into a mass scale unmatched in the earlier period. This, of course, is not to say that there is a direct correlation between the spread of a do-it-yourself legal culture and the topics dealt with in the texts considered here or, more broadly, in other artistic fields: simply, we merely record a fact, and a synchrony of events, which is perhaps not without its underlying logic. Of course, if someone – having one of those manuals at home – on returning from an evening at the theatre, had a question about the legal implications of the events represented onstage, he would be likely to find an initial answer. And the very characters who pass by on the following pages would perhaps have found in them their joys, sorrows and failures, as well as their reconciliations, borne out not only in life but also in the rule of law.

---

24   The editions continued almost down to World War I: see. A. MONTI, *La legge*, cit., p. 400, which cites reprints until 1912.

25   *Ibid.*, p. 397, which also examines the development and spread of more specific works intended for given classes of subjects (merchants, notaries, lawyers), a development that was partly present before the nineteenth-century codifications.

II

Le nozze di Figaro
(Wolfgang Amadeus Mozart – Lorenzo Da Ponte)

Promises of marriage

1. *Le nozze di Figaro*, performed in Vienna in 1786, marked the start of the extraordinary collaboration between Wolfgang Amadeus Mozart and Lorenzo Da Ponte. The first of three libretti written by Da Ponte for Mozart was taken, of course, from Beaumarchais' masterpiece,[26] *La Folle Journée ou le Mariage de Figaro*, performed for the first time in Paris, at the Théâtre de l'Odéon, April 27, 1784, and in turn part of a trilogy including *Le Barbier de Séville* (1775) and *La Mère coupable* (1792).[27]

It appears that it was Mozart himself who passed Beaumarchais' text to Da Ponte in Vienna, where they had met in 1781 (the year of their arrival in the capital), in the *salon* of the Jewish Baron Raimund von Wetzlar. At that moment, the idea of turning *La Folle Journée* into an opera appeared to be beset with difficulties. Beaumarchais's text was banned in the Austrian Empire for its allegedly subversive character, and Mozart had to work on the score in great secrecy. Da Ponte was compelled to pare away the original to adapt it to the scope of *opera buffa* (a genre highly appreciated in Vienna in those years[28]), and tone down its political significance. It was not, however, without difficulty that Emperor Joseph II decided to authorize the performance of the opera, which took place on I May 1786, at the Burgtheater in Vienna.

---

26   See, for certain profiles, E. SALA DI FELICE, 'Figaro e Susanna: dal "Mariage" alle "Nozze di Figaro"', in M. TATTI (edited by), *Dal libro al libretto. La letteratura per musica dal '700 al '900*, Roma: Bulzoni, 2005, pp. 123-182.

27   For an analysis of Beaumarchais' trilogy (in particular, *La Folle Journée*), in terms of cultural history, an essential reference is S. SCHAMA, *Citizens. A Chronicle of the French Revolution*, New York: Alfred A. Knopf, 1989, pp. 123-182.

28   See the essays in M. HUNTER, J. WEBSTER (edited by), *Opera Buffa in Mozart's Vienna*, Cambridge: Cambridge University Press, 2008, and, in particular, P. GALLARATI, *Mozart and Eighteenth-Century Comedy*, pp. 98-111.

Le nozze di Figaro remains very close to Beaumarchais's work, although Da Ponte deviated from it in various respects, mainly in order to tighten the pace of the narrative. This is sometimes dilated in Beaumarchais' play, making it difficult to adapt to the requirements of an opera libretto. Hence Da Ponte simplified various steps in the plot, reduced the number of main characters, and drastically compressed the number of scenes. Da Ponte's skill lay in reworking the original, not just in removing various parts without affecting the coherence of the whole, but also his skill was directed at heightening certain themes – such as eroticism – which were present in Beaumarchais, but emerge boldly in Mozart's masterpiece.

Certainly both Mozart and Da Ponte had close affinities with Beaumarchais' play in terms of content and structure. In some ways, *La Folle Journée* is a hybrid text, which seems almost made to be turned into an opera. In the play (as in the *Barbier de Séville*), Beaumarchais exposed the structures and patterns of spoken theatre to the influence of *opéra comique* and the *genre dramatique*, or *drame*, which had been spreading in France since the 1760s. He included several songs (interludes, *vaudevilles*, small romances) in the play, not for purely decorative purposes, but to dramatic effect: in *Le Mariage de Figaro* there is a striking example of this in the romance entrusted to Cherubino (Act II.4), and set to the tune of one of the best-known popular songs of the period: *Malbrough s'en va-t-en guerre*.[29] So *Le nozze di Figaro* turned a text conceived for the playhouse, but already containing hybrid elements, into an extraordinary opera libretto.

2. The events in Da Ponte and Mozart's opera that concern us here revolve around the relationship between Marcellina and Figaro. Figaro, the central character in the opera, is about to marry Susanna, but the marriage is beset with difficulties. Count Almaviva is trying to revive the old feudal law known as *ius primae noctis*. Other complications arise: the relationship between the count and his wife are under strain from his acknowledged in-

---

29   See, for the theoretical reasons that led Beaumarchais in this direction, his own preface to *Le Mariage de Figaro*. More in general, on Beaumarchais' relations with the opera house, see T.B. CUILLÉ, 'From the Comédie Française to the Opéra: Figaro at the Crossroads', in R. MONTEMORRA MARVIN, D.A. THOMAS (edited by), *Operatic Migrations. Transforming Works and Crossing Boundaries*, Aldershot: Ashgate, 2006, pp. 41-64.

fidelities; the countess clearly feels attracted to Cherubino (a 'lad', as he is called in the libretto, though his hormones are clearly raging); Marcellina, the no longer youthful housekeeper, is enamoured of Figaro and attempts in various ways to wreck his marriage to Susanna. Marcellina is at the heart of the story examined here. At some indefinite time in the past, it appears that Figaro had borrowed a sum of money from her. Figaro promised to repay the debt and heedlessly engaged to marry her if he failed to do so. Repayment (the conditions and the due date are not mentioned, but we later learn that the sum was '2000 pezzi duri'[30]) is being claimed by Marcellina, now that Figaro's marriage to Susanna is imminent. The timing is clearly not accidental. Marcellina, who is in love with Figaro, wishes to prevent the wedding (scheduled for the same day). Her interest is largely to win the personable Figaro rather than obtain repayment.

In Act I.2, Marcellina prepares her strategy: she tells the scheming Bartolo (identified in the libretto by Da Ponte as a 'physician of Seville') about the situation and seeks his help. Bartolo is happy to assist here, because – as we know from a previous episode in the trilogy, *Le Barbier de Seville* – Figaro's machinations had led to Rosina (the Countess, formerly Bartolo's ward) marrying Count Almaviva instead of her guardian.

In Da Ponte's libretto, when Bartolo speaks, there has already been a previous discussion with Marcellina, and the text plunges the reader *in medias res*:[31]

BARTOLO

Ed aspettaste il giorno
fissato alle sue nozze
per parlarmi di questo?

---

30   The 'pezzi duri' or 'pezzi di Spagna' were Spanish coins minted before 1818. Since *Le nozze di Figaro* is set in Seville, this explains the reference to the local currency in use at the time.
31   The text adopted in this chapter is that of the original libretto of 1786 (*LE NOZZE | DI FIGARO | Comedia per musica | tratta dal francese | in quattro atti. | Da rappresentarsi | nel Teatro di Corte | l'anno 1786. | In Vienna, | presso Giuseppe Nob. De Kurzbek, | stampatore di S.M.I.R.*), a specimen of which is reproduced in E. WARBURTON (edited by), *The Librettos of Mozart's Operas*, vol. 3, New York: St Louis, 1992, pp. 1103. In comparing the libretto and score, the reader is referred to the critical edition: L. FINSCHER (edited by), *Le nozze di Figaro, opera buffa in vier Akten. Text von Lorenzo Da Ponte. KV 492*, Kassel: Bärenreiter, 1973 (Neue Mozart-Ausgabe, II/5, Band 16). The English version is taken from the website: http://www.murashev.com/opera/Le_nozze_di_Figaro_libretto_English_Italian.

MARCELLINA	Io non mi perdo,
	dottor mio di coraggio:
	per romper de' sponsali
	più avanzati di questo
	bastò spesso un pretesto: ed egli ha meco,
	oltre questo contratto,
	certi impegni... so io... basta... or conviene
	la Susanna atterrir; convien con arte
	impuntigliarla a rifiutare il Conte.
	Egli per vendicarsi
	prenderà il mio partito,
	e Figaro così sia mio marito.
BARTOLO	*(Prende il contratto dalle mani di Marcellina)*[32]

The stage direction that appears in the libretto 'taking the contract from Marcellina', deserves to be examined more closely. In Da Ponte's libretto, Marcellina evidently shows Bartolo 'a contract', in reality it is a loan agreement. Marcellina says that she is the recipient not only of the contractual commitments, but also of 'certain other commitments', later discovered to be a promise of marriage. So Marcellina has two documents: a loan agreement, and a promise of marriage, issued to guarantee the repayment of the money. It is not clear whether, in the interview preceding the Bartolo-Marcellina recitative, Bartolo has been made fully aware of the situation. Probably, he has, since when Bartolo objects, 'And you wait for the very day fixed for the marriate to speak to me about this?' the situation seems to have been clarified already, though Marcellina's subsequent vagueness ('Certain commitments... I know... That's enough!... Now we have to scare Susanna') suggests otherwise. After talking to Marcellina, Bartolo sings a grandiloquent aria, which explicitly refers to the need to take legal action:

---

32   BARTOLO And you wait for the very day fixed for the marriage to speak to me about this? /MARCELLINA I haven't yet lost hope, my dear doctor; to put an end to wedding plans even more advanced than this a mere pretext has often sufficed; and he has, apart from this contract, other obligations to me – but enough of that! Susanna must be frightened and artfully induced to refuse the Count; out of revenge, he will take my part, and thus Figaro will become my husband. / BARTOLO *(taking the contract from Marcellina)*.

BARTOLO   *(Prende il contratto dalle mani di Marcellina)*
Bene, io tutto farò: senza riserve
tutto a me palesate. (Avrei pur gusto
di dar per moglie la mia serva antica
a chi mi fece un dì rapir l'amica.)

La vendetta, oh la vendetta!
è un piacer serbato ai saggi:
Obbliar l'onte e gli oltraggi,
è bassezza, è ognor viltà.
Coll'astuzia... coll'arguzia...
col giudizio... col criterio...
si potrebbe... il fatto è serio...
ma credete si farà.
Se tutto il codice
dovessi volgere,
se tutto l'indice
dovessi leggere,
con un equivoco,
con un sinonimo
qualche garbuglio
si troverà.
Tutta Siviglia
conosce Bartolo:
il birbo Figaro
vostro sarà!
(Parte)[33]

At any rate, the delicate situation is clarified in the final scene of Act II, just after the very lively scene XI. Marcellina, firmly intending to balk Figaro's marriage to her rival Susanna, goes to law. She hires Bartolo as her attor-

---

33   BARTOLO *(taking the contract from Marcellina)* Good, I'll do all I can. Be quite frank and tell me everything. *(aside)* I should relish marrying off my former servant to the man who once engineered my ward's elopement / BARTOLO Revenge, oh, sweet revenge is a pleasure reserved for the wise, to forgo shame, outrage is base and utter meanness. With astuteness, with cleverness, with discretion, with judgment, it's possible... The matter is serious; but, believe me, it shall be done. If I have to pore over the law books, if I have to read all the extracts, with misunderstandings, with hocus-pocus he'll find himself in a turmoil. If I have to pore over, *etc.* All Seville knows Bartolo, the scoundrel Figaro shall be overcome! *(He goes.)*

ney, and Basilio, the music teacher, as a witness. The three present themselves before the Court, the responsibility of the Count. Still embroiled in the dispute which had pitted him against Susanna, the Countess and Figaro in the previous scene, the Count will now have Marcellina's case heard by his judges. Given the Count's intentions towards Susanna, he will clearly not object to dealing with the matter and so try to scuttle the impending marriage:

MARCELLINA, BARTOLO E BASILIO	*(al Conte)* Voi signor, che giusto siete, Ci dovete or ascoltar.
CONTE	*(da sé)* (Son venuti a vendicarmi, Io mi sento consolar.)
CONTESSA, FIGARO E SUSANNA	*(da sé)* (Son venuti a sconcertarmi, Qual rimedio ritrovar?)
FIGARO	*(al Conte)* Son tre stolidi, tre pazzi. Cosa mai vengono a far?
CONTE	Pian pianin, senza schiamazzi Dica ognun quel che gli par
MARCELLINA	Un impegno nuziale Ha costui con me contratto: E pretendo che il contratto Deva meco effettuar.
CONTESSA, FIGARO E SUSANNA	Come! Come![34]

Marcellina's revelation stuns everyone ('Come! Come!'). The Count, in keeping with the values of the *Ancien Régime*, which he embodies, is ready to deal with the dispute, taking it under his jurisdiction:

---

34 MARCELLINA, BASILIO, BARTOLO (*To the* Count) You, sir, who are so just, you must listen to us now /SUSANNA, COUNTESS, FIGARO They have come to ruin me, what solution can I find? /COUNT They have come to avenge me. I'm beginning to feel better / FIGARO (*To the Count*) They are all three stupid fools, whatever have they come to do? / COUNT Softly now, without this clamour, let everyone speak his mind / MARCELLINA That man has signed a contract binding him to marry me, and I contend that the contract must be carried out / SUSANNA, COUNTESS, FIGARO What, what?

CONTE	Olà, silenzio:
	Io son qui per giudicar.
BARTOLO	Io da lei scelto avvocato
	Vengo a far le sue difese,
	Le legittime pretese,
	Io qui vengo a palesar.
FIGARO, LA CONTESSA	
E SUSANNA	È un birbante!...
CONTE	Olà, silenzio:
	Io son qui per giudicar.
BASILIO	Io com'uom al mondo cognito
	Vengo qui per testimonio,
	Del promesso matrimonio
	Con prestanza di danar.
CONTESSA, FIGARO	
E SUSANNA	Son tre matti!
CONTE	Lo vedremo,
	Il contratto leggeremo
	Tutto in ordin deve andar.
CONTE, MARCELLINA,	
BARTOLO E BASILIO	(Che bel colpo, che bel caso!
	È cresciuto a tutti il naso,
	Qualche Nume a noi propizio
	Qui li/ci ha fatti capitar.)
CONTESSA, FIGARO	
E SUSANNA	(Son confusa/o, son stordita/o,
	Disperata/o, sbalordita/o.
	Certo un diavol dell'inferno
	Qui li ha fatti capitar.)[35]

Over the protests of Susanna, Figaro and the Countess, the outcome of

---

35   COUNT Hey, be silent! I am here to render judgment / BARTOLO Appointed as her lawyer I am here in her defence, to publish to the world her legitimate reasons / SUSANNA, COUNTESS, FIGARO He is a rogue! / COUNT Hey, be silent! / BASILIO Known as a man of the world, I come here as a witness of his promise of marriage when she loaned him some money / SUSANNA, COUNTESS, FIGARO They are all mad, *etc.* / COUNT Hey, be silent, we'll see about that. We will read the contract and proceed in due order / SUSANNA, COUNTESS, FIGARO I am confused, stupefied, hopeless, dismayed! Surely some devil from Hell has brought them/us here! / MARCELLINA, BASILIO, BARTOLO, COUNT A telling blow, a lucky chance! Victory is right before our noses; some propitious power has surely brought them/us here!

the case is entrusted to the reading and interpretation of the contract. The Count's words emphasize the need to proceed to the 'reading' of the contract – produced, as we already know, in writing – and to deal with the question by proceeding in 'order' ('Il contratto leggeremo /Tutto in ordin deve andar.')

The outcome of the proceedings is not, however, immediate: despite the call to order, the second act closes, amid general confusion, with the magnificent sextet (a true first finale) that involves all the leading characters. Amid general astonishment and amazement, the six characters make their exits.

The question is then resumed in Act III, scene V. In Da Ponte's libretto, unlike Beaumarchais' play, we do not see the case unfolding, but we at once learn the outcome. The judge Don Curzio has found against Figaro: the latter must therefore marry Marcellina, unless the debt is repaid. As can be imagined the case has been quite hectic (because of the behaviour – lively, to say the least – of the characters). The Court calls for silence ('ora ammutite'). Figaro's pleas, calling for the Count to intervene and using the term 'appeal', are in vain:

DON CURZIO	*(tartagliando)* È decisa la lite.
	O pagarla, o sposarla. Ora ammutite.
MARCELLINA	Io respiro.
FIGARO	Ed io moro.
MARCELLINA	*(da sé)* (Alfin sposa io sarò d'un uom che adoro.)
FIGARO	Eccellenza m'appello...
CONTE	È giusta la sentenza:
	O pagar, o sposar. Bravo Don Curzio.
DON CURZIO	Bontà di sua Eccellenza.
BARTOLO	Che superba sentenza!
FIGARO	In che superba?
BARTOLO	Siam tutti vendicati...
FIGARO	Io non la sposerò.
BARTOLO	La sposerai.
DON CURZIO[36]	O pagarla, o sposarla. Lei t'ha prestato

---

36 In the libretto published for the Viennese edition (1786), it is Marcellina, not Curzio, who says 'Io t'ho prestati due mila pezzi duri' (see the original libretto, available online at:

Duemila pezzi duri.[37]

Poor Figaro plays his last card and invokes an unspecified (and unjustified) necessity to obtain his parents' consent to his marriage. To this end, he recalls his fanciful origins of noble descent; he was kidnapped as a child by some robbers. The twist in the plot is impending: it turns out – thanks to a tattoo that Figaro has on his arm – that he is the son of Marcellina and Bartolo. The couple have, of course, never married, but they had a son, whom they both recognize. In this way the recognition scene resolves the root of the dispute; first of all, the question of marriage. Curzio states categorically, 'The marriage cannot proceed.' From what we can presume, though on the point the libretto is not explicit, the judgment also settles the dispute over repayment of the debt: Figaro is obliged to repay it in some way:

FIGARO	Son gentiluomo, e senza
	L'assenso de' miei nobili parenti...
CONTE	Dove sono? chi sono?...
FIGARO	Lasciate ancor cercarli:
	Dopo dieci anni io spero di trovarli.
BARTOLO	Qualche bambin trovato.
FIGARO	No perduto, dottor, anzi rubato.
CONTE	Come?
MARCELLINA	Cosa?
BARTOLO	La prova?
DON CURZIO	Il testimonio?
FIGARO	L'oro, le gemme, e i ricamati panni,

---

http://dme.mozarteum.at/DME/libretti-edition/wrkliste.php?sec=libedi&l=). However, in the score, the words are set to music for the part of Curzio, and of course the words are changed to 'Lei t'ha prestati duemila pezzi duri' (cfr. MOZART, *Le nozze di Figaro. KV 492*, Bärenreiter, 2001, atto III.5). In the score, the emphasis is therefore more on the role of the judge in settling the dispute.
37 CURZIO The dispute has been resolved: Pay her or marry her. No more to be said / MARCELLINA I breathe again! / FIGARO And I'm done for! / MARCELLINA *(aside)* At last I shall be the wife of a man I adore / FIGARO *(to the Count)* My lord, I appeal... /COUNT The ruling is a fair one, either pay up or marry. Well done, Don Curzio / CURZIO Your Lordship is most kind! /BARTOLO What a magnificient ruling! / FIGARO What makes it magnificent? BARTOLO We're all avenged / FIGARO I shan't marry her /BARTOLO You will / CURZIO Either pay her or marry her. She lent you two thousand crowns.

Che ne' più teneri anni
Mi ritrovato addosso i masnadieri,
Sono gli indizi veri
Di mia nascita illustre: e sopra tutto
Questo al mio braccio impresso geroglifico...

MARCELLINA   Una spatola impressa al braccio destro...

FIGARO   E a voi chi 'l disse?...

MARCELLINA   Oh Dio!
È egli...

FIGARO   È ver, son io.

DON CURZIO   Chi?

CONTE   Chi?

BARTOLO   Chi?

MARCELLINA   Raffaello.

BARTOLO   E i ladri ti rapir...

FIGARO   Presso un castello.

BARTOLO   Ecco tua madre.

FIGARO   Balia...

BARTOLO   No, tua madre.

DON CURZIO E IL CONTE   Sua madre!

FIGARO   Cosa sento!

MARCELLINA   Ecco tuo Padre.

(abbracciando Figaro)
Riconosci in questo amplesso
Una madre, amato figlio.

FIGARO   *(a Bartolo)* Padre mio, fate lo stesso,
Non mi fate più arrossir.

BARTOLO   *(abbracciando Figaro)*
Resistenza la coscienza
Far non lascia al tuo desir.

DON CURZIO   (Ei suo Padre, ella sua madre
L'imeneo non può seguir.)

CONTE   Son smarrito, son stordito;
Meglio è assai di qua partir.[38]

---

38   FIGARO I am a gentleman, and without the consent of my noble parents / COUNT Where are they? Who are they? / FIGARO Let me go on looking; after ten years I hope to find them / BARTOLO So you're a foundling? / FIGARO No, lost, doctor, or rather, stolen / COUNT How? / MARCELLINA What? / BARTOLO Any proof? / CURZIO Any evidence? / FIGARO The gold, the gems, the embroidered clothes which, as a baby, were found on me by the robbers, these are

3. In Beaumarchais' text, the question of the promise of marriage and Figaro's subsequent trial is spun out much longer: it runs through four scenes of Act III. So it has a much fuller and more highly articulated development than is found in Da Ponte's libretto. But, as we have seen, the distance between the two texts reflects a basic decision Da Ponte had to take in reworking the original. Beaumarchais's comedy was too variegated, articulated around a large number of characters and stories interlacing with each other, to be used as such in an opera libretto. So Da Ponte reduced the number of characters given a full dramatic role, and cut out the other parts. In this respect, the most significant abridgment concerned some of the figures involved in the story of the promise of marriage, and in particular Basilio, Bartolo and Marcellina. He eliminated some actions that were secondary to the staple of the plot, and in particular the issue here at stake: they include the revelation, included in the play but not in the opera libretto, that Figaro was the father of the youngest son of the judge (in the play called Don Gusman Brid'Oison[39]). The result obtained by Da Ponte was often referred to as the result of censorship in the broad sense: Da Ponte himself, in his memoirs,[40] claims to have personally persuaded the Emperor Joseph II to accept an opera based on a work that had been

---

the real proofs of my noble birth; and, above all, this mark here on my arm / MARCELLINA A spatula stamped on your right arm? /FIGARO Who told you? / MARCELLINA Oh God! It's him! / FIGARO True, it's me! CURZIO Who? / COUNT Who? / BARTOLO Who? / MARCELLINA Raffaello! / BARTOLO And you were stolen by robbers? / FIGARO Near a castle / BARTOLO There is your mother / FIGARO Nurse? / BARTOLO No; your mother. / CURZIO, COUNT His mother? / FIGARO What are you saying? /MARCELLINA There is your father / MARCELLINA *(embracing Figaro)* Recognise in this embrace your mother, beloved son / FIGARO *(to Bartolo)* My father, do the same, and let me no longer be ashamed / BARTOLO *(embracing Figaro)* Resistance, my conscience no longer lets you rule / CURZIO He's his father? She's his mother? It's too late for the wedding now / COUNT I'm astounded, I'm abashed, I'd better get out of here.

39   The name of the judge in Beaumarchais' text (Gusman) is believed to be a caricature of the name of Louis Valentin Goëzman de Thurn, a French jurist and diplomat, whom Beaumarchais had dealings with in a noted legal dispute, one of the many that studded his adventurous life. (See P.-A. C. de BEAUMARCHAIS, *The Follies of a Day; or, the Marriage of Figaro. A Comedy*, translated by Thomas Holcroft, London: G.G. and J.J. Robinson, 1785.) These are the lines in Beaumarchais' text dealing with the paternity of Figaro. 'Guzman. "Ha-ave not I see-een you before, young Man?" Figaro. "Oh yes, Mr. President, I once served your Lady." Guzman. "How lo-ong since?" Figaro. "Nine months before the birth of her last Child—And a fine Boy it is, though I say it." Guzman. "Y-es—He's the F-flower of the Flock".'

40   L. DA PONTE, *Le memorie*, Villasanta: Istituto Editoriale Italiano, 1933, p. 163 ff.

banned by reassuring him that the politically troublesome aspects would be eliminated. Assuming that this was true, Da Ponte still needed to display a degree of theatrical pragmatism to ensure that the structure of the libretto was consistent with the demands of *opera buffa* as a genre. In this context, the cutting of the long legal dispute, linked to the decipherment and interpretation of the promise of marriage, lends itself to being read both ways. Beyond that, and with specific reference to the court scenes, Joseph II could easily accept the staging of a play which ridiculed an aristocrat as corrupt as the Count (especially at a time when the emperor was reaffirming the central power of the monarchy against the excesses of many rebellious noblemen), but not the representation of a long and complex scene in which an aristocrat administers justice for his own purposes (justice, moreover, that was ridiculed and clearly unjust) with the tacit connivance of monarchical power.

In Beaumarchais' text, the court case is rich in comedic and polemical effects, that both reflect the author's controversial dealings with justice, and clichés common in the repertoire of the comic theatre of the time: the incompetent judge, clumsy, befuddled and corrupt, is a *topos* of the genre.

[Act III, Scene 12]
Enter Don Guzman, Marcelina, and Doctor

MARCELINA	I shall be happy, Mr. President, to explain the justice of my Cause.
DOCTOR	To shew you on what grounds this Lady proceeds.
GUZMAN	(*Stuttering*) We-e-e-ell, le-et us exa-a-mine the matter ve-erbally.
MARCELINA	There is a promise of Marriage—
GUZMAN	I co-o-o-ompre—hend! Gi-i-iven by you-ou-ou—to—
MARCELINA	No, Mr. President, given *to* me.
GUZMAN	I co-o-o-omprehend! Gi-ven *to* you.
MARCELINA	And a sum of Money which I—
GUZMAN	I co-o-o-omprehend! Which you-ou ha-ave received.
MARCELINA	No, Mr. President, which I have lent.
GUZMAN	I co-o-o-omprehend!—It is re-e-paid.
MARCELINA	No, Mr. President, it is *not* repaid.
GUZMAN	I co-o-o-omprehend—The m-m-man would marry you to pay his de-de-de-bts.

MARCELINA	No, Mr. President, he would neither marry me, *nor* pay his debts.
GUZMAN	D-d-do you think I d-d-d-don't co-o-omprehend you?
DOCTOR	And are you, Mr. President, to judge this Cause?
GUZMAN	T-t-t-to be sure—Wha-at else did I purchase my Place for thi-ink you (*Laughs stupidly at the supposed folly of the Question*) And where is the De-fe-e-endant?

Enter Figaro.

FIGARO	Here, at your service.
DOCTOR	Yes, that's the Knave.
FIGARO	Perhaps I interrupt you.
GUZMAN	Ha-ave not I see-een you before, young Man?
FIGARO	Oh yes, Mr. President, I once served your Lady.
GUZMAN	How lo-ong since?
FIGARO	Nine months before the birth of her last Child— And a fine Boy it is, though I say it.
GUZMAN	Y-es—He's the F-flower of the Flock'—And the cau-ause betwee-een—
FIGARO	A Bagatelle, Mr. President! A Bagatelle.
GUZMAN	(*Laughs.*) A Ba-ag-a-telle! A pro-o-mise of Ma-a-arriage a Ba-a-gatelle! Ha! ha! ha!—And dost thou hope to ca-ast the Pla-aintiff?
FIGARO	To be sure, Mr. President! You being one of the Judges.
GUZMAN	(*With stupid dignity*) Ye-e-es! I am one of the Judges!— Hast thou see-een D-D-Doublefee, my Se-ecretary?
FIGARO	Yes, Mr. President! That's a duty not to be neglected.
GUZMAN	The young Fellow is not so si-i-imple I thought.

Enter Cryer of the Court, Guards, Count, Counsellors and Vassals.

CRYER	Make room there, for my Lord, the Count.
COUNT	Wherefore in your Robes, Don Guzman? It was unnecessary for a mere domestic matter like this.
GUZMAN	Pa-a-ardon me, my Lord! Those who would tre-e-emble at the Clerk of the Court in his Robes, would la-augh at the Judge without 'em.' Forms! Forms! are sacred things.

(The Count and the Court seat themselves.)

COUNT	Call silence in the Court.
CRYER	Silence in the Court.
GUZMAN	Read 'over the Causes', D-D-Doublefee.
DOUBLEFEE	The Count de los Altos Montes di Agnas Frescas, Senor di Montes Fieros, y otros Montes, Plaintiff, against Alonzo

	Calderon, a Comic Poet. The question at present before the Court, is, to know the Author of a Comedy that has been damned; which they mutually disavow and attribute to each other.
COUNT	They are both very right in mutually disavowing it; and be it decreed, that if, hereafter, they should produce a successful Piece, its Fame shall appertain to the Count, and its Merit to the Poet—The next.
DOUBLEFEE	Diego Macho, Day-labourer, Plaintiff, against Gil-Perez-Borcado Tax-gatherer, and receiver of the Gabels, for having violently dispossessed the said Diego Macho, Day-labourer, of his Cow.
COUNT	This Cause does not come within my Jurisdiction; but as it is probable the Day-labourer will never obtain Justice, do thou see, Figaro, that another Cow be sent him, lest his Family should be starved—The next.
DOUBLEFEE	Marcelina-Jane-Maria-Angelica-Mustacio, Spinster, Plaintiff, against—(*To Figaro*) Here's no surname!
FIGARO	Anonymous.
GUZMAN	Ano-o-onymous—I never heard the Name before!
DOUBLEFEE	Against Figaro Anonymous. What Pr'ession?
FIGARO	Gentleman.
COUNT	Gentleman!
FIGARO	I might have been born a Prince, if Heaven had pleased.
DOUBLEFEE	Against Figaro Anonymous, Gentleman, Defendant. The Question before the Court relates to a promise of Marriage; the Parties have retained no Council, contrary to the ancient and established practice of Courts.
FIGARO	What occasion for Council? A race of Gentleman who are always so very learned, they know every thing, except their Briefs! Who insolently interrogate Modesty and Timidity, and endeavour, by confusing, to make Honesty forswear itself; and, after having laboured for hours, with all legal prolixity, to perplex self-evident Propositions, and bewilder the understandings of the Judges, sit down as proud as if they had just pronounced a Phillipic of Demosthenes—(*Addressing himself to the Court*) My Lord, and Gentlemen—The Question before the Court is—
DOUBLEFEE	(*Interrupting him*) It is not you to speak, you are the Defendant—Who pleads for the Plaintiff.

DOCTOR	I.
DOUBLEFEE	You! A Physician turn Lawyer?—
FIGARO	Oh yes, and equally skilful in both.
COUNT	Read the Promise of Marriage, Doctor.
GUZMAN	Re-e-ead the Pro-o-omise of Marriage.
DOCTOR	(*Reads*) I acknowledge to have received of Marcelina-Jane-Maria-Angelica-Mustachio, the sum of two thousand Piasters, in the Castle of Count Almaviva, which sum I promise to repay to the said Marcelina-Jane-Maria-Angelica-Mustachio, *and* to marry her. Signed, Figaro. (*Addressing himself to the Count*) My Lord, and Gentlemen! Hem! Never did cause more interesting, more intricate, or in which the Interest of Mankind, their Rights, Properties, Lives and Liberties were more materially involved, ever claim the profund Attention of this most learned, most honourable Court, and from the time of Alexander the Great, who promised to espouse the beauteous Thalestris—
COUNT	Stop, most formidable Orator; and ere you proceed, enquire whether the Defendant does not contest the validity of your Deed.
GUZMAN	(*To Figaro*) Do you co-ontest the va-va-va-va-lidity of the Dee-eed?
FIGARO	My Lord and Gentlemen! Hem! There is in this Case, either Fraud, Error, Malice, or mischievous Intention, for the Words of the Acknowledgment are, I promise to repay the said Marcelina-Jane-Maria-Angelica-Mustachio, the said sum of two thousand Piasters *or* to marry her, which is very different.
DOCTOR	I affirm it is AND.
FIGARO	I affirm it is OR.
DOCTOR	Well, suppose it.
FIGARO	No Supposition, I will have it granted.
COUNT	Clerk, Read you the Promise.
GUZMAN	Re-e-ead the P-P-P-Promise, D-D-D-Double-fee.
DOUBLEFEE	(*Reads*) I acknowledge to have received of Marcelina-Jane-Maria-Angelica-Mustachio, the sum of two thousand Piasters, in the Castle of Count Almaviva, which sum I promise to repay the said Marcelina-Jane-Maria-Angelica-Mustachio, *and*—*or*—*and*—*or*—*or*— The Word is blotted.

DOCTOR	No matter; the sense of the Phrase is equally clear. This learned Court is not now to be informed the word or particle, *Or*, hath various significations—It means *otherwise* and *either*—It likewise means *before*—For example, in the language of the Poet.

Or 'ere the Sun decline the western Sky,
'Tis Fate's decree the Victims all must die.

FIGARO — This was the language of Prophesy, and spoken of the Doctor's own Patients.

COUNT — Silence in the Court.

CRYER — Silence in the Court.

DOCTOR — Hence then, I clearly deduce (granting the word to be *Or*) the Defendant doth hereby promise, not only to pay the Plaintiff, but marry her *before* he pays her—Again, the the word *Or* doth sometimes signify *Wherefore,* as another great and learned Poet hath it,

Or how could heav'nly Justice damn us all,
Who ne'er consented to our Father's Fall?

That is *wherefore?* For what reason could heavenly Justice do such an unjust thing? Let us then substitute the adverb *Wherefore,* and the intent and meaning of the Promise will be incontestable; for, after reciting an acknowledgement of the debt, it concludes with the remarkable words, *Or* to marry her, that is, wherefore, for which reason, out of gratitude, for the Favour above done me, *I will marry her.*

FIGARO — Oh most celebrated Doctor? Most poetic Quibbler!

Hark with what florid Impotence he speaks,
And as his Malice prompts, the Puppet squeaks,
Or at the ear of Eve, familiar Toad,
Half froth, half venom, spits himself abroad
In legal Puns, *or* Quibbles, Quirks, *or* Lies,
Or Spite, *or* Taunts, *or* Rhymes, *or* Blasphemies.

What think you we know not Quotations, and Poets, and *Ands,* and *Ors,* and *Whys,* and *Wherefores.*

What Drop *or* Nostrum, can such Plagues remove,
Or which must end me, a Fool's Wrath—*Or* Love?

(Pointing first to the Doctor, and then to Marcelina.) We have neither forgot our Reading nor our Syntax, but can easily translate a dull Knave into a palpable Fool— My Lord,

and Gentlemen, You hear his Sophisms, Poetical, and Conundrums, Grammatical.

COUNT	Yes, yes, we hear.

(*Count and the Counsellors rise and consult together.*)

ANTONIO	I'm glad they have put an end to your prating.
MARCELINA	Their Whisperings and wise Grimaces forebode me no good. That Susan has corrupted the chief Judge, and he is corrupting all the others.
DOCTOR	It looks devilish like it.

(*The Count and Counsellors resume their seats.*)

DOUBLEFEE	Silence in the Court.
CRYER	Silence in the Court.
COUNT	The judgment of the Court is, that since the validity of the promise of Marriage is not well-established, Figaro is permitted to dispose of his Person.
FIGARO	The Day's my own.
MARCELINA	I thought how it would be.
COUNT	But as the Acknowledgement clearly expresses the words, *Which sum I promise to pay the said Marcelina-Jane-Maria-Angelica-Mustachio, or to marry her,* the said Figaro stands condemned to pay the two thousand Piasters to the Plaintiff, or marry her in the course of the Day.
FIGARO	I'm undone!
MARCELINA	I am happy!
COUNT	And I am revenged!
ANTONIO	Thank your noble Lordship! Most humbly thank your noble Lordship!—Ah ha! I'm glad thou art not to marry my Niece! I'll go and tell her the good news! (*Exit.*)
CRYER	Clear the Court.

(*Exeunt Guards, Counsellors, and Vassals.*)

4. The question of the legal validity and implications of a promise of marriage has deep roots. Ever since ancient times, the problem has arisen of how to strike a balance between the principle of the freedom of marriage and the effects that may possibly emanate from prenuptial commitments, especially in the light of the expectations that a proposal might raise in its recipient. Despite the social transformations that history brings and which, in recent years, have led to far-reaching changes in the basis of the law of marriage or other comparable relationships, marriage promises, variously

configured and formalized, continue to be of concern to legislation, doctrine and jurisprudence. Even the institution of betrothal, with or without the exchange of gifts, maintains an undeniable social vitality even today. Significantly, the promise of marriage has been described as an institution that resembles 'certain living fossils in the world of nature, belonging to distant geological eras and yet still present in our own, organisms wonderfully adapted, but curiously also marked by the course of the centuries.'[41]

Through a development traversing centuries, spanning Roman law, the High and Late Middle Ages, the upheaval of the Protestant Reformation and the Council of Trent, and spreading into modern codifications, the law's approach to marriage promises twists and turns in the light of a basic, enduring principle, represented by the traditional inadmissibility of *all forms of compulsion in marriage*.[42] For our present purposes, and given the context in which Beaumarchais' comedy developed, followed by Mozart's opera, it is essentially useful to picture the solution of the problem of the validity and effects of promises of marriage under the old French law, shortly before the codification of 1804. This is the sphere in which Figaro's story was conceived and developed, and its legal implications have, first of all, to be examined.[43]

5. French law under the *Ancien Régime* – before the enactment of the Civil Code (the Napoleonic Code of 1804) – recognized the validity of betrothal agreements (called *fiançailles*), believing that they should be regarded as consensual contracts, valid and efficacious as a result of agreement between both parties. An engagement, in short, was a serious matter. There were no formal requirements, except for evidentiary purposes. An earlier *Ordonnance* of Louis XIII of 26 November 1639 (art. 7) requiring that the

---

41 I. SPADA, 'In tema di sponsali', in *Il Diritto Ecclesiastico*, 1960, II, p. 198. A. MANIACI observes that this 'fossil' belongs to the dawn of legal culture, there being clear references to the institution already in the Bible. (*La promessa di matrimonio*, in *Il Codice Civile. Commentario*, founded by P. Schlesinger and edited by F.D. Busnelli, Milan: Giuffrè, 2004, p. 5).

42 For an exception, see the case of the Netherlands, where, in the seventeenth century, a promise of marriage not fulfilled would be legally enforced, for which see MANIACI, *La promessa*, cit., p. 11.

43 For wider considerations on law in the Mozart-Da Ponte Trilogy see G. MAGRI, *Tra diritto, giustizia e regole sociali. La Trilogia Mozart-Da Ponte*, available on the website www.lawandliterature.org.

fiançailles should be put into writing, in the presence of four relatives, was considered a precept valid only for evidentiary purposes, in case one of the parties tried to disavow the engagement.[44]

Already under the *Ancien Régime*, it was strongly emphasized that an engagement, to be valid, had to take place without any constraint on the parties, without violence, threats, and in full awareness. Robert-Joseph Pothier, in his *Traité du contrat de mariage* (1771), stressed that the demonstration of free and unconditional consent was particularly important in the case of an engagement, since it was a matter that affected the most personal sphere of the individual.[45] The only exception, of course, was to require the consent of the people who, by law, were required to grant it in particular cases (for example, parents in the case of minors). Consent, however, could even be given tacitly, as in the case – observed by Pothier – if a father engaged his daughter in her presence, without the girl objecting or opposing what her father was doing. Consent could also come from a unilateral declaration, accepted by the recipient, provided that the parties were certain and definite. Like all contracts, the effectiveness of the promise of marriage could also be subjected to conditions, as it is in fact in the case of Figaro and Marcellina, where the condition is represented by the non-repayment of a loan of money.

Since it was a contract, if disputes arose, the competence to decide lay with the secular Courts, and not with the Church. Pothier, however, notes that in France, since the subject was closely bound up with that of marriage, the jurisdiction of the ecclesiastical Courts was also recognized. The competence of the latter, however, was limited. The Church could only rule on the validity or otherwise of the marriage vows, but not on a possible award of damages in the event of non-fulfilment. In particular, when the Church passed judgement on the promise, once the validity of the engagement was

---

44 The *Ordonnance* of Louis XIII confirmed, however, a precept of an edict of Henry IV in 1606, as well as the earlier *Ordonnance de Blois* of Henry III, which introduced rules similar to those in France approved by the Council of Trent on clandestine marriages. A later edict of Louis XIV in 1697 confirmed the rule (see. M. GUYOT, *Répertoire universel et raisonné de jurisprudence civile, criminelle, canonique et bénéficiale*, tome III, Paris, 1784, p. 543).

45 R.-J. POTHIER, *Traité du contrat de mariage*, Paris: Chez Debure Père, 1771, parte II, Ch. I, no. 3: 'Ce consentement, qui forme les fiançailles, doit être un consentement parfait, qui n'ait point été extorqué par violence ou par menaces, et qui n'ai pas été surpris.'

verified, the only possible remedy for non-compliance (breach of promise) was the request to the party to perform what had been promised. If the party still refused, coercion was not permitted: in the face of a continued refusal to comply, the engagement had to be declared dissolved and, at most, the party who broke the engagement or refused to get married, would be sentenced by the ecclesiastical Court to perform an act of penitence.[46] The ordinary Courts, however, still had jurisdiction to rule on compensation for damages caused by the breach of promise of marriage. As a rule, this was limited to the costs contracted for the wedding preparations, or possibly the need to compensate the loss of time resulting from the failure to respect the engagement. In exceptional circumstances, the affront suffered, or damage to the honour of the party who suffered the breach, might be taken into account. But the Court was strictly prohibited from offering marriage as an alternative to the obligation for compensation: this was deemed immoral, as contrary to the principle of freedom of wedlock.

From the above, as is intuitive, important consequences arose: the *fiançailles*, under the old French law, were true contracts and, as such, they had to be executed between two parties, both free to decide and capable of freely expressing their consent and will. There could be no engagement without reciprocity: this point was strongly stressed, among others, again by Pothier, who drew a further consequence, reflecting a hypothesis corresponding to what is discussed in *Le nozze di Figaro* and its source in Beaumarchais. According to Pothier, when a document containing a promise of marriage is in the hands of one of the two parties, unless the other party also has an original, the contract is invalid. The solution (which, in my opinion, can hardly be reconciled with the affirmation of the freedom of form in the promise of marriage) is justified on the basis that the party that holds the only original can always refuse to perform the promise by destroying the document, so depriving the consent of reciprocity.

It seems clear that, in terms of the law, the promise of marriage in the hands of **Marcellina** is devoid of any value and that, accordingly, the judg-

---

46   Pothier observes that 'tout le pouvoir du juge d'église se borne à imposer cette pénitence; il ne peut statuer sur les dommages intérêts résultans de l'inexécution des fiançailles: s'il le faisait, il yaurait lieu à l'appel comme d'abus' (R.-J. POTHIER, *Traité*, cit., § 52).

ment delivered by Don Curzio ('either marry her or pay') lacks any legal basis. Even before he discovers marriage is impossible, due to the filial relationship that binds him to Marcellina, Figaro had no obligation to fulfil the promise of marriage for the simple fact that the promise was null.

If it were to be considered a valid promise, it would have been a promise conditional on the non-repayment of the debt. Even in this case, however, Figaro would not have had to marry Marcellina. And perhaps she could have claimed damages on the basis of a breach of promise of marriage, *despite the fulfilment of the condition* (namely, the non-repayment of the debt). The above argument concerns the promise of marriage, but not the loan agreement, which we know was the object of a separate deed from the promise of marriage. Marcellina, therefore, regardless of the fate of the promise, could take legal action to claim payment of the debt. But traces of this point are lost, both in Beaumarchais' play and in Da Ponte's libretto.

5.1. With the codification of French law, and the enactment of the Napoleonic Code in 1804, the debate over the validity and effectiveness of wedding vows revived, in particular with regard to the question of the consequences of a broken engagement. The Revolution had repudiated the institution, considered contrary to the fundamental freedoms of the individual. The Napoleonic Code ignored promises of marriage. It did not mention them, did not recognize them, did not regulate them. The matter seemed to no longer interest the law. Yet promises of marriage continued to exist, and engagements continued to be broken off, just as before. Hence the system had to examine the consequences of the matter, in the changed legislative framework following codification. The solution to the question again required the legal nature of marriage vows to be identified beforehand and, in particular, to establish whether they gave rise to actual contractual obligations (as, for instance, Pothier earlier believed), or whether they amounted to a commitment that was only significant on the moral plane. The difference between the two views lay, of course, in the different social value that French society accorded to the freedom of matrimonial ties. The incursion of the French Revolution, the affirmation of the principle of the irreducibility of marriage to any form of legal compulsion, ended by reviving the question in new terms. Faced with this principle, would it be correct to say that a breach of promise of marriage, even in cases of intent or malice, was totally irrelevant to the law? Obviously, this conclusion was repugnant to a social consciousness that continued to see betrothal and marriage vows as part of the complex process that led two people to be united in marriage.

Now, if promises are held to have a contractual nature, their breach would open the door to the remedies appropriate to contract law, in which damages arising from non-fulfilment are significant. This contractual vision – still supported by some jurists in the early nineteenth century – was definitely set aside by a famous ruling of the Cour de Cassation of 30 May 1838,[47] in which the Court, going well beyond the arguments derived from the tradition,[48] excluded that the promise of marriage could be assimilated to a contractual arrangement, and stated that any promise of marriage was null and void. The judgment observed that marriage is an absolutely free and personal choice, and that promises of marriage conflict with this principle. This means that any commitments made during the engagement would not be binding, but would, at most, constitute mere moral obligations or *engagements de conscience*.

Given that a broken engagement did not constitute a failure to fulfil a contract, there remained the fact that the moral implications of the obligations it entailed could lead to compensation for damages:[49] not for breach of promise, but as a tort. In this case, the damages arise from the general rule contained in art. 1382 of the Civil Code concerning tortious liability (the counterpart of art. 2043 of the Italian Civil Code), by which 'Tout fait quelconque de l'homme, qui cause à autrui un dommage, oblige celui par la faute duquel il est arrivé à le réparer.'

In French law, tortious liability requires three conditions: a fault or intent

---

47   The decision can be readily found online, in one of the various commentaries. For the original source, see Cass. Civ., 20 mai 1838, in S., 1838, I, p. 492.

48   It is interesting to note that the Court of Cassation, in the decision cited in the footnote above, stated that its finding was perfectly aligned with the tradition prior to the Code, hence being inspired by a principle of public policy 'qui, soit avant, soit depuis la promulgation du code civil, a toujours été consacré par la jurisprudence'.

49   Breach of an engagement or a promise of marriage may raise the question of the allocation of the gifts exchanged between the betrothed couple: this aspect is considered in connection with the case of Bellini's *La sonnambula*: see below, Chap. V.

on the part of the author of the offence; damage to the victim of the act; a causal link between the act and the damage. By applying this scheme, even after the 1838 decision, the French Courts often recognized the right to compensation for the benefit of the jilted party. In this context, the Court would establish the existence of guilt when an engagement was 'brutally' broken off, by which was meant that it happened capriciously, without adequate reasons (so the decision of the French Supreme Court, *Cass. Civ.*, 18 January 1973, in *JCP* 1974 II, 17794); or if it happened in the days immediately prior to the marriage (for a case when the marriage was broken off five days before the wedding, see *Cass. Civ.*, 2 July, 1970, in *D.*, 1970, 743), or on the eve of the wedding (*Trib. civ. Seine*, 10 May 1932, in *D.H.*, 1932, 390; *Riom*, 12 June 1934, in *D.H.*, 1934, 549) or, finally, on the wedding day itself (*Trib. Paris* 3 December 1976, in *D.S.*, 1978, 339, with note by Foulon-Piganiol). Hence it is interesting to see how the system arrives at conclusions not far from those which applied prior to codification, but based on different assumptions: firstly, because the promise is no longer considered to be in any way comparable to a contract; secondly, because compensation is, basically, recognized when the engagement is broken off wilfully or due to gross negligence, on the basis of the general rule of tort liability, but negligence or wilful misconduct must be involved. Changing one's mind and deciding not to fulfil a promise of marriage does not, therefore, give rise to any liability, unless it happens in particular ways or circumstances. As for the damages that the Courts recognize, it is usually limited: for example, being enough to cover the price of the bridal gown, the cost incurred in sending out invitations, or to purchase furniture for the home. On the other hand, the disappointed party cannot obtain reparation for damages resulting from failure to obtain benefits or advantages that would have arisen from the marriage, such as those that might result from marrying a wealthy person. Jurisprudence has also recognized, always in the sphere of non-contractual liability, the right to obtain compensation for moral damages: for example, one that may affect the reputation of the 'disappointed' party, or even for injury to the affective sentiments (*Cour de Riom*, 12 June 1934[50]).

---

50   The judgment is published in *D.H.*, 1934, p. 549.

In order to win damages, the plaintiff must provide evidence of a promise of marriage. Although wedding vows are not a contract, the *Cour de Cassation* ruled, after the Code entered into force, that the proof of a promise of marriage had to be in writing, in accordance with art. 1345 of the *Code Civil*. This position – sharply criticized in doctrine – has been abandoned in more recent times, partly in the light of developments that occurred in the rules of assessing biological fatherhood, and was most recently rejected by the Court of Cassation in a judgment of 3 January 1980.[51] In this decision, the Court acknowledged that, to prove the existence of the promise, witnesses or prima facie evidence may be accepted (such as statements that the person in question intended to get married made to friends and family, or the purchase of goods with a view to the couple's life together, etc.).

5.2. The situation in Austria, where the first performance of *Le nozze di Figaro* was held, was less favourable to promises of marriage than under French law during the *Ancien Régime*. At that time the Empire was being changed by Joseph II's reforms, including those concerning the institution of marriage and its discipline. Emperor Joseph II's reforms clearly tended to secularize the institution, whose discipline fell under the State, with freedom from the Church. In this context, the institution of betrothal itself was repealed, with the law ascribing no value to it. So even in Austria, Figaro would not have had to worry about the promise of marriage to Marcellina; and for those who attended the opening night of Mozart's opera, and applied the schemes of the legislation then in force in Vienna, the story of the promise would have seemed absurd, or at least quite singular.

The same approach was maintained in Austria even after codification. While, as we have seen, the Napoleonic Code ignored the promise of marriage, the Austrian Code of 1811 (*Allgemeines bürgerliches Gesetzbuch– ABGB*), reflects the heritage of Josephine legislation and expressly excludes the binding nature of such promises, or of any clauses and penalties contained in them, by limiting the consequences of breach of promise to payment of damages.

---

51 The text of the decision can be found at the following address: http://www.legifrance.gouv.fr/affichJuriJudi.do?idTexte=JURITEXT000007004781.

§ 45 of the Austrian Code[52] provides that 'Betrothal, or a promise to marry, in whatever circumstance or conditions made or accepted, produces no legal obligation either to contract marriage or fulfil what has been stipulated if the promise is not fulfilled.'[53] Of particular interest, though, especially in the context of the story of *Le nozze di Figaro*, is the express reference to what may be agreed for breach of promise: any commitment made to that effect is without any effect. It is evident, in short, that under Austrian law, Marcellina would have had no right to marry Figaro, or even to demand repayment of the loan, *on the basis of a promise of marriage made to her*. However, from both Beaumarchais and Da Ponte, we learn that the debt does not arise from the promise, but from a distinct contract, which therefore remains valid and does not come under the rigid provisions of § 45 *ABGB*.

5.3. The Italian Civil Code of 1942 also chose to expressly formulate the principle of freedom of marriage and the inefficacy of matrimonial agreements. Art. 79, and art. 53 of the Civil Code – similarly to the previous 1865 Civil Code of the Kingdom of Italy – states that, 'The promise of marriage does not compel to contract marriage or to execute whatever was agreed in the event of non-compliance.' This is a provision that applies to any 'promise of marriage', irrespective of its form, of whether it has been given a solemn character or not, and whether expressed explicitly or tacitly. The rule is also intended to apply to a promise of marriage granted unilaterally, without reciprocity, as in the case of that given by Figaro to Marcellina. Obviously, this approach might concretely raise the issue of whether certain situations can actually be considered as a 'betrothal' (leaving aside, for the moment, the so-called 'solemn' promises, governed by art. 81, for which see below). Of course this also raises the question of proof, requiring to be resolved case by case.

The rule laid down in art. 79 c.c. must be read in the light of the general

---

52   Throughout this volume, the translation of the articles of the *ABGB* in English is an unofficial courtesy translation by the Author.

53   *ABGB*, § 45: 'Ein Eheverlöbnis oder ein vorläufiges Versprechen, sich zu eheliche, unter was für Umständen oder bedingungen es gegeben oder erhalten worden, sieht keine rechtliche Verbindlichkeit nach sich, weder zur Schließung der Ehe selbst, noch zur Leistung desjenigen, was auf den Fall des Rücktrittes bedungen worden ist.'

principle of matrimonial freedom, which, in the Italian system, is numbered among the inviolable rights of the individual, and is therefore also covered by Constitutional guarantees. In law, the application of this measure has repeatedly led to the affirmation of the absolute freedom of the individual to contract marriage or not: the unilateral dissolution of a promise of marriage reflects a fundamental human right, protected by articles 2 and 29 of the Italian Constitution. Art. 79 is the expression of a principle of public policy, endowed with the strong guarantee that, under Italian law, is given to the protection of the rights of the person.[54] This protection is strengthened by its recognition at the supranational level. Art. 16 of the Universal Declaration of Human Rights, of 10 December 1948, provides, among other things, that 'Marriage shall be entered into only with the free and full consent of the intending spouses.' Art. 12 of the European Convention for the Protection of Human Rights and Fundamental Freedoms (ECHR), which the European Union, in addition to the individual Member States, may embrace since 2009, provides that, 'Men and women of marriageable age have the right to marry and to found a family, according to the national laws governing the exercise of this right.' Art. 23, par. 2 of the International Covenant on Civil and Political Rights, adopted in New York on 16 December 1966 and ratified in Italy by law no. 881 of 25 December 1977 provides, likewise, that 'The right of men and women of marriageable age to marry and to found a family shall be recognized.' Art. 9 of the Charter of Fundamental Rights of the European Union (Nice, 7 December 2000 and the Treaty of Lisbon, December 1, 2009) has the same legal status as the European Union treaties. It stipulates that, 'The right to marry and the right to found a family shall be guaranteed in accordance with the national laws governing the exercise of these rights.' In short, art. 79 of the Civil Code, and the principle of the non-binding nature of the marriage vows, is embedded in a context of Constitutional and supranational status, which tends in the same direction: to ensure the freedom of marriage agreements.[55] The right to marry and the right to found a family shall be

---

54   For further references on this point, and for confirmation of the analogous doctrinal position, A. MANIACI, *La promessa*, cit., pp. 19 ff.

55   For interesting reflections on the specific scope of the protection stemming from the provisions

guaranteed in accordance with the national laws governing the exercise of these rights.

Art. 79 of the Civil Code stipulates the nullity not only of promises of marriage themselves, but also of any guarantees given to reinforce the fulfilment of the promise, as – to cite an extreme case, the subject of a judicial ruling – the issuance of promissory notes to ensure compliance with the promise of marriage.[56] In the same way, the undertaking to compensate the jilted party, in case of breach of promise of marriage, beyond the limits established by law and, in particular by art. 81 of the Civil Code, is null. The damages that can be recovered in this case are determined strictly by law and cannot, therefore, be agreed preventively by the parties. Likewise illegal are all conditions (whether suspensive or resolutive) that have the purpose of affecting freedom of marriage. In this respect, then, under Italian current law, Marcellina could not rely on the failure to repay the debt as a condition to force Figaro to fulfil the wedding promise.

If the effects of the promise of marriage can clearly be derived from art. 79 of the Civil Code, the law – in seeking to achieve that delicate balance between the freedom of matrimonial ties and protecting the trust of the other party – recognizes that, in the event of breach of promise, there may be some consequences. We will return to this question in greater detail in relation to Vincenzo Bellini's *La sonnambula*, but here it is at least necessary to remember two general points. First, art. 80 of the Civil Code states that, if the marriage is not contracted, the promisor 'may require the return of gifts made due to promise of marriage'. But the application 'cannot be made after one year from the day on which the refusal to celebrate the marriage was received or the date of the death of one of the promisors'. In *Le nozze di Figaro* it does not appear that Figaro and/or Marcellina have donated anything in relation to the wedding promise and, therefore, this rule is not relevant.

Secondly, the broken promise may open the prospect (as we saw in the case

---

cited, see 'La tutela dei diritti fondamentali nelle Carte costituzionali, ovvero del difficile dialogo tra Carte e Corti', in *Diritto di famiglia e delle persone*, 2013, pp. 173 ff.; G. DI ROSA, 'Commento sub Art. 79', in *Commentario del codice civile*, edited by E. Gabrielli, Turin: UTET, 2010, pp. 23 ff.

56   See App. Napoli, 13 February 1974, in *Giur. It.*, 1976, I, 2, pp. 168 pp., with note by F. FINOCCHIARO, 'Nullità della caparra come negozio accessorio alla promessa di matrimonio'.

of French law) to the obligation of providing compensation. The matter of compensation for damages resulting from the breaking of an engagement is regulated in the Italian system more analytically and precisely than in French jurisprudence or the Austrian *ABGB*. Art. 81 of the Code expressly provides that a promise of marriage made mutually by public act or private agreement by a person of age or a minor permitted to marry under art. 84, or resulting from the request for a reading of the banns, obliges the promisor who unjustifiably breaks off an engagement it to pay compensation for the damages caused to the other party for any expenditure made and the obligations contracted as a result of that promise. The damages payable must be within the limits of expenditure and obligations corresponding to the financial means of the parties. Compensation to the same degree is payable by the party who by a culpable action has given just cause for rejection to the other. The application cannot be made after one year from the day of refusal to celebrate the marriage.

Among the greatest differences from the other systems analysed, the first is that damages are recoverable only in relation to promises to marry that meet certain requirements: they must be 'mutual promises' written in the manner laid down (namely by public deed or private agreement). In this respect, the scope of the rule sanctioned in art. 81 of the Civil Code is narrower than that of art. 79. This is not surprising, since the law, precisely because of the general principle of freedom of the marriage bond, limits the scope for compensation for breach of promise to *certain cases*.

Secondly, in Italy, the rule of limitations of compensation to only those expenses and obligations contracted because of the promise is – unlike the other systems analysed – specified by law and expressly limited as to the *object* (only expenditures incurred and obligations contracted because of the promise) and as to *amount*: the compensation is recognized within the limits that correspond to the economic and social status of the parties. Such a precise definition of the damage compensable clearly appears as the result of the need to find a balance – to be honest, not an entirely consistent one – between the principle of matrimonial freedom, on the one hand, and responsibility for damages on the other.[57]

---

[57]   On this point, G. DI ROSA, 'Commento sub Art. 81', in *Commentario del codice civile*, cit., p. 35,

Art. 81 of the Civil Code also introduces a rule which provides expressly for the recoverability of damages caused by those who, by their own fault, have given just cause for withdrawal by the other party. Finally, a further distinction concerns the application of a maximum period of one year from the refusal to celebrate the marriage to bring the action: this term is not present in either the French or the Austrian system.

6. In conclusion, all the systems under review would lead to the decision of the non-enforceability of the wedding vows by Marcellina. So there is no way she could have compelled Figaro to marry her. Marcellina might, however, be able to secure damages (within the time limits variously identified), with limited protection – under the Italian Civil Code currently in force – of one year after the breaking of the promise of marriage. Breaking the promise to marry Marcellina could not itself give rise to an obligation for Figaro to repay the debt, as this question would have to be examined solely on the basis of the loan agreement. Application for repayment would have involved a legal action, based on the specific contract. The court case described by Beaumarchais, and replicated by Da Ponte, therefore has no basis in law, either according to the original sources, or those in force in the place of the first performance of the literary source, or its operatic version. It is, ultimately, pure invention, the functional representation of the limitations and flaws of justice, ridiculed through the figure of incompetent, or at least far from impartial, judges and rapacious lawyers, in keeping with a panoply of characters and figures already common in the repertoire of eighteenth-century comic theatre. There remains, however, the question whether the representation of these events reflects Beaumarchais' urge to engage in real social criticism, or merely satisfies an overriding concern for theatrical effect. Or perhaps, finally, it is a reflection of his many personal struggles with the Courts of the Kingdom of France, experienced on many occasions during his adventurous life.[58]

---

which also illustrates the difficulties that follow identification of the exact nature of the responsibility arising from art. 81 (non-contractual liability; pre-contractual liability; liability *ex lege*).

58   The most complete biography of Beaumarchais at present is the one by M. LEVER *Pierre-Augustin Caron de Beaumarchais*, 3 vols., Paris: Fayard, 1999-2004.

III

Così fan tutte
(Wolfgang Amadeus Mozart – Lorenzo Da Ponte)

Civil marriage and the Josephine reforms

1. The last work in the trilogy by Da Ponte-Mozart is a masterpiece that still (in fact, especially) today never fails to disclose prospects of different interpretations and keys to new readings, while eluding all attempts at classification.[59] Apart from combining elements from different sources, the work is a kind of kaleidoscope of the human soul. It constantly returns shifting and ever-changing visual images depending on the light that strikes it. *Così fan tutte* is a mock-comic opera: in reality it is a fierce work. It lays bare the weaknesses and vulnerability of the human, as very few other works have done.

The story concerns an exchange of couples: Dorabella and Fiordiligi are two sisters ('ladies' in the stage directions) of Ferrara. Their lovers are respectively Ferrando and Guglielmo, who appear to be madly in love. The two young men are assured of the loyalty of their fiancées, but Don Alfonso, an elderly, cynical philosopher, challenges their certainty. He persuades them to accept a bet, to show them the fallacy of their ideal of fidelity, and so the true nature of the female soul or, rather, of the human soul in general.[60] The two young men agree: the wager requires them to pretend to go to war and return soon after, disguised as Albanians; in this guise, each woos the other's fiancée.

---

59   The history of the reception of *Così fan tutte* is complex, and characterized, at least throughout the nineteenth century, by deep suspicion for a text that was not easy to classify. The criticisms focused above all on the libretto, which was actually judged by some as 'silly', and saved 'only' by Mozart's music. On this topic, also for further references, S. KUNZE, *Il teatro di Mozart*, Venice: Marsilio, 2006, pp. 528 ff.

60   This aspect is aptly stressed by A. ARBLASTER, *Viva la libertà! Politics in Opera*, London: Verso Books, 1997, p. 32.

The facts speak for themselves. After some initial resistance, and the eventful finale of Act I, Dorabella and Fiordiligi yield. Despina (their artful and disenchanted maid) helps Don Alfonso by encouraging the two ladies to indulge the advances of the two bogus Albanians, and they finally agree to marry them. A fake wedding is staged, in the middle of which the two lovers reappear suddenly, exposing the women's infidelity. The opera closes with the reconciliation of the original couples, but it is not exactly a happy ending. The couples patch things up, but their harmony skates over the surface. What happened in those few hours reveals unsuspected depths and leaves an enduring sense of disquiet.

In this extraordinarily ambiguous interplay of mockery, steeped in irony,[61] the culmination of the intrigue devised by Don Alfonso is the sham marriage between the pairs of exchanged lovers. The whole plot unfolds in a single day.[62] It takes only a few hours to shatter the illusions about fidelity and love initially harboured by the characters. In the wedding scene, Despina, disguised as a notary, simulates a civil wedding between the lovers disguised as Albanian nobles and the two sisters, before the veil of deception falls and the truth is revealed.

2. The staging of the sham marriage takes place at the very end of the opera (at the end of Act II) and many things emerge as we retrace its course. It is first of all Don Alfonso who announces the arrival of Despina as the notary to celebrate the marriage (Act II.17):[63]

---

61   For this point C. FERTONANI, 'Ironia, citazioni e richiami in "Così fan tutte"', in *Teatro alla Scala. Così fan tutte. Stagione 2013-2014*, Milan: Edizioni del Teatro alla Scala, 2014, pp. 89 ff. Paolo Gallarati speaks of an opera with a 'sphinx-like face on which bitterness and smiles alternate', in P. GALLARATI, *L'Europa del melodramma. Da Calzabigi a Rossini*, Alessandria: Edizioni dall'Orso, 1999, p. 233.

62   Without invoking the Aristotelian unities, the fact that the whole chain of events begins and is resolved in a single day is brought out by Fiordiligi's words (Act II.10): 'Ma non so come mai | si può cangiar in un sol giorno un core.' ('But I do not know how | in one day a heart may change') To which Dorabella replies: 'Che domanda ridicola! siam donne!' ('What a ridiculous question! We are women!'). This point, together with others that may seem implausible (the fact, for example, that the two girls fail to recognise their lovers disguised as Albanians) has at times elicited unfavourable judgments about *Così fan tutte* in terms of structure and dramatic cogency: on these positions, and for a review of them, see P. KIVY, *Osmin's Rage. Philosophical Reflections on Opera, Drama and Text*, Princeton: Princeton University Press, 1988.

63   The passages from the libretto are taken from that of the Viennese premiere (*COSÌ FAN*

DON ALFONSO	Miei signori, tutto è fatto.
	Col contratto nuzïale
	il notaio è sulle scale
	e *isso fatto* qui verrà.
GLI AMANTI	Bravo, bravo! Passi subito.
DON ALFONSO	Vo a chiamarlo: eccolo qua.[64]

Despina enters, disguised as the 'notary Beccavivi'. She reads out the marriage contract, to the appreciation of all present, who are in a hurry to get the matter over, under the pressure of an obvious erotic drive that now has to find an outlet:

DESPINA	Augurandovi ogni bene
	il notaio Beccavivi
	coll'usata a voi sen viene
	notariale dignità!
	E il contratto stipulato
	colle regole ordinarie
	nelle forme giudiziarie,
	pria tossendo, poi sedendo,
	clara voce leggerà.
TUTTI	Bravo, bravo in verità!
DESPINA	Per contratto da me fatto,
	si congiunge in matrimonio
	Fiordiligi con Sempronio,
	e con Tizio Dorabella
	sua legittima sorella,
	quelle, dame ferraresi,
	questi, nobili albanesi.
	E, per dote e contradote...

TUTTE | O SIA | LA SCUOLA | DEGLI AMANTI| Dramma giocoso | in due atti | da rappresentarsi | nel Teatro di Corte l'anno 1790, Vienna, Presso la Società Tipografica); for a modern edition, see G. GRONDA, P. FABBRI (edited by), *Libretti d'opera italiani dal Seicento al Novecento*, Milan: Mondadori, 1997, pp. 885-959, based on the same work. The English text is taken from the translation by W. WEAVER available on the following website: http://www.murashev.com/opera.
64   DON ALFONSO Ladies and gentlemen, all is done; the notary is on the stairs with the marriage contract and will come here *ipso facto* / FIORDILIGI, DORABELLA, FERRANDO, GUGLIELMO Bravo! Bravo! Let him come in at once / DON ALFONSO I'll go to call him. Here he is.

GLI AMANTI	Cose note, cose note, vi crediamo, ci fidiamo: soscriviam, date pur qua. *(Solamente le due donne sottoscrivono)*
DESPINA E DON ALFONSO	Bravi, bravi in verità! *(La carta resta in man di Don Alfonso. Si sente gran suono di tamburo e canto)*[65]

It should be noted that the scene of the fake marriage contains certain details that prove decisive for the course of the following scene, which closes the work. In particular, the contract is signed only by the two women and the document remains in Don Alfonso's hands. The first trick is of paramount importance, to bring out the betrayal by the two women. The second device is functional to the moment when Don Alfonso displays the text of the contract to the two men, apparently unaware of what had occurred in their absence. Immediately after signing the marriage contract a 'great sound of drumming and singing' is heard: it is none other than the same military band that, a few hours earlier, had come to fetch Guglielmo and Ferrando and carried them off to the battlefield. That sound, which we hear, with memorable dramatic effectiveness, even before the reappearance of the two young men in their normal clothes, immediately casts a shadow over the happy wedding party. The military band immediately plays as an alarm signal, but though the reason is clearly recognizable, all the characters initially exclaim, using a typical self-defence mechanism, 'What a din! What song is this!'

The storyline is plunging headlong towards conclusions that no one can yet foresee. Don Alfonso goes impassively to the window to see what is happening. Continuing the charade, he announces the arrival of 'your

---

65 DESPINA Wishing you every good thing, the notary Beccavivi comes to you with his usual notarial dignity! And the contract, drawn up with the ordinary rules in the legal forms, first coughing, then sitting down, he will read out loud and clear / FIORDILIGI, DORABELLA, FERRANDO, GUGLIELMO, DON ALFONSO Bravo! Bravo! Really! / DESPINA According to the contract drawn by me, united in matrimony are Fiordiligi with Sempronio, and with Tizio, Dorabella, her legitimate sister. The former are Ferrarese ladies; the latter, Albanian noblemen, and as dowry and counter-dowry... / FIORDILIGI, DORABELLA, FERRANDO, GUGLIELMO These things are known! We believe you, we trust you, we'll sign. Hand it over / DESPINA, DON ALFONSO Bravo! Bravo! Really! *(The contract remains in Don Alfonso's hand. A loud sound of a drum is heard.)*

spouses'. Havoc breaks loose: the nuptial party immediately breaks up, the table laid for the wedding breakfast is swept away, and the 'musicians leave'.[66] With great excitement Fiodiligi and Dorabella lead their two fake Albanian spouses into an adjoining room. Don Alfonso takes the notary (Despina) into another room. The two young men then secretly leave their room; Don Alfonso returns to the stage, alone with the two girls, and seeks to reassure them, but unsuccessfully:

DON ALFONSO	Rasserenatevi...
LE DONNE	Numi, consiglio!
DON ALFONSO	Ritranquillatevi...
LE DONNE	*(quasi frenetiche)*
	Chi dal periglio
	ci salverà?
DON ALFONSO	In me fidatevi,
	ben tutto andrà.
LE DONNE	Mille barbari pensieri
	tormentando il cor mi vanno,
	se discoprono l'inganno,
	ah di noi che mai sarà?[67]

In the next scene (Act II.18), which closes the opera, the following events take place:
– Ferrando and Guglielmo enter, no longer disguised as Albanians, but dressed as soldiers. They find the sisters stunned;
– The servants bring in a trunk and Guglielmo asks it to be put in the room where he has hidden the Notary-Despina;
– Despina leaves the room and reveals her disguise;
– Don Alfonso drops the marriage contract signed by the two women on the floor, and calls on the two young men to pick up the document;

---

66   The libretto bears the following stage direction: 'I servi portano via la tavola, e i suonatori partono in furia.' ('The servants take the table away, and the players leave in haste').
67   DON ALFONSO Be reassured! / FIORDILIGI, DORABELLA Gods, counsel! / DON ALFONSO Calm yourselves! / FIORDILIGI, DORABELLA Who will save us from danger? Who? / DON ALFONSO Trust in me. All will go well! / FIORDILIGI, DORABELLA A thousand barbarous thoughts are tormenting my heart; if they discover the deceit, whatever will become of us!

– Ferrando and Guglielmo, seemingly horrified, read the marriage contract and make as if to enter the first room (the one from which they had secretly come out). The two girls stop them, but Don Alfonso calls out to let them in;[68]

– Ferrando and Guglielmo 'enter the room for a moment, then emerge without hats, cloaks and moustaches, but in their fake garments. They ridicule the women and Despina'.

So the story moves towards its bitter-sweet ending, filled with references to the 'true' significance of the opera. It is up to Don Alfonso to break the tension and reveal to the two girls the deception he had practised on them:

DON ALFONSO   V'ingannai, ma fu l'inganno
                  disinganno ai vostri amanti,
                  che più saggi omai saranno,
                  che faran quel ch'io vorrò.
                  (Li unisce e li fa abbracciare)
                  Qua le destre, siete sposi:
                  abbracciatevi e tacete.
                  Tutti quattro ora ridete,
                  ch'io già risi e riderò.[69]

The comedy closes with the famous sextet:

TUTTI   Fortunato l'uom che prende
                  ogni cosa pel buon verso,
                  e tra i casi e le vicende
                  da ragion guidar si fa.
                  Quel che suole altrui far piangere
                  fia per lui cagion di riso,
                  e del mondo in mezzo i turbini
                  bella calma troverà.[70]

---

68 Referring to Don Alfonso's conduct, the libretto has the stage direction 'Accenna la camera dov'erano entrati prima gli amanti.' ('He points to the room where the lovers entered').

69 DON ALFONSO I deceived you, but my deceit was undeceiving for your lovers, who will be wiser now and will do what I wish. Give me your hands: you're bride and groom. Embrace and be silent. Now all four of you laugh; I've laughed already and will laugh.

70 ALL Fortunate is the man who takes everything for the best, and in all events and trials allows

2. In the structure of *Così fan tutte*, the fake marriage is fundamental: it is the culmination of all Don Alfonso's machinations. Marriage, as ceremony, ritual, is the ideal moment which concentrates the unveiling of the plot, with the unexpected reappearance of the two lovers before the sisters' astonished eyes. So it is not a simple masquerade (just as the whole story concocted is neither a masquerade nor a futile occasion), but an essential element of the plan rationally designed by Don Alfonso to demonstrate his theorem: fidelity in love is an invention, and the erotic drives – the 'chemistry of the passions', so admirably depicted in Goethe's *Elective Affinities* – will finally gain the upper hand. What unites the two couples exchanged is a strong physical attraction. However convincing the disguise of the two 'Albanians', it is legitimate to suppose that this turns on drives that already existed before the start of the story invented by Don Alfonso and elicits them. In this respect, whether the disguise was plausible or implausible, and the women could recognize their lovers in the guise of the two Albanians or not – a point in the libretto that has been repeatedly criticized – appears a false problem.

3. *Così fan tutte* premiered at the Burgtheater in Vienna on 26 January 1790. Unlike the other two works that comprise the Mozart-Da Ponte trilogy, the story of its composition is little known, if not completely unknown. Apart from uncertainty over how the commission originated, the literary sources of the libretto are not clearly identifiable, though for some years now, many references which Da Ponte seems to have used have been traced.[71] In his memoirs, Da Ponte only made a brief reference to the subject, referring to one of the arias written for his partner, the soprano Adriana Ferrarese, who starred in the role of Fiordiligi on the opening night in Vienna. He never explicitly stated whether it was his own original creation or adapted from earlier sources, as was his custom.[72]

---

himself to be led by reason. What usually makes others weep is, for him, a source of laughter, and in the midst of the world's whirlwinds he will find a lovely calm.

71   V.I. WOODFIELD, *Mozart's 'Così fan tutte': A Compositional History*, Woodbridge: The Boydell Press, 2008, pp. 99 ff. According to some commentators, the 'silence' surrounding the opera's composition was due in part to the moral condemnation the text has aroused since its appearance: see in particular, A. STEPTOE, 'The Sources of "Così fan tutte". A Reappraisal', in *Music & Letters*, LXII (1981), pp. 281-294.

72   L. DA PONTE, *Le memorie*, Villasanta: Istituto Editoriale Italiano, 1933, p. 192. Obviously, the

On the day following the premiere, in Vienna there were rumours that the libretto was based on a true story that had happened a few years earlier in Trieste, and Joseph II himself had suggested the subject to Mozart and Da Ponte.[73] The conjectures about the source of the story have not yet been fully assessed.[74] The question I would like to raise here concerns the scene briefly described in the previous section, concerning the particular way Da Ponte represents the marriage between the fake Albanians and the two young women. In particular, the scene takes place in the presence of a (fake) notary, and therefore represents a civil, and not a religious, marriage. Then, unlike what is found in other texts (see, for example, Bellini's *La sonnambula* below), there is no mention of a religious marriage (which generally followed the signing of the marriage contract).

Da Ponte-Mozart's choice deserves notice, firstly on the plane of dramatic effectiveness. A *mise en scène* with a priest and all the trappings of a religious ceremony would perhaps have had a far more spectacular effect. Instead of dressing up as a notary, Despina might have disguised herself as a priest, and the scene could have been enriched with altar boys, chaplains and priests, with religious music interspersed at various points as the ceremony unfolded. So why a notary? A first answer to this question would depend on the real meaning that was intended for the scene – or rather that the audience at the first performance might have attributed to it. If it is supposed that what takes place in the scene is simply an engagement, then the question does not arise.

However, this reading of the scene in Act II.17 does not seem entirely correct, and this is because Despina as notary uses words that seem to make it clear that what is being celebrated is a true marriage:

---

reference is to *Le nozze di Figaro* and *Don Giovanni*, but it also applies to almost all the other works by Da Ponte, as noted by A. STEPTOE, *The Sources*, cit., P. 282.

73   See C. OSBORNE, *Guida alle opere liriche di Mozart*, Florence: Sansoni, 1991, pp. 353 ff.

74   See, among the conjectures that have aroused most interest, that by E.H. GOMBRICH, '"Così fan tutte" (Procris included)', in *Journal of the Warburg and Courtauld Institutes*, XVII/3-4, 1954, pp. 372-374, who saw the text as derived from Ovid; and that by A. STEPTOE, *The Sources*, cit., p. 283, who identifies it in the so-called wager theme, common in the European literary canon (including Boccaccio and Shakespeare): namely, the theme of a bridegroom's wager on the fidelity of his wife. Steptoe, however, finds it plausible to assume that Da Ponte derived the theme also from *La novela del curioso impertinente* by Cervantes, interpolated in *Don Quixote*.

DESPINA　　　　　　　　Per contratto da me fatto,
　　　　　　　　　　　si congiunge in matrimonio
　　　　　　　　　　　Fiordiligi con Sempronio,
　　　　　　　　　　　e con Tizio Dorabella
　　　　　　　　　　　sua legittima sorella,
　　　　　　　　　　　quelle, dame ferraresi,
　　　　　　　　　　　questi, nobili albanesi.
　　　　　　　　　　　E, per dote e contradote...[75]

We then have to imagine the possible reasons why Da Ponte chose to represent a false civil marriage and not a religious one, naturally assuming that this choice is the one that in the context of the first performance in Vienna would, or might, have seemed the most natural. Given that on this point no records of the period are available, and the two authors have not left any relevant information, we are essentially left having to formulate conjectures. One possible reason for the staging of a civil and not religious marriage might lie in what has been named by some as a convention of eighteenth-century comic opera. This theory suggests it would not have been appropriate, or even permitted, to represent a prelate or religious ceremony on the stage of the Burgtheater in Vienna.[76] This is plausible, though it requires corroboration. Certainly, the representation of a religious ceremony at the theatre, in comic terms like the wedding scene in Così fan tutte would have run the risk of creating embarrassment and misunderstandings: even in the Vienna of the Josephine reforms, a notary might be mocked, but not a priest.

An alternative or supplementary reading of the matter could, however, start from the particular historical context in which the first performance of Così fan tutte took place, in this case with the development of the legal framework of marriage in Vienna in 1790. The broad project of state reforms devised by the Emperor Joseph II was one of the distinctive features of his reign (1764-1790), among the most representative of enlightened absolut-

---

75　DESPINA According to the contract drawn by me, united in matrimony are Fiordiligi with Sempronio, and with Tizio, Dorabella, her legitimate sister. The former are Ferrarese ladies; the latter, Albanian noblemen, and as dowry and counter-dowry...

76　A. DI PROFIO, 'Un sujet à la mode. "Il matrimonio segreto" et ses emprunts,' in L'Avant-Scène-Opéra, 175 (1997), pp. 92-101.

ism in eighteenth-century Europe. Joseph II's reforms, particularly of the law, include numerous measures that were, to say the least, courageous, even for an 'enlightened' monarch of the day: the *Zivil Gerichtsordnung of 1781*, a particularly advanced Civil Code for the period; the continuation, with the *Josephinisches Gesetzbuch*, of the Maria Theresa's *Codex* project; and the project for a penal code, strongly marked by Enlightenment principles, handed down to history as *Josephinisches Strafgesetz* (1787), which never went into force because of the emperor's death. Also related to Joseph II's reforms was the 1788 *Kriminalgerichtsordnung (KGO)*, one of the earliest examples of a code of 'modern' criminal procedure, modelled on principles that favoured the accused in ways that were very advanced for the day.

Joseph II's reforms also encroached markedly on the activities of the Church. Numerous measures were intended to emphasise the secularity of the State and to claim sectors for the State that had traditionally been reserved, at least in part, to the Church. In particular, during his reign he suppressed monasteries and curbed the contemplative and religious orders. He promoted the foundation of State institutions to educate the clergy and public colleges. In 1781, the 'Patent of Toleration' (*Toleranzpatent*) enshrined the abolition of religious discrimination against Protestants and Jews.[77]

This was the context for the reform of marriage law, entrusted to the *Ehepatent* of 1783. It clearly defined marriage as a contract; private law and jurisdiction of the State applied to all marriages in the territories of the Empire.[78] In accordance with the *Toleranzpatent*, which accorded to non-Catholic confessions some, albeit limited, freedom of worship, the

---

77 For a summary see the reconstruction by E. WANGERMANN, *The Austrian Achievement. 1700-1800*, London: Thames and Hudson, 1973, especially pp. 107 ff.

78 'Die Ehe an sich selbst, als ein bürgerlicher Vertrag (Contract) betrachtet, wie auch die aus diesem Vertrage herfließenden, und den Vertrag errichtenden gegen einander zustehenden bürgerlichen Gerechtsame und Verbindlichkeiten erhalten ihre Wesenheit, Kraft und Bestimmung ganz und allein von den landesfürstlichen Gesetzen; die Entscheidung der hierüber entstehenden Streitigkeiten gehört also für die landesfürstlichen Gerichtsstellen' (The passage is taken from *Das Ehepatent vom 16. Jenner 1783, mit allen hinnach ergangenen dahin gehörigen allerhöchsten Verordnungen. In einem planmässigen Zusammenhange zum allgemeinen Gebrauche*, Graz: Im Verlage bei Kaspar Zaunrith, 1788, pp. 9-10).

Ehepatent applied not only to marriages between Catholics, but also those between Protestants, as well as unions between Protestants and Catholics. Although the *Ehepatent* assigned competence on the subject of marriage exclusively to the State, Joseph II's measure did not establish compulsory civil marriage. The *Ehepatent* allowed Catholic marriages to continue to apply the canon law. Despite this, the *Ehepatent* was an important step in the development of civil marriage, because it was the first measure in Europe (hence preceeding the reforms introduced in France in the revolutionary period) to sanction the separation between civil marriage and the religious sacrament. The rules of the *Ehepatent* would be transferred a few years later into the body of the Austrian Civil Code of 1811 (*ABGB*). The fact that the French Civil Code had meanwhile introduced the institution of compulsory civil marriage on the basis of the Revolutionary legislation[79] did not, therefore, make a substantial impact on the forms of Austrian law in this area.

Albeit in the context of such a highly articulated and innovative period of reforms, in the latter part of Joseph II's reign, the climate that had characterised the decade 1780–1790 had begun to change. Austria's financial difficulties, problems encountered in Hungary, the Netherlands and – most important of all – the signals coming from revolutionary France that threatened the very survival of the great European monarchies, had led to a rapid change in the atmosphere that had been breathed until then in Vienna.

At the Burgtheater in Vienna, on the evening of 26 January 1790, Joseph II was not present. The emperor died shortly after, on 20 February, following the Ottoman war. However, if he had been able to see the last, prodigious product of the collaboration between Lorenzo Da Ponte and Mozart, he might have grasped and appreciated the care shown by the two Authors in representing marriage celebrated by a notary, instead of a priest.

---

79   In France, civil marriage was introduced with the Constitution of 1791, and especially with the later law of September 20, 1792, which also introduced divorce.

IV

Il matrimonio segreto

(Domenico Cimarosa – Giovanni Bertati)

A secret marriage

1. *Il matrimonio segreto* is one of the most successful works in the repertoire of *opera buffa*, and one of the most widely represented of all time from its first performance, on 7 February 1792 at the Burgtheater in Vienna, where it had a triumphant reception. The two authors, Giovanni Bertati (Martellago, 1735 – Venice, 1815) and Domenico Cimarosa (Aversa, 1749 – Venice, 1801) were at that time at the height of their career. Bertati had been working in Venice for many years, a leading librettist at the Teatro San Moisè, and had taken the place of the court poet in Vienna held until 1791 by Lorenzo Da Ponte. Cimarosa was a highly celebrated composer: over the years his operas had gained a wide following, well beyond Naples, where he began his career. He was a cosmopolitan composer: his travels and the pan-European dissemination of his works make him one of the most representative figures of the typical model of 'itinerant composer' in eighteenth-century Europe, as well as definitely one of the most representative of the genre of *opera buffa* at the time.

Bertati and Cimarosa had met in Vienna during Cimarosa's stay in 1791, on returning from his trip to St. Petersburg, where he had been invited in 1787 by Catherine II of Russia. The broad popularity enjoyed by *opera buffa* in Vienna at that time was in itself an incentive to produce works of good compositional workmanship, adapted to the public taste.

The structure of his work is faithful to the canons of the genre: the subject matter, the distribution of the parts, the structure and style of *recitativo secco*, the construction of the acts, intended to climax with vibrant finales, are all elements that unequivocally place *Il matrimonio segreto* in the mainstream of eighteenth-century *opera buffa*. Though it was composed after the Da Ponte-Mozart trilogy (which deviates from tradition in several important respects), Cimarosa's masterpiece adhered much more closely to the schemes of what, rightly, has often been described as the veritable industry of comic opera in the eighteenth century: a style, a form, clearly recognisable, and basically rigid, albeit with considerable margins of adaptability depending on the demands of the public and patrons.[80]

Bertati's libretto was inspired first of all by *The Clandestine Marriage*, a play by George Colman and David Garrick, performed for the first time at Drury Lane, London, in 1766. In its turn highly successful, two French translations were also in circulation: a first version by Marie-Jeanne de Laboras (aka Madame Riccoboni), published in 1768, and a second by the Baroness De Vasse, dating from 1784. The two translations had already served as the basis for texts intended for musical theatre. Madame Riccoboni herself had turned it into a libretto for an *opéra comique* titled *Sophie ou Le mariage caché*, set to music by Joseph Kohaut (1738–1777), and produced at the Comédie-Italienne in 1768. In 1790 it was the turn of *Le mariage clandestin*, to a libretto by Joseph-Alexandre Ségur (1756–1805) with music by François Devienne (1759–1803), also performed in Paris, at the Théâtre de Montansier.[81]

The deep sources of Bertati's libretto, however, are more complex: the subject was, first of all, itself a *topos* of stage plays and operas.[82] In addition, the text has roots also in other artistic forms, in particular the famous series of paintings entitled *Marriage à la Mode* by William Hogarth,[83] painted in

---

80   See in particular, for a comparison between *Il matrimonio segreto* and the operas of the Da Ponte-Mozart trilogy, in the context of the genre's development in the late eighteenth century, P. GALLARATI, *Musica e maschera. Il libretto italiano del Settecento*, Turin: EDT, 1984, pp. 162 pp., to which add R. IOVINO, *Tutto nel mondo è burla! Appunti per una storia dell'opera comica italiana*, Genoa: De Ferrari Editore, 1998, pp. 55 ff.

81   The Théâtre de Montansier, sited close to the north-west wing of the Palais-Royal, opened in 1784, as the Théâtre des Beaujolais, and was originally used for presenting puppet shows. In 1790 it was taken over by Mme de Montansier and was given her name: the house was expanded and used to perform French works, and Italian operas translated into French. After various vicissitudes, in 1852 the theatre was given the name of the Théâtre du Palais-Royal, and it is now active as a repertory theatre.

82   See in this respect A. DI PROFIO, 'Un sujet à la mode. "Il matrimonio segreto" et ses emprunts', in *L'Avant-Scène Opéra*, 175 (1997), pp. 93 ff. To offer a few brief references, the theme of the secret marriage was dealt with by, for instance, Leonardo Leo, with *Il matrimonio nascosto* (1727); Gioacchino Rossini, with *La scala di seta* (1812); Pasquale Anfossi, with *Il matrimonio per inganno* (1779); Gaetano Donizetti, with *L'ajo nell'imbarazzo* (1824).

83   On relations between Hogarth and *The Clandestine Marriage*, and in particular on the

about 1743. The latter 'source' is, in fact, expressly mentioned by David Garrick – he was a friend of Hogarth's, who painted several portraits of him – in the Prologue to *The Clandestine Marriage*.

Il matrimonio segreto was staged at the Burgtheater in Vienna on 7 February 1792, the day of the signing of the Austrian alliance with Prussia against the French revolutionary government. Tradition relates it was a great success, though with some variations. The predominant version has it that the Emperor Leopold II, after attending the performance and offering the artists a hearty meal, actually wished the work to be repeated. An alternative version, judged unreliable, states that Leopold II was unable to attend the premiere of the work, but that the episode of the encore occurred at the second performance.[84] Regardless of which is the correct version, there is no doubt that the work was a resounding success, and has remained in the repertoire of opera houses worldwide ever since.

2. As we have seen, the story of *Il matrimonio segreto* is highly characteristic of the *opera buffa* genre, with characters who reflect its stereotypes. Geronimo, a wealthy merchant in Bologna, has two marriageable daughters, Elisetta and Carolina, and he clearly hopes to find noble, wealthy husbands for them. But Paolino, a young man who works in Geronimo's shop, and Carolina have already been secretly married for two months, and are in great perplexity over how to break the news to him. Paolino seeks to persuade Count Robinson, his friend, to propose marriage to Elisetta, so hoping to make the discovery of his marriage to Carolina more palatable. But as soon as Count Robinson sees Carolina, he falls in love with her and has no wish to marry Elisetta. He even offers to give up half the dowry promised by Geronimo if he gives her permission to marry Carolina instead of Elisetta. In her turn, Fidalma, a wealthy widow and Geronimo's sister, is in love with Paolino. Faced with a plot that becomes ever more tangled, Carolina and Paolino decide to flee, but the attempt fails: their plan is discov-

---

different approaches adopted by Garrick and Colman, see F. DEGRADA, *Dal 'Marriage à la mode' al 'Matrimonio segreto': genesi di un tema drammatico nel Settecento*, in *Il palazzo incantato. Studi sulla tradizione del melodramma dal Barocco al Romanticismo*, Fiesole: Discanto Edizioni, 1979, vol. II, pp. 19 ff.

84   R. IOVINO, *Domenico Cimarosa operista napoletano*, Milan: Camunia, 1992, pp. 150 ff.

ered, but in the end, everything ends happily. Hence the secret marriage is both the basis of the action and a trigger to all the other events, finally leading to the denouement, when the union between the two young people is revealed.

3. The opera opens in a saloon in Geronimo's house. On stage are Carolina and Paolino, and the delicate question of their secret relationship is immediately recounted. But Carolina wishes to free herself from the burden of their secret and reveal all to her father:[85]

PAOLINO	Cara, non dubitar,
	mostrati pur serena.
	Presto avrà fin la pena
	che va a turbarti il cor.
CAROLINA	Caro, mi fai sperar.
	Mi mostrerò più lieta.
	Ma sposa tua segreta
	nasconderò il dolor.
PAOLINO	Forse ne sei pentita?
CAROLINA	No, sposo mio, mia vita.
PAOLINO	Dunque perché non mostri
	il tuo primier contento?
CAROLINA	Perché vieppiù pavento
	quello che può arrivar.
	Se m'ami, deh! t'affretta
	l'arcano a palesar.
PAOLINO	Sì, sposa mia diletta,
	ti voglio contentar.
(a 2)	Se amor si gode in pace
	non v'è maggior contento;
	ma non v'è egual tormento
	se ognor s'ha da tremar.[86]

---

85   The text represents the libretto of the first performance: *IL MATRIMONIO SEGRETO* | *dramma giocoso* | *per musica* | *in due atti* | *da Rappresentarsi* | *nel Imperial Teatro di Corte,* | *l'anno 1792.* | *In Vienna.* The English translation is taken from the edition of *Il Matrimonio Segreto*, Cetra Opera Series, 1950, adapted to the version of the libretto used as a reference in the text.
86   PAOLINO Beloved! Beloved, have no doubts. Look calm once again. Soon the grief will end that so disturbs your heart / CAROLINA Beloved! Beloved, you give me hope. I'll try to look

Carolina trusts, perhaps somewhat too confidently, to her father's common sense, and tries to persuade Paolino to reveal their relationship:

CAROLINA	Lusinga, no, non c'è. La nostra unione
	lungo tempo segreta
	non può restar. E se si scopre avanti
	di quel che ha da scoprirsi,
	quale schiamazzo in casa,
	qual bisbiglio di fuori, o sposo amato!
	Né un trasporto d'amor sarà scusato.
PAOLINO	Dici il ver; vedo tutto.
CAROLINA	Il padre mio
	è un uom rigido è ver; ma finalmente
	è d'un ottimo cor. In sulle furie
	monterà al primo istante
	che saper gliel farai;
	ma dopo qualche dì certa poi sono,
	che pien d'amor ci accorderà il perdono.
PAOLINO	Sì; questa sicurezza
	la sola fu che a stringere c'indusse
	il nodo clandestino.
	Ma senti: oggi la sorte
	occasion propizia a me presenta
	di svelare il segreto
	con meno di timore.[87]

The revelation of the secret marriage (now two months old) takes place in

---

happier: but still, as your wife in secret, I'll be hiding my sorrow / PAOLINO Perhaps you regret it? / CAROLINA No, my husband, my life / PAOLINO Why then don't you appear as happy as you were before? / CAROLINA Because I'm even more afraid of what may now occur. Ah, if you love me, make haste to reveal the secret / PAOLINO, Yes, my darling bride, I want to comfort you / BOTH If love is savored peacefully, there is no greater joy; but there's no torment worse than being in constant fear.

87   CAROLINA Have no illusions. Our union cannot remain a segret much longer / And if what needs to be discovered is discovered too early, what a row in the house, what gossips outside, oh my beloved husband! / PAOLINO You're right; I see it all / CAROLINA My father is a stern man, it's true, but basically he has a heart of gold. He'll fly into a rage, at first, when you tell him the news; but after a day or so, I'm certain, full of love, he'll grant us his pardon. / PAOLINO Yes, this certainty was the only thing that led us to tie the clandestine knot; but listen: today Fate offers me a lucky chance to reveal our secret with less fearfulness.

the last scene of Act II, shortly before the final reconciliation that closes the opera:

CAROLINA, PAOLINO	Ah, signore, ai vostri piedi a implorar veniam pietà!
CONTE, CAROLINA	Oh che vedo! resto estatico!
ELISETTA, FIDALMA	Quest'è un'altra novità.
CAROLINA	Cosa s'intende?
FIDALMA	Cosa vuol dire?
CAROLINA, PAOLINO	Vi supplichiamo di compatire, che d'amor presi... son già due mesi... il matrimonio fra noi seguì.
CAROLINA, FIDALMA	Il matrimonio!
CAROLINA, PAOLINO	Signori sì.
GERONIMO	Ah, disgraziati! Qual tradimento! Andate, o tristi: pietà non sento. Più non son padre: vi son nemico. Io vi discaccio, vi maledico, raminghi andate lontan da me.
CAROLINA, PAOLINO	Pietà, perdono. Colpa è d'amore.
FIDALMA	Pietà non s'abbia d'un traditore.
CONTE, ELISETTA	Deh! Vi calmate. Deh! Vi placate, rimedio al fatto più già non c'è.
FIDALMA	Sian discacciati. Sian castigati. Azion sì nera punir si de'.
CONTE	Ascoltate un uom di mondo, qui il gridar non fa alcun frutto: ma prudenza vuol che tutto anzi s'abbia d'aggiustar. Il mio amor per Carolina m'interessa a suo favore. Perdonate a lor di core. Ch'io Elisetta vo a sposar.
LISETTA	M'interesso anch'io signore, deh! Lasciatevi placar.
CAROLINA	*(a Fidalma)* Voi che dite?
FIDALMA	Voi che fate?
CONTE, PAOLINO, CAROLINA, ELISETTA	*(tutti inginocchiati)* Perdonate, perdonate.

FIDALMA	Già che il caso è disperato,
	ci dobbiamo contentar.
GERONIMO	Bricconacci! Furfantacci...!
	Son offeso, son sdegnato...
	Ma... vi voglio perdonar.
PAOLINO, CAROLINA,	Che trasporto d'allegrezza!
CONTE, ELISETTA	Che contento! Che dolcezza!
	Io mi sento giubilar!
TUTTI	Oh che gioia! Oh che piacere!
	Già contenti tutti siamo!
	Queste nozze noi vogliamo
	con gran pompa celebrar.
	Che si chiamino i parenti,
	che s'invitino gli amici,
	che vi siano gli strumenti.
	che si suoni, che si canti.
	Tutti quanti han da brillar.[88]

4. The question of the forms and modes of celebrating marriage has marked the changes, ever since classical law, in the institution of marriage, affecting customs, the ecclesiastical discipline of marriage and State legislation. In its lengthy evolution, which it is impossible to retrace here, it

---

88 CAROLINA, PAOLINO Ah! Sir, we fall at your feet to beg for mercy! / COUNT, CAROLINA Oh what do I see! I remain ecstatic / ELISETTA, FIDALMA This is another piece of news / CAROLINA What do we mean? / FIDALMA What does she mean? / CAROLINA, PAOLINO We beg you to have compassion; since, driven by or love, two months ago we were married / FIDALMA, GERONIMO Married! / CAROLINA, PAOLINO Yes, sir! /GERONIMO Ah! Wretches! What a betrayal! Go, villains, I feel no pity! Father no more, I'm your enemy. I cast you out, and curse you; go and roam far from me! / CAROLINA, PAOLINO Pity, pardon. Love is to be blamed. FIDALMA No pity for a traitor / COUNT, ELISABETTA Pray, calm down! Pray, be pacified, there is no remedy to the facts / FIDALMA Be they chased. Be they punished. Such a dark action must be punished / COUNT Listen to a man of the world. Shouting now will do no good; and prudence suggests that everything should, in fact, be set to rights. My love for Carolina interests me in her behalf: forgive her with all your heart. I'm going to marry Elisetta / ELISETTA I'll take her part too, sir, pray be pacified / CAROLINA (to Fidalma) What do you say? FIDALMA What do you do? COUNT, PAOLINO, CAROLINA, ELISETTA (all kneeling) Pardon, pardon, since the case is desperate, we must be content / GERONIMO Rascals, scoundrels! I am offended, I am angry, but I'm willing to forgive you / PAOLINO, CAROLINA, COUNT, ELISETTA Oh what joy! What delight! What sweetness! I feel happy! /ALL Oh what joy! What delight! Now all of us are happy! We want to celebrate the wedding with great pomp. Le the relatives be summoned, let our friend be invited, let there be music and singing, everyone must sparkle.

also dealt with, and gradually settled, the question of the so-called secret marriage, meaning the marriage celebrated without the observance of any particular forms, or without any public act.[89] The problem of clandestine marriage is, actually, a fascinating subject, as it is affects issues concerning both the right of the person and fundamental human rights, as well as those affecting religion and the State. If marriage is the most natural expression, the culmination of the feelings that bring two people together in a stable relationship, this institution is at the centre of issues that lie at the crossroads of faith, religions, public interests, economic matters, the safeguarding of the 'weak' party (the children, typically), and many other matters.

In classical law, the *Decretum Gratiani* (c. 1140–1142) indicates marriage as an institution that belongs to natural law. The *ius connubii*, or marriage as a place of the natural manifestation of the affection of man, clearly emerges as the foundation of the canonical matrimonial system. As the expression of a natural right, authority respected it, defended it, and sought to address the many practical problems that inevitably arose (the capacity to contract marriage; the validity of the tie; conditions and limits on the right to contract a new marriage in the event of invalidity of the first, and so forth). With regard, in particular, to the form of the celebration of marriage, already in the Middle Ages the Church had introduced a compulsory liturgical form, in order to endow marriage with legal certainty and oppose the celebration of clandestine weddings, whose existence was difficult to prove: the form provided for the veiling of the woman, the exchange of rings, the joining of hands and celebration by a priest. It should, however, be noted that failure to comply with these forms did not invalidate marriage. From this arose a delicate balance between the opposed requirements: on the one hand, to recognise the freedom of the bond, and, on the other, to ensure a certain discipline.[90] This situation gave rise to a number of rules, which revealed a rift between the substantial reality, and the formal rules, by which, if there was a clandestine marriage, even if not proven, it continued to be

---

89   The following considerations are restricted to the Catholic discipline, since the Protestant tradition, ever since the Reformation, has followed different lines of development, although opposition to secret marriages is also a regular feature of the Reformed systems.

90   P. SCOPONI, *I divieti matrimoniali in casi singoli*, Rome: Editrice Pontificia Università Gregoriana, 2011, pp. 28 ff.

valid. If one of the spouses were to remarry, he or she would be committing adultery. However, in the case of a marriage of doubtful existence, the subsequent marriage, celebrated according to the required forms, would take precedence in external relations.

The question of clandestine marriages was long debated at the Council of Trent (1545–1563).[91] The settlement of this point by the Council confirmed the validity of clandestine marriages celebrated hitherto, and rejected the need for parental consent for the marriage to be valid, reducing the scope of the requirements previously set out. At the same time, the Council introduced the so-called 'canonical form' of marriage: consent to marriage must therefore be expressed in the presence of the two spouses (*de praesenti*) before the parish priest and in the presence of two witnesses. Under the new rules, before a marriage was contracted, the curate of the parish in which each of the two being married would reside, also had to read the banns three times in church during High Mass, on three consecutive feast days.[92] After the reading of the banns, if there was no legitimate opposition, the marriage could take place in the presence of the parish priest with two or three witnesses and, as proof of the ceremony, the compilation of the marriage deed was required. Establishing a form *ad validationem* made it possible to introduce a clearer discipline of the clandestine marriages, the disclosure of which had not been discouraged under the previous system. Starting from the Council of Trent (in the countries that accepted the rules it established) matrimonial contracts held without a public ceremony, corroborated by a formal deed recording its celebration, were null.

During the Council, discussion of clandestine marriages was, however, very intense, and many of the council fathers (about fifty in all) opposed the approval of the final measure: the so-called *Tametsi Decree* of 11 November 1563, which would regulate religious marriages until the adoption

---

91 See generally, on the issue of secret marriages both before and after the Council, D. LOMBARDI, *Storia del matrimonio. Dal Medioevo ad oggi*, Bologna: Il Mulino, 2008, pp. 38 ff. For some related issues, see the volume by various authors edited by S. SEIDEL MENCHI and D. QUAGLIONI, *Trasgressioni. Seduzione, concubinato, adulterio, bigamia (XIV-XVIII secolo)*, Bologna: Il Mulino, 2004.

92 The institution of the reading of banns appears to have originated in Carolingian France. On this point see A. RENDA, 'Commento sub art. 93', in *Commentario del codice civile*, edited by E. Gabrielli, Turin: UTET, 2010, p. 108.

of the 1917 Code of Canon Law. Even after the Council, in any case, there were rumours that in the Church strongly stressed the natural right of every man to marry. This is what Leo XIII did, for example, in 1880 in the encyclical *Arcanum Divinae sapientae*, with regard to the exclusive authority of the Church in the wedding of the baptized;[93] a position that was then reaffirmed in 1891 in the encyclical *Rerum Novarum*, in which the pope stated that the matrimony was a natural right, which could not be restricted by the laws of man, nor denied to anyone.

In the 1917 Code of Canon Law, canon 1035 stated that 'Omnes possunt matrimonium contrahere, qui iure non prohibentur.' The point where this provision is placed, at the beginning of the section on impediments to marriage, rather diminished its general application, even if it provided a significant confirmation in canon law of the principle that marriage is a fundamental human right. In the 1983 Code, the same canon (now 1058) was inserted among the preliminaries to the whole legislation about marriage, so placing it in the nature of a general principle; the right to marriage is, therefore, among the basic grounds of the marriage law of the Catholic Church.

The story of *Il matrimonio segreto* thus touches on a classic theme of marriage law and, in general, of family law.

5. In Vienna, at the time of the first performance of *Il matrimonio segreto* (1792), Joseph II's reforms had caused an upheaval in the institution of marriage,[94] largely because of the priority accorded to civil marriage as an institution independent of religious marriage, being subject only to State jurisdiction. The reform of marriage introduced into Austria an analytical form of publication of the banns, which had to be given out three times at the parish church of the future spouses.[95] These were measures

---

93   The text of the encyclical can be found at the following address: http://w2.vatican.va/content/leo-xiii/it/encyclicals/documents/hf_l-xiii_enc_10021880_arcanum.html.

94   See, in this volume, the chapter devoted to *Così fan tutte*.

95   'Jede Ehe soll, bevor sie geschlossen wird, in der Pfarrkirche der Brautleute an einem Sonntage oder gebothenen Feyertage zur Zeit der Predigt, oder wenn sonst das Volk hinlänglich versammelt ist, öffentlich aufgebothen (verkündiget), bey dieser Verkündigung beyde Brautleute mit Tauf- und Geschlechtsnahmen, Geburtsort und Stand deutlich bezeichnet, und dieses Aufgeboth (Verkündigung) noch an zwey folgenden Sonn- oder Feyertagen wiederhohlet werden,

intended to combat clandestine marriages, clearly compatible with, and fully justified by, the wider process of 'nationalization' that marriage was undergoing as a result of the reforms introduced by Joseph II. The theme of Cimarosa's opera was therefore topical, in addition to having long been a subject of debate.

6. In England and Scotland – which provided the frame of reference of the primary source for *Il matrimonio segreto* – the question of clandestine marriages had been the subject of specific attention and widespread debate in the very years preceding the composition of *The Clandestine Marriage*. The question, in particular, had undergone significant developments after a court case, which broke out in Scotland in 1746, came before the House of Lords and caused a considerable stir. Traditionally, the regulation of marriage, in both England and in Scotland, did not provide specific forms for the wedding: the only thing necessary for a marriage to be recognized in law was the free consent of the parties, provided that the age of the engaged couple was at least 12 for males and 14 for females. It was also required that marriages should take place between persons not related by close family ties, and the couple should not be bound by a previous marriage. The validity of the marriage required neither the consent of parents nor the presence of witnesses. In order to prove the existence of a marriage it was possible to proceed by a declaration of both parties (*verba de praesenti*), or by a promise of marriage which was followed by sexual intercourse (*verba de futuro*). Given the difficulties which often arose, in order to clearly establish these facts, the practice had led to the recognition of less secure evidence, such as correspondence sent by the man to the woman, in which the former addressed the latter as his 'wife', or the circumstance of the couple's cohabitation, or their being socially recognized, in their circle, as husband and wife.[96]

---

damit ein jeder ein ihm etwa bekantes, dieser Ehe im Wege stehendes Hinderniß gehörig zuentdecken, Zeit gewinne': *Das Ehepatent vom 16. Jenner 1783, mit allen hinnach ergangenen dahin gehörigen allerhöchsten Verordnungen. In einem planmässigen Zusammenhange zum allgemeinen Gebrauche*, Graz: Im Verlage bei Kaspar Zaunrith, 1788, § 31, pp. 9-10.

96   For a highly articulated reconstruction, R.B. OUTHWAITE, *Clandestine Marriage in England*, 1500-1850, Rio Grande: Hambledon Press, 1995.

In the first half of the eighteenth century, the phenomenon of irregular marriages grew significantly, both in England and Scotland. Moreover, even if the presence of a minister of the church was not necessary to ensure the validity of the marriage, the betrothed couple often still preferred some ceremony to be performed and to receive a 'certificate of marriage', so that actual professional wedding celebrators began to spread, who made their living by officiating weddings around the country. These people were often far from scrupulous; for example, they frequently failed to ascertain the identity of the spouses, or to examine their marital status. Their certificates, therefore, were not considered decisive in the Courts when evidence was weighed, but were taken into consideration in the formation of judgment.

On the social level, there is no evidence that irregularly married couples were considered somehow less 'regular' than those who had married according to law. Difficulties naturally arose, however, when one party claimed to be married to another, and the latter denied it. Another case was that of the recurring appearance of a unexpected, self-styled, 'second' wife, after the death of a husband, when the question of inheritance was raised. The case that triggered the reform of English law arose in 1746. Captain John Campbell of Carrick, who died at the Battle of Fontenoy, had lived with his wife Jean Campbell – whom he had married, in 1725, with an irregular marriage – for about twenty years. After his death, one Magdalen Cochran made application to be recognized as the beneficiary of the Captain's pension, claiming to be the wife of the deceased. The legal dispute lasted until January 1753, when it was decided definitively by the House of Lords: Magdalen Cochran's claims were rejected, but the Lords pressed for a law to be passed against clandestine marriages. The judgment was therefore followed by legislative action: in 1753 Parliament approved the Marriage Act, 'For the Better Preventing of Clandestine Marriage'. The measure, banning illegal marriages in England, would become better known by the name of Lord Hardwicke's Marriage Act (named after Philip Yorke, first Earl of Hardwicke, who proposed the law in Parliament).[97]

---

97   See L. LENEMAN, 'The Scottish Case That Led to Hardwicke's Marriage Act', in *Law and History Review*, vol. 17, no. 1, 1999, pp. 161 and ff.

The law, however, was applied in England but not in Scotland, where the question was long debated.

The Marriage Act provided that, with regard to marriages entered into from 1754 on, the only legal form of marriage would be one preceded by the reading of banns and performed in a parish church (except in the case of a special license). However, marriages concluded according to Scottish law would continue to be recognised in England. Even seventy years after the Marriage Act, the Scottish Courts refused to apply the principles of the law, on the basis of a rather curious point: it was argued that the fact of getting married in one parish would not prevent one of the spouses from showing up, some time later, in another parish, and so celebrating a second wedding. In short, the Marriage Act, according to the Scots, was quite unnecessary, and so could not be applied. What should have been established was a national system of civil marriage registration, but this was introduced only in 1836 by the Births and Deaths Registration Act.

7. In current legislation in Italy, marriage is governed by arts. 93-101 of the Civil Code, as amended most recently by Presidential Decree (D.P.R.) of 3 November 2000, no. 396. The celebration of marriage, under art. 93, has to be preceded by the publication by the registry officer; the publication has to be requested by both spouses or by a person who has received a special commission from them (art. 96 of the Civil Code). Since D.P.R. no. 396/2000 repealed art. 95 c.c. (which established that the deed of publication must be affixed to the door of the town hall for at least eight days, including two successive Sundays), the duration of the publication is now deduced from art. 99 c.c., according to which a marriage cannot be celebrated before the fourth day after the publication itself. This general rule is subject to two exceptions: the Court may, for good cause, shorten the period or, 'for the gravest reasons', actually authorize omission of the publication. In the latter case, the bride and groom, in front of the clerk of Court, declare under their sole responsibility that none of the impediments established by the law (see articles 85 to 89 c.c.) exists in the case of their marriage. The clerk of Court must precede the declaration by a reading of these articles and advise the registrants of the importance of their attestation and the severity of the possible consequences.

In addition to this, by force of art. 101 c.c., in a case of imminent danger to the life of one of the spouses, the registrar of the locality may proceed with the marriage without prior publication (and without consent, if this is required), provided that the couple swear that there are no impediments that are not susceptible to dispensation. In the deed of marriage, the registrar declares how imminent danger of life was ascertained.[98]

Note that, if these details are omitted from the publications, the marriage that is celebrated by the registrar is simply *irregular*, but is not invalid. From this it follows that a marriage, in which there are no discernible causes of invalidity (such as kinship; incapacity for marriage, etc.), which has however not respected the need for publication, is subject to an irregularity which gives rise to administrative sanctions on the spouses and/or registrar who nonetheless celebrated it,[99] but it remains, in fact, valid and efficacious.[100]

Without prejudice to what has been said with of the formalities that precede the celebration of marriage, art. 130 c.c. provides that 'no one may claim the title of spouse and the effects of marriage, without presenting the marriage certificate excerpted from the civil registries. Possession of the marriage state, though affirmed by both spouses, does not dispense them from presenting the marriage certificate.' This is a measure that, in the preceding perspective, gives absolute importance, for the existence of the marriage bond itself, to the marriage certificate, as drawn up and transcribed in the public registers. Hence this measure definitively deprived of recognition, under the private law, all marriages not contracted in the way and with the formalities required by law, and it constituted the full expression of the long evolution of the marriage laws, in the context which provides the setting of the story recounted in Cimarosa's masterpiece.

---

98   It should be noted, also in relation to other sections of this volume (see in particular the analysis of *La sonnambula*), that the application to the registrar for publication by an engaged couple amounts to a formal promise of marriage, with the consequences that follow from this under article 81 c.c.

99   The omission of publication may be a legitimate reason for the registrar to refuse to celebrate a marriage (see. A. RENDA, 'Commento sub art. 94', in *Commentario del codice civile*, cit., p. 118).

100   On this subject, see, *ex multis*, A. RENDA, *Commento sub Art. 93*, in *ibid.*, pp. 118 ff., with references also to the Court of Cassation in the sense indicated in the text.

8. The opera by Bertati and Cimarosa, in dealing with a case of clandestine marriage, is a typical example of a libretto that dealt very effectively with an issue deeply rooted in the social fabric of its time, but which today leaves us almost indifferent, in the wake of the disruptive social changes that have relegated the theme of the secret marriage to outworn antiquities. Carolina and Paolino's secret marriage is not just a clever device by the librettist and composer to create a comic opera which parades the stock characters and situations of the genre. It also mirrors a phenomenon that, for a long time, kept legislators and the Church hard at work seeking practical solutions.

Today clandestine marriages have been replaced by other problems and other sensitivities: cohabitation, unmarried couples, civil unions, new techniques and methods of procreation, atypical families. And the law, in all this, labours to catch up with civil society, in an attempt, in the name of order and the common good, to pigeonhole the most intimate human passions in their protean manifestations.

V

La sonnambula

(Vincenzo Bellini – Felice Romani)

Engagement rings and wedding vows

1. Is it reasonable to demand the return of a wedding ring, when an engagement is broken off? In Vincenzo Bellini's *La sonnambula*, the setting of a libretto by Felice Romani, Elvino signs a marriage contract bestowing all his goods on Amina, including the ring that belonged to his mother. Shortly after, Elvino is convinced Amina has been unfaithful to him, having surprised her, before their religious marriage, in Count Rodolfo's bedroom. Unaware that she suffers from somnambulism, he takes back the ring in a fit of rage. In the end, the mistake is cleared up, but the nub of the question that emerges in the opera lies in these simple facts: a contract of marriage, the gift of the wedding ring, and the revocation of the gift. Is the revocation, performed in a fit of rage and jealousy, legitimate? And what were the relevant laws at the time of when the opera was composed? And what significance did the system ascribe, in general, to pre-nuptial or wedding gifts? And, today, what are the rules that are followed, and how do they differ from those in force at that time?

2. The libretto has complex origins. Its most direct precursor is a ballet-pantomime in three acts, *La somnambule, ou L'arrivée d'un nouveau seigneur*, with music by Ferdinand Hérold, performed for the first time at the Académie Royale de Musique in Paris on 19 September 1827.[101] The plot

---

101   On the sources of *La sonnambula* and, in particular, the ballet from which it is taken, se J.-C. YON, 'L'Arrivée d'un nouveau seigneur, ou "La somnambule" avant Bellini', in *L'Avant-Scène Opéra*, no. 178, 1997, pp. 56 ff.; Q. PRINCIPE, *'La sonnambula' di Vincenzo Bellini. Invito all'opera*, Milan: Mursia, 1991, pp. 35 ff., which also presents an interesting analysis of the text, identifying five archetypes in it: the person defamed; the character in a disturbed psychic state; incest avoided; the 'new master'; the woman jealous of a younger rival. Principe also gives the Italian translation

of the ballet was devised by two famous French authors of the early nineteenth century: Eugène Scribe (for the scenario) and Jean-Pierre Aumer (collaboration on the scenario and the choreography). Hérold's ballet, however, was not an entirely original work, since it was derived in its turn[102] from another text, La somnambule, also written by Scribe, in partnership with Germain Delavigne, and performed with considerable success at the Théâtre de Vaudeville[103] a few years before, on 6 December 1819.[104] Apart from these antecedents, recent studies have shown that Romani's libretto was influenced by a work following Hérold's pantomime-ballet, notably La Villageoise somnambule, ou Les deux fiancées: a comédie-vaudeville by François-Victor-Armand d'Artois (also called Dartois) and Jean-Henri Dupin, performed on 15 October 1827 at the Théâtre des Variétés in Paris.[105] This comédie is, in effect, a reworking of Hérold's ballet and has many similarities with the Romani text, so lending plausibility to the conjectural existence of this third source of the libretto, which Romani would have been inspired by. For instance, on a point relevant to our text, i.e. the fact that the ring, which he gives to Amina, belonged to Elvino's mother does not appear in the traditional sources cited but in the comédie-vaudeville, which is slightly later than Hérold's pantomime ballet.

The opera by Bellini and Romani, set in a mountainous region of Switzer-

---

of the ballet script, of particular interest in identifying points of contact and deviation between the source and Romani's libretto.

102   In the vaudeville, for instance, the protagonist is a somnambulist who marries the character corresponding, in La sonnambula, to Count Rodolfo. In general, however, the whole situation of the vaudeville – a bourgeois setting – is remote from that of the 1827 ballet, set in Provence; see, in this respect, the clarifications by P. BRUNEL, Vincenzo Bellini, Paris: Fayard, 1981, p. 213.

103   On the genre of vaudeville, see the classic work by E. LINTILHAC, Histoire générale du théâtre en France. La comédie, de la Révolution au Second empire, 5 vols., Paris: Flammarion, 1904-1911, and, most recently, A. VIALA, Histoire du théâtre, Paris: PUF, 2014.

104   A curious point, in the highly successful vaudeville, is that at one point the protagonist engages in a contredanse from the opera Nina, ou la Folle par amour, a comédie mêlée d'ariettes by Marsollier and Dalyrac, composed in 1786, which in its turn inspired the celebrated Nina by Paisiello (1787), as well as a ballet by Milon and Persuis, performed at the Paris Opéra in 1813. The disorder suffered by the character of Nina has more than a few points of contact with the psychology of the various sleepwalking women populating the opera house, including the protagonist of Bellini's opera: on this topic see, for further reference, Q. PRINCIPE, La Sonnambula, cit., pp. 36 ff.

105   See S. MORABITO, 'Contesti della Sonnambula di Bellini', in Bollettino di Studi Belliniani, I, 2015, pp. 38 ff.

land,[106] opens with a festive scene.[107] Amina and Elvino are getting married, and the whole village is celebrating (except the inn-keeper Lisa who is in love with Elvino and burns with jealousy). The ritual uniting the two lovers includes, as is fitting, the signing of a marriage contract, drafted by a notary, followed the next day by the religious wedding to sanctify the union of the two young people.

The notary's arrival is announced by the peasant choir ('Viene il Notaro', Act I.3). Amina, seeing the notary, impatiently awaits the groom's arrival (Act I.4):[108]

AMINA	Il notaro? Ed Elvino non è presente ancor?
NOTARO	Di pochi passi io lo precedo, o Amina: in capo al bosco io lo mirai da lungi.
CORO	Eccolo.
AMINA	Caro Elvino! alfin tu giungi![109]

On arriving, Elvino announces the drafting of the contract and establishes the exchange of gifts between the parties (Act I.5). Amina does not have much to give to Elvino, except her love ('il cor soltanto'):

ELVINO	Siate voi tutti, o amici, al contratto presenti.
NOTARO	*(si dispone a stendere il contratto)*

---

106   The stage direction at the beginning of the libretto reads: 'The scene is set in a village in Switzerland'.

107   These are the stage directions in the libretto: 'As the curtain rises, we hear from afar pastoral sounds and distant voices shouting: "Viva Amina." It is the villagers coming to celebrate her wedding'.

108   The passages in this chapter are taken from the libretto of the 1831 premiere in Milan (*LA |SONNAMBULA | Melodramma | di | Felice Romani. | Da rappresentarsi | nel Teatro Carcano | la quaresima del 1831. | Milano | per Antonio Fontana | M.DCCC.XXXI*), compared with the critical edition of the score (V. BELLINI, *La sonnambula. Melodramma in due atti di Felice Romani*, edited by A. Roccatagliati and L. Zoppelli, Milan: Ricordi, 2009). The English translation is taken from the one available on http://www.murashev.com.

109   AMINA The notary? And Elvino isn't here yet? /NOTARY He's right behind me. From above the woods I saw him in the distance / CHORUS Here he is. AMINA Dear Elvino, here at last!

	Elvin, che rechi
	alla tua sposa in dono?
ELVINO	I miei poderi,
	la mia casa, il mio nome,
	Ogni bene di cui son possessore.
NOTARO	E Amina?...
AMINA	Il cor soltanto.
ELVINO	Ah! tutto è il core!

(Mentre la madre – di Amina, n.d.a. – sottoscrive, e con essa i testimoni, Elvino presenta l'anello ad Amina)[110]

Having sealed the contract and, in this case, the donation (note, signed also by the bride's mother and witnesses),[111] Elvino hands the wedding ring to Amina, accompanying the gesture with a famous cavatina, in which we immediately grasp everything that makes Bellini's style's so instantly recognizable. To a simple, sweet melody, with long, soaring notes, Elvino expresses his complete devotion to his beloved. The melodic line, set off by the entrance of the wind instruments, thus accompanies his gift of the ring:

ELVINO

Prendi: l'anel ti dono
che un dì recava all'ara
l'alma beata e cara
che arride al nostro amor.
Sacro ti sia tal dono
come fu sacro a lei;
sia de' tuoi voti e miei
fido custode ognor.[112]

---

110   ELVINO And now, friends, all of you, witness our betrothal contract. *(The notary prepares everything for the signatures.)* / NOTARY Elvino, what gifts do you bring to your wife? ELVINO My farms, my house, my name, everything that I possess / NOTARY And Amina?... / AMINA Only my heart / ELVINO Ah! the heart is everything! *(As Amina's mother and the witnesses sign, Elvino presents a ring to Amina.)*

111   Light is shed on the solemn character of the situation accompanying the gift by P. BRUNEL, *Vincenzo Bellini*, cit., p. 219. Note the accuracy sometimes found in librettos when dealing with legal details, though not strictly necessary, except for the evident desire to ensure the performance is faithful to the facts.

112   ELVINO Here, receive this ring that the beloved spirit who smiled upon our love wore at the alter. Let this gift be sacred as it was to her let it always be witness of our trust.

Note that Elvino clearly states the ring's origin: it is the engagement ring that belonged to his mother, and he now gives it to Amina. This fact, which serves on the dramatic plane to make the moment of betrothal even more solemn, and colours the ring with a special significance, has, however, precise effects on the plane of law, because for Elvino the ring is an heirloom ('family jewel'), to which French jurisprudence specifically attributed a special value, as we shall see.

After Elvino's aria, there follows a beautiful duet between the two lovers: a moment of joy and tenderness, following their formal union, reprising the central motif of the cavatina. After which Elvino himself is the first to emphasize they are now united ('Sposi or noi siamo'), and, shortly after, he recalls that the religious marriage ceremony will be celebrated the day after:

ELVINO	Sposi or noi siamo.
AMINA	Sposi!...
	Oh tenera parola!
ELVINO	*(le dà un mazzetto)*
	Cara! nel sen ti posi
	questa gentil vïola.
AMINA	*(lo bacia)* Puro, innocente fiore!
	[omissis]
ELVINO	Domani, appena aggiorni,
	ci recheremo al tempio, e il nostro imene
	Sarà compiuto da più santo rito.[113]

The continuation of the story all centres on the pathology of Amina's sleep-walking, and the misunderstandings it creates. For some time, the villagers see a figure wandering through the village at night, and many of them are frightened, believing it to be a ghost. In reality it is Amina, who on the very night before the religious marriage is solemnized, wanders into Count Rodolfo's bedroom.[114] Here she is discovered, and, consequently, ac-

---

113   ELVINO Now we are betrothed / AMINA Betrothed!... Oh sweet word! / ELVINO *(giving her a bouquet)* Beloved, upon your heart let this violet stay /AMINA Flower, pure and innocent! / ELVINO May it remind you of me. [omissis] / ELVINO Tomorrow, when day comes, we'll go to the church, and our vows will be solemnised.
114   On the character of Rodolfo and its implications, see S. MORABITO, *Contesti*, cit., p. 43, who

cused of shameless betrayal. The poor thing is, apparently, indefensible. Confronted with what appears to be the terrible evidence of Amina's infidelity, Elvino decides to dissolve the betrothal. In a dramatic exchange with Amina – who protests her innocence, confirmed by Count Rodolfo himself – Elvino, carried away by rage, tears the engagement ring from her finger (Act II.4):

CORO	Buone nuove!
	Dice il Conte ch'ella è onesta,
	che è innocente; e a noi già move.
ELVINO	Egli! oh! rabbia.
TUTTI	Ah! placa l'ira...
ELVINO	L'ira mia più fren non ha.
	(le toglie l'anello)
AMINA	Il mio anello!... oh! madre!...[115]

Amina's words – their drama heightened by lack of musical accompaniment – are followed by the chorus, which scathingly rebukes Elvino's impulsive gesture.

The ring is restored to Amina only after the clarification, in part thanks to the efforts of Rodolfo, who had immediately realized he was Amina's father[116]. Elvino himself sees Amina sleepwalking on the edge of the mill

---

sheds light on the emblematic feature of a phenomenon of the Restoration, namely the return of noble landowners to their own countries after the French Revolution. A similar character is found (as there observed) in Scribe and Boïeldieu's *opéra comique, La Dame blanche*, 1825. From Romani's drafts for the libretto, the author deduces that the reason for Rodolfo's disappearance from the village is as follows: the scion of the noble family, he first seduced a young woman (Amina's mother), abandoning her when she was pregnant; then he was sent abroad by his family until the matter blew over. Clearly, if this inspiration had been developed in the libretto, it would raise quite a few issues on the legal plane.

115   CHORUS Happy news! The Count says she is pure, innocent. He's coming to us / ELVINO He! oh rage! / ALL Stay your wrath! / ELVINO No! I must leave. My wrath has no bounds. *(He takes the ring from Amina.)* / AMINA My ring! Oh, mother!

116   Rodolfo's recognition of Amina, seeing her likeness to her mother, is rather veiled in Romani's libretto. The plot would have enabled Romani and Bellini to expand it, developing a typical recognition scene. On the possible reasons (mainly of a theatrical order) which led to the opposite choice, see S. MORABITO, *Contesti*, cit., pp. 39 ff. The relationship between Rodolfo and Amina implies, however, the theme of incest avoided, as observed by Q. PRINCIPE, *La Sonnambula*, cit., p. 69, where he gives account of the cuts made to the original libretto on this point.

roof, in precariously balance, and realizes (with all the other villagers) that his beloved is innocent. So everything falls into place: Elvino returns the ring to Amina, and the prospect to a happy ending appears:

AMINA	A me t'appressi? oh! gioia!
	L'anello mio mi rechi?
RODOLFO	*(ad Elvino)*
	A lei lo rendi.
	(Elvino le rimette l'anello)
AMINA	Ancor son tua: tu mio tuttor... Mi abbraccia,
	tenera madre... io son felice appieno![117]

Elvino and Amina can finally celebrate the marriage, reconciled and happy (Act II.9):

TUTTI	Innocente, a noi più cara,
	bella più del tuo soffrir,
	vieni al tempio, e a' piè dell'ara
	incominci il tuo gioir.[118]

Although the plot of Felice Romani's libretto turns on the episode of sleep-walking and Amina's alleged betrayal, the story of the ring is a highly significant moment, brought out strongly by the stress Bellini lays on it, starting from the magnificent cavatina by the tenor that accompanies Elvino's gift to his beloved. The gift seals the pact between the spouses; its reappropriation by Elviro consecrates his (alleged) knowledge of Amina's infidelity; its return to Amina finally marks the end of the rupture and leads to the happy finale. But what is the significance of all this on the legal plane?

3. In addressing the questions posed by the work, and in particular the matter in hand, we have to examine two different traditions and legal sys-

---

117   AMINA You're near me? Oh joy! Have you brought my ring? / RODOLFO *(to Elvino)* Give it back to her. *(Elvino puts the ring on her finger)* / AMINA I'm yours once more; you're mine... Dear mother, embrace me... my joy's complete!
118   ALL Innocent Amina, so dear to us, made lovelier by your grief, come to the church and there, at the alter, begin your joy.

tems: the French and Austrian. As it turns out, the libretto of the opera is of French origin. However, the opera was performed for the first time, at the Teatro Carcano in Milan on 6 March 1831, at that time under Habsburg rule.[119] The work was immensely successful, partly due to inspired performances by the two outstanding protagonists: Giuditta Pasta[120] and Giovanni Battista Rubini, two of the greatest and most celebrated singers in all nineteenth-century opera history.

The case of the engagement ring should then first be dealt with on the basis of the laws concerning marriage and donations, contained in the 1811 Austrian Civil Code (*ABGB*), declared applicable 'in all the provinces under the Government of Milan, in the place of any other law or custom',[121] with effect from 1 January 1816.

Under Austrian law in the period, the question of donations between affianced couples was regulated by § 1247 *ABGB*, which ruled that 'jewels, gems and other precious things pertaining to dress, which a husband gives his wife, are considered in case of doubt as not given as a loan but a gift. If then one of the future spouses promises to the other, or if a third party promises or gives one of them something in contemplation of the future marriage, the gift can be revoked if the marriage does not take place through no fault of the donor'.[122]

This measure partly derogated from § 1246, which stated that 'the validity or invalidity of donations between married parties is judged according to the laws in force for donations in general', and § 946, which established, as a general rule, the irrevocability of donations.[123] The exception concerns

---

119   The opera was first performed soon after (24 October 1831) in Paris at the Théâtre Italien.

120   The other great singer to appear in the role of Amina in the nineteenth century was Maria Malibran: for a summary, see A. ORLANDINI, 'In mia man... Pasta, Malibran e Grisi alla conquista di Norma e Amina', in P. MIOLI (edited by), *Malibran. Storia e leggenda, canto e belcanto nel primo Ottocento italiano*, Bologna: Patron Editore, 2010, pp. 312 ff.

121   So established by the edict of 28 September 1815.

122   For the sake of completeness, it should be noted that – again on the subject of donations between spouses or a betrothed couple – § 1232 *ABGB* also defines the so-called 'morganatica', which can be assilimilated to gifts: 'The gift that her husband promises to give to his wife on the morning after the wedding is termed the *morganatica*. If it has been promised, it is presumed that in case of doubt it was actually given in the first three years of marriage.'

123   § 946 *ABGB* 'Donations are generally irrevocable.'

the question of the revocability of a donation which, as in this case, is permissible if the marriage is not celebrated 'through no fault of the donor': namely (in the case of *La sonnambula*), if the failure to perform the marriage is not attributable to the groom. In practice, if the groom gives his bride an engagement ring, and the marriage is not celebrated without the responsibility for this lying with the groom, the ring has to be returned.[124]

The legislation contained in the *ABGB* is the outcome of a long historical tradition, which was embodied in Roman law in European codifications of the nineteenth century, but through different rules.

On the subject of prenuptial donations, in the wake of Roman law and in particular of Justinian tradition, essentially two types of donations had emerged, in the period before the nineteenth-century codifications: what were termed *donationes simplices* (simple donations) and *donationes propter nuptias* (nuptial gifts).[125] The distinction between them lay precisely in their relation to marriage: simple donations were those made between betrothed couples, following a simple promise of marriage; matrimonial gifts were made (either by the couple or by third parties) as a function of marriage itself, and therefore became effective only when the marriage was celebrated. The provisions of § 1247 *ABGB* clearly envisaged both the above situations. The wording 'in contemplation of future marriage' ('in Rücksicht auf die künftige Ehe') is clearly regarded as covering both the hypothesis of simple donations between lovers and those subordinated to the marriage.

As already mentioned, in the nineteenth-century codes, the above division between the two types of donations, derived from Roman law, was dealt with differently, and this leads us to the French tradition, to which the text of *La sonnambula* belongs, given the literary sources on which it draws. The Napoleonic Code of 1804, unlike the Austrian, does not recognize two forms of donation, and formulates an express rule *only for wedding gifts*. In particular, according to art. 1091 *Code Civil*: 'Les époux pourront, par con-

---

124   Note, however, that § 1247 *ABGB* formulates a specific rule for the husband's position: in fact, the jewels and items of value 'given' by the husband to his wife are to be understood – if the title is not clearly stated – as gifts.

125   P. FERRETTI, 'La misteriosa ratio dell'Article 80 del Codice civile italiano', in G. SANTUCCI (edited by), *Fondamenti del diritto europeo. Seminari trentini*, Naples: Jovene, 2012, pp. 149 ff.

trat de mariage, se faire réciproquement, ou l'un des deux à l'autre, telle donation qu'ils jugeront à propos, sous les modification ci-après exprimées.' Art. 1088 of the *Code Civil* specifies in turn that 'Toute donation faite en faveur du mariage sera caduque, si le mariage ne s'ensuit pas.'

As traditionally observed, the Napoleonic Code regulated gifts made between betrothed couples *by means of* a marriage contract;[126] gifts made in other contexts – i.e. outside the marriage contract – were regulated by ordinary law, and, as such, they were generally irrevocable.[127] The Napoleonic Code, departing from the bipartition established in Justinian law, was generally justified in the light of the clear desire of the legislator not to attribute any specific significance to marriage vows, also in the case of the effects of donations. This is a significance that (since the *ABGB*, and the codes of the German area in general also govern gifts between betrothed couples) promises of marriage did possess in other codes.

Hence there is a particularly large gap between the Austrian Civil Code and the Napoleonic Code. In the wake of the revolutionary legislation, the latter did not recognize promises of marriage, not even in part,[128] with the result that gifts made with a view to marriage had to be returned, for obvious reasons of coherence. However, in France, the general rule was subjected to two exceptions as a result of case law: gifts of modest value, *cadeaux d'usage*, were withdrawn from the rules requiring restitution; and, as we will see, the engagement ring, by virtue of its recognized sentimental value, was subject to special rules.

Unlike the French Code, therefore, the *ABGB* seems to almost to be inclined to impose a 'penalty' in the case of non-fulfilment of the promise of marriage, if the donor were at fault. If the marriage was not celebrated

---

126   In this respect, *ex multis*, F. LAURENT, *Principi di diritto civile*, vol. XV, Naples: Vallardi, 1884, p. 158; G. BAUDRY-LACANTINERIE, M. COLIN, *Delle donazioni fra vivi e dei testamenti*, in *Trattato teorico-pratico di diritto civile*, Milan: Vallardi, 1882, p. 882.

127   P. FERRETTI, *La misteriosa*, cit., p. 171.

128   The French system, however, does not seem to have ever fully assimilated the solution adopted, firstly, in the revolutionary period and then the Napoleonic Code. Even in more recent years, disputes arising out of broken engagements and breaches of promise of marriage have been lively, and resolved by applying – with all the uncertainties of the case – the general clause on liability in torts (art. 1382 *Code Civil*). See RUBELLIN-DEVICHI, 'Fiançailles', in *Rivista trimestrale di diritto e procedura civile*, 1989, p. 277 and, for further observations, G. OBERTO, 'La promessa di matrimonio', in *Trattato di diritto di famiglia*, edited by P. Zatti, Milan: Giuffrè, 2011, vol. I, pp. 331 ff.

because of acts imputable to the donor, the donation was not revocable. The Austrians, in short, took donations made during an engagement more seriously than the French did.

4. In *La sonnambula*, Elvino and Amina follow the traditional procedure for their wedding: first, by the marriage contract, the spouses settle the civil and patrimonial aspects of their union; the religious wedding will then be celebrated in church.[129]

Applying Austrian law, § 1247 ABGB provides the right for Elvino to demand and obtain the return of the ring if, without any fault on the part of the donor, the marriage does not take place.[130] But from this point of view Elvino's position is doubtful: he accuses Amina of infidelity on the basis of evidence that would definitely merit further discussion, and Elvino's decision not to proceed with the marriage appears, in fact, somewhat hasty. Elvino is sentimental, impulsive; he stops at appearances, he does not reflect, he refuses to trust what Rodolfo himself repeatedly tells him, and breaks off the engagement without wishing to listen to reason. Now, from a purely legal point of view, it is, however, true that the application of § 1247 ABGB does not require proof of the *guilt* of the future spouse (in this case, Amina), but only the lack of any misconduct on the part of the donor, and this seems to be true of Elvino. There is, in short, no proof of Amina's guilt (she was not caught engaging in sexual intercourse!). But this is not actually necessary. It is, however, doubtful at least that Elvino can be considered as at *fault*: after all, his decision to break the engagement is based on an objective fact, which he may interpret hastily, but it is difficult to accuse him of being at fault. Ultimately, the overall situation is not clear.

Also, Elvino is confirmed in his opinion because, on the night following the marriage contract, before the religious wedding, Amina is found in Count Rodolfo's bedroom. Hence, at that moment the suspicion of be-

---

129   See, for some interesting points – though referred to Belgium, but still related to the *Napoleonic Code* – P. GODDING, 'Les contrats de mariage dans la première moitié du 19ème siècle: fidélité à la coutume ou adoption sans reserve du Code Napoléon?', in *Revue belge d'Histoire contemporaine*, no. 1-2, 1983, pp. 91 ff.
130   § 1247 ABGB: '... wenn die Ehe ohne Verschulden des Geschenkgebers nicht erfolgt...'

trayal is legitimate. Elvino's decision to break off the engagement and take back the ring appears without fault.

5. Under French law, as has already been observed, art. 1091 of the *Code Civil* only governs donations made 'par contrat de mariage', declaring them forfeit if the marriage contract is not followed by celebration of the wedding (art. 1088). The solution of Amina and Elvino's case would therefore be the same as that envisaged by the Austrian Code, but with two different shades of interpretation, which are far from secondary:
– if Elvino had donated the ring not with the marriage contract, but as a simple donation, under French law the gift would remain subject to the general rules on donations, and thus apparently irrevocable. By contrast, as we have seen, the Austrian law would *in any case* have covered it under § 1247 *ABGB*, as one of the wedding gifts;
– while § 1247 *ABGB* required that the gift should be revoked, given the absence of any misconduct on the part of the donor, the *Code Civil* (art. 1088) – in the case of a donation granted 'par contrat de mariage' – states that the gift is revocable solely because of failure to celebrate the wedding, *regardless of consideration of whether one of the parties is at fault.*

6. While the above considerations remain valid, in the French system, on the basis of long-established judicial interpretation, there are particular deviations from the general rules specifically for the *engagement ring.*
First deviation: in principle, and following the general rule, the engagement ring should be returned to the person who gave it if the marriage is not celebrated; however, the ring should not be returned if it is a gift of modest value, so being classed among what are called 'customary gifts'.
Second deviation (from the first...): if the donee has committed misconduct (as in *La sonnambula*, Elvino has some justification for believing, at least temporarily, is Amina's case), the Courts have held that the party acting in good faith can recover the ring.
Third deviation: this is the situation in which the engagement ring is a 'family jewel' (heirloom), like a ring that has belonged to the fiancé's mother, and is given to the bride. In this case, if the engagement is broken, the ring is always returned. However, the classification of a ring as a 'family

jewel' is not always easy. Sometimes, in Court decisions, it seems to depend on whether it is a jewel from a family with long traditions; at others, the classification simply rests on its origin (i.e. the ring was not bought new, but belonged to the latter's family, without involving further distinctions or criteria).

Fourth deviation: if the engagement ring has a considerable value compared to the patrimony of the person who donates it, case law is inclined to conclude that, if the engagement is broken, the ring must be returned. Note that French law also applies these rules concerning the engagement ring in the case of divorce.[131]

Now, in the case of Amina and Elvino, we saw that the ring was a 'family jewel': if the rule just mentioned were applied, on breaking off the engagement, the disappointed fiancé could rightly claim restitution. Similar conclusions would be reached in cases where, regardless of whether the ring constitutes or not a family jewel, the Court found Elvino to be the victim of Amina's reprehensible conduct. Finally, Elvino could, in any case, reclaim the ring, if it had had a significant value: on this point, however, the conclusions are at best dubious, since we know nothing of the ring's true value, either as an absolute figure or in relation to Elvino's patrimony.

7. In the Italian Civil Code currently in force,[132] the general rule applied is that of the irrevocability of donations,[133] except in the case of ingratitude[134]

---

131   See, on this subject, the leading case Cass. civ. I, 19 December 1979, in *Bull. Civ.*, I, 270. The maxim is formulated as follows: 'Justifie légalement sa décision rejetant la demande de restitution de la bague de fiançailles formée par le mari à la suite du divorce des époux la Cour d'appel qui, après avoir exclu le caractère de souvenir de famille du bijou litigieux, estime souverainement que la remise de la bague à la fiancée constituait en l'espèce, compte tenu des facultés respectives des époux et de leurs familles un présent d'usage, qui ne pouvait comme tel, donner lieu à restitution'.

132   With regard to the solution reflected in the pre-unification Civil Code of 1865, see P. FERRETTI, *La misteriosa*, cit., pp. 175 ff.: the Code adopted a formulation that gave rise to uncertainty, even though the prevalent interpretation tended to hold that the solution to be adopted was not dissimilar to that in the Napoleonic Code.

133   Art. 800 c.c. (*Cause di revocazione*): 'Gifts may be revoked for ingratitude or the supervention of children.'

134   Art. 801 c.c. (*Revocazione per ingratitudine*): 'The application for revision for ingratitude cannot be presented except when the donee has committed one of the acts referred to under the numbers 1, 2 and 3 of art. 463, namely has been guilty of grievous injury to the donor or has wilfully caused material injury to the donor's estate or wrongly refused alimony due under arts. 433, 435 and 436.'

or a couple with upcoming children.[135] There are, however, exceptions to the general principle in the specific case of donations between betrothed couples (art. 80 c.c.) and donations 'with regard to marriage' (art. 785 c.c.): two rules that are not, in reality, easy to reconcile to each other.

In particular, according to art. 80 c.c. (entitled *Restituzione dei doni*): 'The promisor may demand the return of gifts made because of the promise of marriage, if this has not been contracted. The request is not practicable after one year from the day in which the refusal to celebrate the marriage was received or the date of the death of one of the promisors.'[136]

Art. 80 of the Italian Civil Code differs from both the model provided by the Austrian Code of 1811 and the Napoleonic Code of 1804.

Compared to the Austrian Code, the difference lies above all in the fact that art. 80 c.c. permits the return of gifts, *irrespective of the reason why the marriage was not concluded*, provided that such gifts were made on the basis of a commitment that can be termed a 'promise of marriage' in the technical sense: in law, it has been established that to produce the expected effects of art. 80 c.c., it is necessary for there to be an 'official engagement', namely that there exists a 'statement, explicit or implicit, normally made public in the circle of the couple's relations, friends, and acquaintances, of wishing to frequent each other with the serious intention of getting married, a useful test period in which each of the betrothed can acquire the maturity required in order to reach a responsible decision to celebrate the marriage.'[137] The reason for this particular approach has been the object of various re-

---

135   Art. 803 c.c. (*Revocazione per sopravvenienza di figli*): '1. Gifts made by one who had not or did not know he had children or descendants at the time of the donation, may be revoked on the supervention or discovery of a child or descendant of the donor. They may also be revoked by the recognition of a child, unless it be established that at the time of the gift the donor knew of the existence of the child. 2. Application may also be made for revocation if the child of the donor was already conceived at the time of donation. (The text quoted is the one in force, replaced by Art. 88, paragraph 1 of Legislative Decree no. 28 December 2013, no. 154, in force as of February 7, 2014).'
136   It is common ground in both doctrine and jurisprudence, that the 'promise of marriage' pursuant to art. 80 c.c. should not be endowed with special formal or substantive characteristics: thus, for example, Cass., 3 May 1983, no. 3015, in *Il Foro italiano*, 1983 I, p. 1593. On another level, therefore, rests the discipline in art. 81 c.c. (*Risarcimento dei danni*), which implies a promise of marriage made by public deed or written private agreement.
137   See. G. DI ROSA, 'Commento sub art. 79', in *Commentario*, cit., pp. 23 ff., who on this point refers to the decision of the Court of Cassation of 2 May 1983, no. 3015, in *Giustizia Civile*, 1983, pp. 1370 ff.

constructions. According to some commentators, the rule is intended to protect the donor, to prevent the latter falling a prey to 'facile speculation' by the donee, who might break the promise made substantially in order to retain the gifts made.[138] According to another interpretation, the purpose is rather the result of the legislature's desire to erase any sign of the broken promise of marriage, so making it easier to form new affective ties.[139] Some have seen art. 80 c.c. as a special case of the revocation of gifts, due to the disfavour with which cases of a breach of promise of marriage should be treated.[140]

Regardless of how the approach reflected in art. 80 c.c. is to be interpreted, it makes the right to obtain restitution of pre-nuptial gifts dependent solely on the objective fact of the failure to marry.[141] Misconduct by the donor or the donee is not relevant, nor are any other limitations or conditions, except those related to the nature of the goods donated: if, for example, they have been worn or have deteriorated, and so cannot in practice be fully recovered.[142] Art. 1247 of the 1811 Austrian Code, however, does treat misconduct on the part of the donor as a relevant factor. In its approach, the ItalianCode in force seems to have shifted the 'pressure' resulting from the decision to break off an engagement onto the donee: the latter, in fact, might be conditioned as a result of the fact that, by refusing to consent to the marriage, the donation would be revoked. Hence some commentators see it as a measure that cannot easily be reconciled with the principle of matrimonial freedom.[143] A further element of distinction compared to the solution

---

138   Thus G. TEDESCHI, 'Matrimonio (promessa di)', in *Novissimo Digesto Italiano*, edited by A. Azara and E. Eula, vol. X, Turin: UTET, 1964, p. 424.

139   See Cass. 8 February 1994, no. 1260, in *Giustizia Civile*, 1994, I, pp. 1192 ff. On this decision, and in general on art. 80 c.c., see L. GATT, 'I doni fatti a causa della promessa di matrimonio: natura giuridica e limiti al diritto di restituzione', in *Rivista di diritto civile*, 1995, II, pp. 383 ff.

140   F. SANTOSUOSSO, 'Il matrimonio', in W. BIGIAVI (founded by), *Giurisprudenza sistematica civile e commerciale*, Turin: UTET, 2007, p. 34.

141   In doctrine and in law it has rightly been pointed out that the provisions of art. 80 c.c. are not configured as a condition for recission. The restitutory effect, in other words, does not occur automatically as a function of the failure to perform the marriage, but presupposes the exercise of the power of revocation on the part of the donor.

142   So Cass. 8 February 1994, no. 1260, cited above.

143   Thus P. FERRETTI, *La misteriosa*, cit., p. 180. Art. 80 c.c., however, raises the problem of distinguishing gifts that fall within this provision, and customary gifts, of modest value, regulated by art. 770 paragraph 2, c.c. On this point see L. GATT, *I doni fatti*, cit., pp. 393 ff.

earlier adopted by the Austrian Code is the term of one year within which the lawsuit must be undertaken to obtain restitution pursuant to art. 80 c.c. Art. 785 c.c. deals, in its turn, as we have seen, with a different case. According to this article (*Donation in respect of marriage*), 'The donation made in respect of a particular future marriage, both between the spouses and by others in favour of one or both spouses or of their unborn children, is concluded without the need for it to be accepted; but it does not take effect until the wedding.' It is believed that this provision regulates what are commonly called 'wedding gifts'.[144] The distinction of this rule compared to art. 80 c.c. has aroused extensive discussion and continues to do so, since it is not clear when one or the other case applies. According to some, the distinction should be sought in the relatively modest value of the goods that are given,[145] compared to the far from modest value of those attributed to the gifts under art. 785 c.c. This is, however, a debatable opinion, since this distinction is not apparent from the wording of the two provisions. 'Gifts' between a betrothed couple (as expressed in the art. 80 c.c.) are not, therefore, according to this thesis, gifts, but *liberalità d'uso* (customary donations) because of their modest value.[146] However, this argument is not convincing, since it is not always necessarily true that gifts between a betrothed couple are always of modest value.[147] Some commentators have proposed a distinction between the two cases, based upon the *justifying reasons* for the gifts: the gifts made under art. 785 c.c. would be only those made with specific regard to the future marriage, and as a function of the latter. By contrast, the gifts that come under art. 80 c.c. are only those made to ratify, to represent, a commitment to contracting matrimony in future (a promise of marriage).[148] However, this argument is also criticized, since the distinction proposed leaves areas of uncertainty: a person who makes

---

144   See A. GIANOLA, 'Commento sub art. 785', in *Commentario al codice civile*, edited by P. Cendon, Milan: Giuffrè, 2009, pp. 663 ff.

145   A. TORRENTE, 'La donazione', in *Trattato di diritto civile e commerciale*, edited by A. Cicu and F. Messineo, Milan: Giuffrè, 1956, p. 120.

146   G. OPPO, *Adempimento e liberalità*, Milan: Giuffrè, 1947, pp. 40 ff.; G. OBERTO, *La promessa*, cit., p. 337.

147   *Ex multis*, G. AUTORINO STANZIONE, *Il diritto di famiglia nella dottrina e nella giurisprudenza: trattato teorico-pratico*, vol. I, Turin: Giappichelli, 2011, p. 55.

148   Thus L. GATT, *I doni fatti*, cit., pp. 403 ff.

a gift in consideration of a promise of marriage, in fact, generally makes the gift 'in consideration of the promise, namely of marriage', and the two cases end up by becoming confused.[149]

The distinctions made by the Courts appear clearer, although not without problematic aspects. According to a relatively recent ruling on the question (Trib. Taranto, 28 June 2013), art. 80 c.c. deals with gifts which engaged couples give each other when the donation is animated by a serious intention to marry, with the exclusion, however, of donations of real estate and land. For the Court of Cassation, 'a gift with a view to marriage, contemplated in art. 785 c.c., is a formal and typical negotiation, characterized by the express mention, in the public deed that contains it, that the patrimonial donation made by one of the "spouses" by or a third party is performed "with a view to a determinate future marriage".'[150] Previously, the Court of Cassation had also stated that 'For a donation to be considered a nuptial gift, it is necessary that the deed should make reference to a clearly identified marriage, so as to exclude that it falls under the scheme dealt with by art. 785 c.c. a patrimonial donation made only with a general and accidental prospect of marriage. (In this case, it is believed that the judge had properly excluded the nature of a donation with regard to marriage of several acts of generosity between two people who had long lived together as husband and wife, having found that the cohabitation prior to marriage, which had lasted for about twenty years, and the recurrence of the donations, were logically irreconcilable with the specific reference to marriage required by art. 785 c.c.).'[151]

Thus it appears that in jurisprudence, when we need to distinguish between art. 80 and art. 785, the emphasis is placed on the structure of the negotiation and its contents, which, in order for art. 785 c.c. to apply, must be clearly identifiable.

8. As evinced by the above comparison between the Italian Civil Code and the Austrian Code of 1811, certain differences are also to be found between

---

149   Thus G. OBERTO, *La promessa*, cit., p. 335.
150   Cassazione civile, sez. II, 12 July 2006, no. 15873.
151   Cassazione civile, sez. II, 7 December 1989, no. 5410.

the Italian and the French system. The Italian system is different from the French one, primarily because it subordinates the act of restitution to a precise time-limit (one year), which is not envisaged in the Napoleonic Code. Furthermore, the definition of the 'gifts' to be returned in case of failure to marry encompasses – by a constant interpretation of doctrine and case law – all donations made free of charge, regardless of the value or the nature of the good given: hence no rules apply specifically to the engagement ring.

9. In conclusion, the issue of the ring, in the context of *La sonnambula*, appears likely to be treated in the same way by the various systems considered, although by paths and approaches that are not perfectly coincident. Under Austrian law, in force in Milan in 1831, the ring is subject to return unless Elvino's 'fault' happens to be proven (§ 1247 *ABGB*). According to the Napoleonic Code, and thus the tradition from which the libretto derives, the revocation of the gift would be decided by art. 1088 of the *Code Civil*, as a consequence stemming from a *contrat de mariage*, when the wedding failed to take place: there are a number of different reasons for this (a 'family jewel'; Amina's fault; the significant value of the ring with respect to Elvino's patrimony). Under the present Italian Civil Code, revocation would be possible under art. 80 c.c., within one year after donation. If, however, the donation were to fall under art. 785 c.c., it would not take effect until the marriage was celebrated.

The case, in short, is intricate, and the solutions variable. Fortunately, we are assured of a happy ending to the opera: Elvino marries Amina, amid joy and general rejoicing. And the engagement ring, as in the best tradition, remains with the bride, and the couple live happily ever after.

VI

L'elisir d'amore

(Gaetano Donizetti – Felice Romani)

A case of contractual fraud

1. *L'elisir d'amore* (first performance in Milan, Teatro alla Canobbiana, 12 May 1832) is one of Gaetano Donizetti's greatest and most enduring successes. The opera belongs to the class of Donizetti's less serious works. The premiere was followed by a run of thirty-two performances and it has remained continuously in the programme of almost all the world's opera houses ever since. The most famous arias – embodying Donizetti's typically fluent melodies – colour the work with a vein of melancholy, with smiles prevailing over laughter,[152] although there are moments more directly reminiscent of the *opera buffa* repertory, such as Dulcamara's grand opening aria ('Udite, udite, o rustici', Act I.5).

In *L'elisir d'amore*, the story revolves around the sale of an allegedly miraculous love potion: it is actually a contractual scam, perpetrated against the protagonist (Nemorino), at a time when 'consumer protection' did not exist as a legal category. The intricate question still raises various legal problems.

2. Donizetti composed the opera in a tearing hurry,[153] urged on by the impresario Lanari, who was frantically looking for a work to replace a gap that

---

152   Unsurprisingly, Donizetti subtitled the work as a 'melodramma giocoso' and not an 'opera buffa'. For an assessment of *L'elisir d'amore* in the context of the development of the genre of *opera buffa* in the 1830s-40s, see F. IZZO, *Laughter Between Two Revolutions. Opera Buffa in Italy, 1831-1848*, Rochester: University of Rochester Press, 2013, pp. 21 ff., who emphasizes the aspects of Donizetti's opera that differ from the great preceding *opera buffa* repertoire, including works by Rossini. Still a standard work on Donizetti is W. ASHBROOK, *Donizetti and his Operas*, Cambridge: Cambridge University Press, 1982.

153   According to the account passed down by Romani's widow, Donizetti composed the work in just a fortnight. The statement is generally questioned by musicological studies, but the fact remains that Lanari was hurrying Donizetti, who proved capable of rising to the challenge.

had opened at the last minute in the programme at the Teatro alla Canobbiana. For the same theatre, Donizetti had already written *Le convenienze e inconvenienze teatrali* (1831), so he knew the theatre well. To speed up the work, Lanari told Donizetti to apply to Romani for the libretto of the new opera: in addition to being a member of the élite of the theatre of the day, Romani knew Donizetti well, having worked with him on five operas already.[154]

He soon decided to accept the commission. Perhaps to gain time, Romani suggested adapting a French opera: this was *Le philtre*, a collaboration between Eugène Scribe and Daniel François Esprit Auber. In the hands of the two Italians, Scribe and Auber's opera (refashioned without any concern for international copyright, which was practically non-existent at the time[155]) became tinged with a rather melancholy sentimentality, absent from its source, which is more directly comic, as well as adapting the traditions of the Commedia dell'Arte. After the première at 12 May 1832, in Milan, *L'elisir d'amore* proved a great success, and so entered history.[156] Re-

---

154   They were *Chiara e Serafina, ossia I pirati* (1822), *Alina, regina di Golconda* (1828) and *Gianni di Parigi* (1828), *Anna Bolena* (1830), *Ugo, Conte di Parigi* (1832). After *L'elisir d'amore* the two authors worked together again on *Parisina d'Este* (1833), *Lucrezia Borgia* (1833) and *Rosmonda d'Inghilterra* (1834).

155   According to S. ROLLET, 'L'elisir d'amore, entre France et Italie', in *L'Avant-Scène Opéra*, no. 288, 2015, p. 80, *Le philtre*'s copyright was not valid beyond the borders of France: Scribe and Auber, essentially, could not have claimed royalties for the reuse of their work in Italy. But the matter changed when *L'elisir d'amore* began to be performed in Paris. In particular, it seems that Scribe and Auber received and split the royalties from the performances of Donizetti's opera in France (this appears from the *Catalogue général des oeuvres dramatiques et lyriques faisant partie du répertoire de la Société des auteurs et compositeurs dramatiques*, Paris: L. Peragallo, 1863, p. 117). Scribe may have attained this through the urging of Victor Hugo, who, as is well known, was one of the leading proponents of copyright protection in nineteenth-century France (thus S. ROLLET, cit.). Scribe's widow was much more energetic: in 1865 she brought a suit against the Théâtre-Italien to secure recognition of her right to authorize beforehand every performance of *L'elisir d'amore*, reputed to be a 'falsification' of *Le philtre*. S. ROLLET believes this was one of the factors that led the theatre to slow down performances of Donizetti's opera from 1870 on.

156   While passing through Milan, Hector Berlioz attended one of the first performances, though he did not share the flattering opinions of the work. In a letter dated 25 May 1832 addressed to his friend, the lawyer and librettist Jean-Jacques-Humbert Ferrand, Berlioz offered some stinging criticisms of it: 'A Milan, j'ai entendu, pour la première fois, un vigoureux orchestre; cela commence à être de la musique, pour l'exécution au moins. La partition de mon ami Donizetti peut aller trouver celles de mon ami Paccini et de mon ami Vaccaï. Le public est digne de pareilles productions. On cause tout haut comme à la Bourse, et les cannes font sur le plancher du parterre un accompagnement presque aussi bruyant que celui de la grosse caisse': H. BERLIOZ, *Correspondance générale*, vol. 1, edited by Pierre Citron, Paris: Flammarion, 1972, p. 554.

vival of the opera at the Théâtre Italien in Paris on 17 January 1839 was a foregone conclusion,[157] because of the success it received at other European opera houses[158] and the dialectical relationship between the two traditions, Italian and French, which characterized much of the history of musical theatre in the two countries during the nineteenth century.[159]

3. *L'elisir d'amore* opens with the peasant chorus followed by Nemorino's famous romanza. As he watches Adina read aloud the story of Tristan and Isolde, he sings a sweet melody, written in *larghetto*, skilfully built up on passing notes:[160]

NEMORINO *(osservando Adina che legge)*
Quanto è bella, quanto è cara!
Più la vedo e più mi piace...
Ma in quel cor non son capace
lieve affetto ad inspirar.
Essa legge, studia, impara...
Non vi ha cosa ad essa ignota...
Io son sempre un idiota,
io non so che sospirar.
Chi la mente mi rischiara?

---

157   Thus A. DI PROFIO, 'L'opera francese in Italia e l'opera italiana a Parigi: "L'elisir d'amore" o il crocevia di due tradizioni', in *La Fenice prima dell'Opera*, no. 6, 2010 p. 26. On the concurrent performances of the two works in Paris, on the stage at the Théâtre-Italien (Donizetti) and the Académie Royale (Auber), in 1839-1870, see S. ROLLET, *L'elisir d'amore*, cit., pp. 76 ff. On the reception of Donizetti's work in Paris, and certain reviews which insisted on the supposed aesthetic superiority of Auber's music over Donizetti's, see E. SALA, 'Finzione e sentimento', in *Teatro alla Scala. L'elisir d'amore. Stagione 2014-2015*, Milan: Edizioni del Teatro alla Scala, 2015, p. 65.
158   Until the Parisian date, the opera was performed several times in Italy and abroad: at La Fenice in Venice (2 March 1833), San Carlo in Naples (15 August 1835), La Scala in Milan (27 September 1835), the Lyceum Theatre in London (10 December 1836).
159   A. DI PROFIO, *L'opera francese*, cit., brings out the many stylistic affinities between *L'elisir d'amore* and the French tradition, almost as if Donizetti had already prepared for his opera's performance in Paris.
160   The passages from the libretto are based on the edition printed for the opening performance in Milan: *L'ELISIR | D'AMORE | melodramma giocoso in due atti | da rappresentarsi | nell'I. R. Teatro alla Canobbiana | la primavera dell'anno 1832 | Milano | per Gaspare Truffi e comp.* The English translation is based upon *The Elixir of Love*, Boston: Oliver Ditson Company, 1885, available at https://archive.org/details/cu31924098674538, amended in order to follow the version of the libretto used as reference in the text.

His attempts to gain her attention are fruitless ('Ma in quel cor non son capace | lieve affetto ad inspirar'). Adina, a well-to-do young woman,[162] seems indifferent to (literally) poor Nemorino. She is, however, interested in Belcore (described in the libretto as a 'a sergeant with the garrison in the village'), though she has not yet decided to yield to the dandy's flattery and marry him (Act I.2):

BELCORE	Or se m'ami, com'io t'amo,
	che più tardi a render l'armi?
	Idol mio, capitoliamo:
	in qual dì vuoi tu sposarmi?
ADINA	Signorino, io non ho fretta
	Un tantin pensar ci vo'.[163]

Nemorino is downcast, to say the least. The plot is further entangled by one Dr. Dulcamara, who turns up in the village. An itinerant quack, travelling from village to village, he ensnares the gullible and the ingenuous, selling his miraculous nostrum which, so the self-styled doctor declares, can cure all ills:

DULCAMARA	Ei move i paralitici,
	spedisce gli apopletici,
	gli asmatici, gli asfitici,
	gl'isterici, i diabetici,
	guarisce timpanitidi,
	e scrofole e rachitidi,

---

161   NEMORINO Ah! how lovely, ah! how dear to me! While I gaze, I adore more deeply. Oh! what rapture that soft bosom with a mutual flame to move; But, while she's her mind improving, I my own am not illuming. I am but an idiot still, and can only sigh.

162   Among the characters in the book, Adina is called a 'rich and capricious tenant farmer' while Nemorino is a 'farmer, a simple young man, in love with Adina.' Significantly, already in the notes to the libretto, the trait that distinguishes Nemorino, in addition to his social position, and his being a 'simple young man', is that he is in love with Adina.

163   BELCORE If thou lovest me as I love thee, why not ground our arms instanter: let capitulation free thee, make thy conqueror thy slave / ADINA Noble sergeant, a few days' leisure, to reflect, I humbly crave.

e fino il mal di fegato,
che in moda diventò.[164]

After hearing him cry up his infallible remedies, in a celebrated and elaborate aria, Nemorino asks Dulcamara whether he has a love philtre like the one Isolde administered to Tristan. Nemorino knows the story, not because he is a reader of books, but because, shortly before, he heard it read by Adina. Dulcamara, sensing a sale, declares he has the very thing, gulling Nemorino into believing he can sell him an elixir capable of winning Adina's heart. For one sequin (his whole wealth) Nemorino buys the miraculous elixir he extols. What Dulcamara sells him is actually a bottle of wine. So begin the vicissitudes of the poor young man (Act I.6):

NEMORINO	Avreste voi... per caso...
	la bevanda amorosa
	della regina Isotta?
DULCAMARA	Ah!... che?... che cosa?
NEMORINO	Voglio dire... lo stupendo
	elisir che desta amore...
DULCAMARA	Ah! sì, sì, capisco, intendo.
	Io ne son distillatore.
NEMORINO	E fia vero?
DULCAMARA	Se ne fa
	gran consumo in questa età.
NEMORINO	Oh, fortuna!... e ne vendete?
DULCAMARA	Ogni giorno, a tutto il mondo.
NEMORINO	E qual prezzo ne volete?
DULCAMARA	Poco... assai... cioè... secondo...
NEMORINO	Un zecchin... null'altro ho qua...
DULCAMARA	È la somma che ci va.
NEMORINO	Ah! prendetelo, dottore.
DULCAMARA	Ecco il magico liquore.
NEMORINO	Obbligato, ah sì, obbligato!
	Son felice, son rinato.

---

164   DULCAMARA This cures the apoplectical, the asthmatical, the paralytical, the dropsical, the diuretical – Consumption, deafness, too, the Richest and the scrofula; all evils are at once upset, by this new and fashionable mode.

DULCAMARA	Elisir di tal bontà!
	Benedetto chi ti fa!
	(Nel paese che ho girato
	più d'un gonzo ho ritrovato,
	ma un eguale in verità
	non ve n'è, non se ne dà.)
	[omissis]
NEMORINO	E il sapore?...
DULCAMARA	Egli è eccellente
	(È Bordò, non elisir[165]).[166]

Dulcamara is well aware of the deception and its legal implications, so he urges Nemorino to be discreet, being concerned about intervention 'by the authorities'. The reference to justice is therefore explicit:

DULCAMARA	Sovra ciò... silenzio... sai?
	Oggidì spacciar l'amore
	è un affar geloso assai:
	impacciar se ne potria
	un tantin l'Autorità.
NEMORINO	Ve ne do la fede mia:
	neanche un'anima il saprà.[167]

---

165   In the French source it is Lacryma Christi (spelt incorrectly in Scribe's libretto, which has 'lachrymachristi'): a well-known Campanian wine, available in three colours: white, red and rosé. According to various sources available online, unverified, the name of the wine comes from the tears shed by God after recognizing, in the Gulf of Naples, a tract of heaven torn off by Lucifer as he hurtled down to the underworld.

166   NEMORINO Have you, by good fortune, the amorous draught of the Queen Isotta? / DULCAMARA Ah! – the what? – what is it? /NEMORINO I mean to say – the miracuolous elixir that can awaken love / DULCAMARA Oh! yes, yes – I understand you now I am the veritable compounder of it / NEMORINO Is it possible! / DULCAMARA I am the only man who can make it. It is in great demand / NEMORINO. Oh! happiness! And do you sell it? / DULCAMARA Daily, sir, to the whole world /NEMORINO And what do you charge for it? DULCAMARA Very little – that is according to – /NEMORINO One piaster is all that I possess /DULCAMARA That's exactly the price of it /NEMORINO Oh! there, take it doctor / DULCAMARA Here, then, is the magic liquid / NEMORINO Thank you kindly! Pleasure's ray beams bright before me: Joy awaits me, hope elates me, – All combines my plans to aid. Thank you kindly! /DULCAMARA In my travels I've met marvels – Fools of every sort and size; But of all the marvelous fools, the biggest stands before my eyes. [omissis] NEMORINO How does it taste? DULCAMARA Oh! Excellent! (And so it ought – for it is Bordeaux wine).

167   DULCAMARA Silence, silence, sir, I pray. Selling love in this queer fashion may no little

The wine at least has the effect of making Nemorino tipsy, which surprises Adina, since for the first time she notices him (Act I.8):[168]

ADINA	(Chi è quel matto?
	Traveggo, o è Nemorino?
	Così allegro! e perché?)
NEMORINO	(Diamine! È dessa...
	(si alza per correre a lei, ma si arresta e siede di nuovo)
	Ma no... non ci appressiam. De' miei sospiri
	non si stanchi per or. Tant'è... domani
	adorar mi dovrà quel cor spietato.)
ADINA	(Non mi guarda neppur! com'è cambiato!)
NEMORINO	La rà, la rà, la lera!
	La rà, la rà, la rà...
ADINA	(Non so se è finta o vera
	la sua giocondità.)
NEMORINO	(Finora amor non sente.)
ADINA	(Vuol far l'indifferente.)[169]

---

trouble bring me. Discovered would it be this sale, they may put me in the gaol /NEMORINO Silent as the grave I'll be, – They'll get no work or look from me

168   On Nemorino's attitude, which is far from 'innocent' see E. SALA, *Finzione*, cit., p. 71. The author sheds light on a usually overlooked aspect of the text, observing that: 'While Nemorino is obviously not enabled to win Adina's love by drinking the elixir (which is actually plain red wine), it does perform a function that goes far beyond being a mere bogus potion sold by a charlatan. What is it a symbol of, then? I would say of the unpredictable, enigmatic, irreducible, illusory and mocking paths and purposes of desire: what the elixir seems to suggest is that fiction and feeling are not just compatible, but are not even very far apart! Before Dulcamara's arrival, the elixir immediately performs its function as intermediator (in René Girard's sense) of Nemorino's desire. The latter, contemplating the object of his impossible desires (Adina) from the sidelines, from beyond, hears from her own lips the story of a "certain elixir of love" that that made the "cruel" Queen Isolde fall in love. This sort of narrative and archaic ballad-cavatina, which tells the story of Tristan and Isolde, is accompanied, by way of a modern dance, with an insinuating slow waltz that turns into a marked mazurka (according to Ashbrook) in the chorus-refrain. This is what can teach Nemorino to make himself loved. The dances can begin.'

169   ADINA Who is this idiot? Do I dream? Or is it indeed Nemorino, thus acting the fool? / NEMORINO (Bless me, there she is) *(he runs towards her, but stops suddenly)*. But no, I will not go to her: my sighs are no longer tiresome to her; I will be silent, for tomorrow her proud heart must succumb to me) / ADINA He does not even look at me: what a change is this? /NEMORINO Lara, lara la, lara! Lara, lara lara! /ADINA (I should like to know whether this mirth is true or only pretended) / NEMORINO (She does not appear to love me yet) / ADINA (Oh! this indifference must be all assumed).

In Act II, Adina finally decides to take the great step. She is about to marry Belcore. Since the love potion seems to be slow in taking effect, Nemorino wants to purchase a second bottle. But he has spent all his money, so he enlists among Belcore's soldiers for the signing-on money, enabling him to pay for it (Act II.2):

NEMORINO	Caro dottor, una bottiglia ancora.
DULCAMARA	Ben volentier. Mi piace
	giovare a' bisognosi. – Hai tu danaro?
NEMORINO	Ah! non ne ho più.
	[omissis]
NEMORINO	Io mi dispero...
	perché non ho denaro... e non so come,
	non so dove trovarne.
BELCORE	Eh! scimunito!
	Se danari non hai,
	fatti soldato... e venti scudi avrai.
NEMORINO	Venti scudi!
BELCORE	E ben sonanti.
NEMORINO	Quando? adesso?
BELCORE	Sul momento.[170]

Suddenly, word gets around in the village that Nemorino has received a large inheritance. This makes him immediately attractive to the village girls, and Amina begins to feel the stirrings of jealousy. Nemorino has not the least of idea of what is happening, and believes it is the effect of the elixir (Act II.4-5):

GIANNETTA	Sappiate dunque che l'altro dì
	di Nemorino lo zio morì,

---

170   NEMORINO Ah! my dear doctor, give me another bottle directly /DULCAMARA With all my heart. Nothing is so delightful to me as to be of service to the unfortunate. How much money have you? / NEMORINO Ah, me! I have not a penny left. *[omissis]* /NEMORINO I am in despair, because I am in immediate want of money – I have occasion for a crown, have not a shilling, and do not know how to procure one / BELCORE Oh, simpleton, if you want money, it is easy enough to get it by enlisting as a soldier. Then you will have twenty crowns / NEMORINO Twenty crowns! /BELCORE And good ones too / NEMORINO When? On the instant? /BELCORE This very minute.

	che al giovinotto lasciato egli ha
	cospicua immensa eredità...
	Ma zitte... piano... per carità.
	Non deve dirsi.
CORO	Non si dirà.
TUTTE	Or Nemorino è milionario...
	è l'Epulone del circondario...
	un uom di vaglia, un buon partito...
	Felice quella cui fia marito!
	Ma zitte... piano... per carità
	non deve dirsi, non si dirà.
	[omissis]
NEMORINO	*(fra sé, meravigliato)*
	(Cos'han coteste giovani?)
GIANNETTA E CORO	Caro quel Nemorino!
	Davvero ch'egli è amabile;
	ha l'aria da signor.
NEMORINO	(Capisco: è questa l'opera
	del magico liquor.)[171]

Only now does Dulcamara reveal he sold the elixir to Nemorino, and Adina at last realizes his feelings for her (Act II.7):

ADINA	(Che ascolto?) E a Nemorino
	voi deste l'elisir?
DULCAMARA	Ei me lo chiese
	per ottener l'affetto
	di non so qual crudele...
ADINA	Ei dunque amava?
DULCAMARA	Languiva, sospirava
	senz'ombra di speranza; e, per avere

---

171 GIANNETTA Know, then, that Nemorino's uncle died the other day, and has left him a considerable inheritance. But silence! Nobody must know it yet / CHOIR Nobody shall know it / ALL Now Nemorino is a wealthy man: he is the richest man in al the neighborhood – he is a worthy man – a good match – happy the girl who may get him. But be silent – nobody must know it yet. *[omissis]* /NEMORINO (marvelling) (What is the matter with these young people?) / GIANNETTA AND CHOIR How dear is that Nemorino! How exceedingly amiable he is! He has quite the appearance of a duke! /NEMORINO (I begin to comprehend: their courtesy is the effect of the magic liquor).

una goccia di farmaco incantato,
vendé la libertà, si fe' soldato.[172]

Adina is persuaded of Nemorino's goodness of heart and deep, true affection. In this way Act II rapidly sees a change in Nemorino's lot. Shortly after he sings the famous romanza 'Una furtiva lagrima' (Act II.8), the couple speak of their feelings for each other, and a happy ending is now assured. Adina redeems the contract by which Nemorino had enlisted in the army, and declares her love:

ADINA   Ah! fu con te verace
                    se presti fede al cor.
            Sappilo alfine, ah! sappilo,
                    tu mi sei caro, e t'amo;
                    quanto ti fei già misero,
                    farti felice or bramo:
                    il mio rigor dimentica;
                    ti giuro eterno amor.
NEMORINO   Oh! gioia inesprimibile!
                    Non m'ingannò il dottor.
              (Nemorino si getta ai piedi di Adina)[173]

Amid the general happiness, Dulcamara is also pleased with the way things have gone, praising his marvellous elixir to the throngs of villagers: a portent, that cures every possible ill and 'corrects every defect' (Act II.10):

CORO   Oh! il gran liquore!
DULCAMARA   Ei corregge ogni difetto,
                    ogni vizio di natura.
                    Ei fornisce di belletto

---

172   ADINA (What do I hear?) And you gave this elixir to Nemorino? /DULCAMARA He asked me for it, that he might try its effects upon some cruel fair one/ADINA Then he was in love? / DULCAMARA He languished, sighed without a ray of hope; and for a draught of the magic elixir, he sold his liberty, and became a soldier.

173   ADINA Ah? my beating heart assures me that he has not ever deceived thee. No! To be for ever sad cannot be the will of fate. If the wrongs that I have done thee, you can from your mind dismsis, then most happy shall I be, and with the fondest love will greet thee / NEMORINO Oh, joy beyond expression! The doctor, then, hath not deceived me! (*He throws himself at the feet of Adina.*)

la più brutta creatura:
camminar ei fa le rozze,
schiaccia gobbe, appiana bozze,
ogni incomodo tumore
copre sì, che più non è... [174]

4. As we have seen, the theme of *L'elisir d'amore* has French origins. Romani's libretto was based directly on *Le philtre*,[175] performed for the first time in Paris, at the Académie Royale de Musique (in the Salle Le Peletier) on 15 June 1831.[176] The authorship of *L'elisir d'amore* is, moreover, explicitly stated by Romani at the head of the libretto.[177] By a curious coincidence, in Paris

---

174   CHOIR Oh, wonderful elixir! DULCAMARA It corrects every imperfection, every natural defect of the person. It gives beauty to the most ugly creature – the hunchback it makes straight – the clumsy full of grace – the lame to run as swift as the wind; and the largest tumours and swellings vanish under its magic influence...

175   The literature has long uncritically handed down the story of the derivation of Scribe's text from an Italian tale, *Il filtro*, by one Silvio Malaperta, due to an account published in 1830 in the *Revue de Paris* by Stendhal. A. GERHARD has already dealt with the inaccuracies of this reconstruction, and cast oubts as to the very existence of the Italian source of Scribe's text, in an article entitled 'Ein missverständener Schabernack: Gaetano Donizettis eigenwilliger Umgang mit Felice Romanis "L'elisir d'amore"', in M. CAPRA (edited by), '*Una piacente estate di San Martino*'. *Studi e ricerche per i settant'anni di Marcello Conati*, Lucca: LIM, 2000, pp. 117-126 and, subsequently, M. EVERIST, 'A Transalpine Comedy. "L'elisir d'amore" and Cultural Transfer', in D. COLAS, A. DI PROFIO (edited by), *D'une scène à l'autre. L'Opéra italien en Europe*, Wavre: Mardaga, 2009, vol. 2, pp. 279 ff.; R. VERDIRAME, 'Dalla Francia all'Italia e ritorno. Percorsi di un libretto d'opera', in A. BENISCELLI, Q. MARINI, L. SURDICH (edited by), *La letteratura degli italiani. Rotte confini passaggi*, proceedings of the XIV Congresso nazionale dell'Associazione degli Italianisti (Genoa, 15-18 September 2010), Genoa: DIRAS, 2012. The latest research confirms that the story published under the name of Malaperta was written by Stendhal, who used a fancy name to 'dignify' his own work (though its contents are different in every way from Scribe's text): the tale first appeared in 1830, actually as by 'Silvia Valaperta', then it was taken up and republished in later collections, where the name was changed to 'Malaperta' and, from there, it was handed down in the subsequent quotations: in this respect, see C. CAZAUX, 'L'Elixir d'amour', in *L'Avant-Scène Opéra*, cit., p. 10. The error is hard to die, as in the recent (and monumental) work in 4 vols. by M. JAHRMÄRKER, *Die Libretto und Opernwerkstatt Eugène Scribe*, Wurzburg: Königshausen & Neumann, 2015, where we still read that Scribe's text derives from Silvio Malaperta's *Il filtro* (see *ivi*, vol. I, p. 181).

176   H. SCHNEIDER gives the date 15 June 1831, also mentioned on the title page of the libretto (*Auber, Daniel-François-Esprit*, in *The New Grove Dictionary of Opera, ad vocem*, edited by Stanley Sadie, London: Macmillan, 1992). The date of 20 June is instead indicated by S. PITOU, *The Paris Opéra: An Encyclopedia of Operas, Ballets, Composers, and Performers. Growth and Grandeur, 1815-1914*, Westport, Connecticut: Greenwod Press, 1990, and confirmed by the site www.chronopera.free.fr.

177   'Il soggetto è imitato dal *Filtro* di Scribe. Gli è uno scherzo; e come tale è presentato ai lettori.' ('The subject is imitated from the *Philtre* by Scribe. It is a joke; and as such it is presented to the readers').

---

on the evening of the first performance, *Le philtre* was put on together with the ballet-pantomime *La somnambule, ou L'arrivée d'un nouveau seigneur*, by Scribe-Hérold, mentioned above. Auber-Scribe's *Le philtre* was a huge success: from the first performance, it ran until 8 January 1862 (the date of the last performance, limited, however, to a single act[178]); the work was presented no fewer than 243 times at the Académie Royale de Musique, always in association with another work, usually a ballet. The première featured the tenor Adolphe Nourrit, a truly legendary figure of the French operatic repertoire in those years, celebrated for his extraordinary vocal talent (which has long since entered the history of musical theatre), as well as for the part he played, together with the leading French authors of the period, in codifying the genre of nineteenth-century *grand-opéra*. Despite appearances, the work is not attributable to the traditional French scheme of *opéra-comique*, as it does not contain the typical alternation of spoken dialogue and sung parts. All the recitatives are in music. Auber significantly intended the work for the stage of the Académie Royale de Musique, where, at that time, there was no place for the *opéra-comique* genre, still considered 'minor'.[179] Probably, as studies have shown, *Le philtre* can be attributed to the development of a genre identified by the term *petit opéra* (like Rossini's *Le Comte Ory*), which the Académie Royale produced to counter the competition of the comic genre.[180]

In Auber-Scribe's opera, Guillaume, 'garçon de ferme', is the counterpart of Nemorino; Terézine, 'jeune fermière' is the counterpart of Adina, and the part of Dulcamara is matched by that of Dr. Fontanarose, a 'charlatan'. The similarity between the French model and Romani's libretto, with particular reference to the issue that concerns us here (the sale of the fake love potion to an ingenuous peasant) is quite marked. Again in *Le philtre*, the quack doctor sings a long, elaborate *aria di sortita*, which Romani drew on directly:

---

178   See J.-C. YON, 'À la source de *L'élixir: Le philtre*, "le seul opéra-bouffe français des temps modernes qui mérite d'être cité"', in *L'Avant-Scène Opéra*, cit., pp. 68 ff.

179   On this point, *ex multis*, see H. LACOMBE, *Les voies de l'opéra français au XIXe siècle*, Paris: Fayard, 1997.

180   See A. DI PROFIO, *L'opera francese*, cit., p. 31.

FONTANAROSE	Prenez, prenez mon élixir!
	Il peut tout guérir
	La paralysie
	Et l'apoplexie
	Et la pleurésie
	Et tous les tourments,
	Jusqu'à la folie,
	La mélancolie
	Et la jalousie
	Et le mal de dents.[181]

As in Donizetti's work, Guillaume asks the doctor if he has a love philtre, and the deal is done:

GUILLAUME	Auriez-vous *le boire-amoureux*
	du beau Tristan de Léonnais?[182]
FONTANAROSE	Hein! qu'est-ce?
GUILLAUME	Un philtre qui faisait qu'on s'adorait sans cesse.
FONTANAROSE	*(froidement)* Dans notre état nous en tenons beaucoup!
GUILLAUME	Il serait vrai!
FONTANAROSE	Chaque jour j'en compose,
	car on en demande partout!
GUILLAUME	Et vous en vendez?
FONTANAROSE	Oui
GUILLAUME	*(avec crainte)* Et combien?
FONTANAROSE	Peu de chose!
GUILLAUME	*(tirant timidement trois pièces d'or de sa poche[183])*

---

181   As for Romani's libretto, the passages from the French version are taken and adapted from a copy of the first performance: *LE PHILTRE | opéra en deux actes, | paroles de M. Scribe, | musique de M. Auber | représenté pour la première fois | sur le théâtre de l'Académie Royale de Musique, | le 15 juin 1831 | Paris. | Bezou, Libraire, | 1831.*

182   This is, in reality, Tristan de Léonois, the hero of the thirteenth-century romance, dating from the period 1215–1230. The manuscript can be viewed online at the site of the Bibliothèque Nationale de France, at the following address: http://gallica.bnf.fr/ark:/12148/btv1b86001746/, although it is more likely that Scribe-Auber knew the edition by Louis-Élisabeth de La Vergne, Comte de Tressan (*Tristan de Lénois* in *Corps d'extraits de romance de chevalerie*, vol.1, Paris: Chez Pissot, 1782, pp. 1183), rather than the manuscript.

183   In *Le philtre*, unlike Romani's text, the quack doctor declares on arriving (Act I.5) the price of his 'miraculous remedy', stating that he will offer a discount of one *écu*: hence the price of the potion will only be three francs.

	J'ai là... c'est tout mon bien, j'ai là trois pièces d'or!
FONTANAROSE	*(les regardant)* Justement, c'est le prix!
GUILLAUME	*(vivement et le lui donnant)* Prenez... et ce breuvage, ce philtre?...
FONTANAROSE	*(tirant de sa poche un petit flacon)* Le voici!

5. For our present purposes, the legal references, in the light of which we will examine the issues that appear significant, range from the 1811 Austrian Civil Code (applicable in Milan at the time of the first performance) to the 1804 French *Code Civil*, which supplies the legal framework in which Auber and Scribe's original is set.

We can start from the point that concerns us here. Nemorino is evidently and deliberately deceived by Dulcamara. The contract which he engages in is characterized by a serious lack of consent: Nemorino believes he has bought a miraculous philtre, while Dulcamara has simply sold a bottle of good wine. It is, in other words, a clear case of contract fraud. Dulcamara acts in bad faith, and even envisages problems with justice. In Romani's libretto, as in Scribe's, it is clear that Nemorino is resolved to purchase the potion on the basis of Dulcamara's hyperbolic claims and repeated assurances of its nature and efficacy. Not only does Dulcamara imply he is a regular producer of the elixir, but regularly claims to sell large quantities 'in the world'. Dulcamara then gives Nemorino precise directions on how to take it and its effects, strengthening the ingenuous farmer's belief that it really is a powerful potion that can make his aloof beloved fall in love with him. Nemorino, for his part, having just heard the tale of Tristan and Isolde, is in a particularly suggestible mood.

The satisfaction with which Dulcamara comments to himself on the deal he has just done emphasizes and reiterates – if it were necessary – his bad faith ('In my travels I've met marvels – Fools of every sort and size; But of all the marvelous fools, the biggest stands before my eyes'). There are, therefore, all the typical elements of contract fraud: deceit, misrepresentation of reality, the inducement to the other party to enter into the contract on the basis of a deception that is clearly crucial to the formation of consent.

The situation in which a contract is entered into under the influence of deceit or fraud exerted by one of the parties is typically regulated, in the nineteenth century codifications that concern us here, as part of the broader regulation of vitiating factors of consent (a subject that includes, in addition to fraud, at least error and violence). Contract fraud differs from other forms of defects of consent (for example, error) in general due to the seriousness of the misconduct, intentionally designed to mislead the other party, and therefore deliberately mischievous. It may also amount to a criminal conduct: contract fraud is therefore sanctioned in many systems – including the Italian – both in criminal and private law.[184]

Here, and for the purposes of our examination of the plot of Donizetti's *L'elisir d'amore*, the focus will be solely on the implications in private law, disregarding – as usual – the criminal law consequences, however significant, that might arise from examination of the facts. Hence we will explore the positions, respectively, of Nemorino and Dulcamara, with specific reference to their contract, having as its object the sale of the purported elixir of love.

6. In the 1811 Austrian Code (*ABGB*), the regulation of contract fraud is formulated in § 871: 'If one of the parties is led into error by the other with false statements, and this error concerns the principal thing or an essential quality of it, on which the intention was primarily directed and explained, the party that was so misled is not bound by the contract.'

Under § 871 *ABGB*, contract fraud is one of the elements that – for example in the Napoleonic Code or in the current Italian Civil Code – supplements the notion of 'manipulation' or 'fraud', inherent in the rules covering contract fraud.

According to § 871 *ABGB*, contract fraud (in the form of 'false statements') causes the invalidity of the contract ('the party ... is not bound'), and this invalidity can be invoked by the party who has suffered the effects of the deception. The consequences are, firstly, restitution, and this also affects the party seeking the remedy (§ 877 *ABGB*: 'The party applying for a con-

---

184   The connection between criminal unlawfulness and invalidity of the contract is subject to interrelations that are complex and in many ways fascinating. The literature is extensive: for a first survey and further references, see A. GRASSO, *Illiceità penale e invalidità del contratto*, Milan: Giuffrè, 2002; M. RABITTI BEDOGNI, *Contratto illecito e norma penale. Contributo allo studio della nullità*, Milan: Giuffrè, 2000.

tract to be declared invalid because of contract fraud, for his part, must return everything that had been awarded to his advantage by the said contract'). The suit for invalidity, in this case, is not subject to a term limit, unlike the provisions of § 1487 *ABGB* for contracts concluded with an error, but without malice, for which, in contrast, it is three years. Subject to the above, under § 874 *ABGB* 'the party that by means of fraud or unjust fear effects a contract is obliged to make reparation for its harmful consequences.'[185]

If restitution is not possible – because, for example, the good has been destroyed, or was consumed, as in the case in question, or if a bottle of wine cannot be found, to replace that consumed – then an equivalent must be provided.[186] Ultimately, according to Austrian law, Nemorino – induced by Dulcamara's 'false statements' (§ 871) to buy the fake elixir – could have invoked the invalidity of the contract. He would have obtained the return of his sequin, and would have had to fulfil the obligation to restitution by providing an 'equivalent'; in this case, the natural consequence would have been the return of one bottle of wine, it being further understood that some adjustment would have been needed if, in making restitution by equivalent, the market price of the bottle had been less than the sequin paid by Nemorino.

7. The situation in which the hapless Nemorino finds himself, regarded in the light of the provisions of the Napoleonic Code (in force in France at the time of the composition of Eugène Scribe's work), would have had implications that were similar, *but not identical*. Art. 1116 of the *Code Civil*, like the provisions of the Austrian Civil Code, takes account of the possibility of contract fraud affecting the validity of the contract. Also in this case, the consequence is the invalidity of the contract: 'Le dol est une cause de nullité de la convention lorsque les manoeuvres pratiquées par l'une

---

185   According to G. CAROZZI, *Giurisprudenza del Codice civile generale della monarchia austriaca*, vol. XX, Milan, 1829, Chap. VI, no. 22, p. 165, 'this satisfaction must then be complete, meaning it has to extend not only to the damage caused, but also loss of profit and compensation for the offence caused.'

186   On this subject, see D. MAFFEIS, *Contratti illeciti o immorali e restituzioni*, Milan: Giuffrè, 1999, pp. 31 ff.

des parties sont telles, qu'il est évident que, sans ces manoeuvres, l'autre partie n'aurait pas contracté. Il ne se présume pas et doit être prouvé.' The conditions are, however, partly different from those established by the *ABGB*. The French Code, for example, gives consideration not only to the 'statements' by the party responsible for fraud, but uses a broader term (*manoeuvres*); the (relative) nullity of the contract is envisaged only in the case that, if there had been no contract fraud, the party who has suffered the effects would not have concluded the contract (this last requirement is not envisaged under Austrian law).[187] For the purposes of recourse to art. 1116, another relevant factor is also incomplete information, if it is done intentionally,[188] even though this question has always raised problems of coordination with the rules on pre-contractual liability. It is instead at least doubtful that the concept of 'statements', used by the *ABGB*, can also cover silence or failure to reveal some relevant information.

According to art. 1304 of the *Code Civil*, in its original version, the action of nullity for contract fraud was subject to a ten-year limitation period, commencing on the day when the contract fraud was discovered.[189] Finally, the French system holds that contract fraud constitutes a tort, and thus allows the person who has been damaged, to take legal measures to obtain compensation: such is the case envisaged by art. 1116 (so-called *dol principal*). Initially, the two actions were alternatives, but today the law recognizes the possibility of a combined action.[190] It follows that the victim of contract

---

187   Duranton notes that, with art. 1116, the *Code Napoléon* fully accepted the measure in Roman law: 'le Code civil, dans l'Article 1116, a aussi adopté la distinction des juriconsultes, entre le dol qu'ils appellent principal [...] et le dol incidente, puisqu'il décide que le dol n'est cause de nullité, que lorsque les manoeuvres pratiqués par l'une des parties sont telles, qu'il est évident que, sans ces manoeuvres, l'autre partie n'aurait pas contracté; ce qui ne veut pas dire, n'aurait point contracté aux mêmes conditions, mais ce qui veut dire, n'aurait point formé le contrat, n'aurait pas contracté du tout' (A. DURANTON, *Cours de droit civil français, suivant le code civil*, Brussels: Hauman, 1835, vol. 6, p. 59).

188   Considering a flaw inherent in the sale of a firm, the Court of Cassation expresses itself as follows: 'Une demande indemnitaire, exclusivement fondée sur la réticence dolosive reprochée au cédant d'un fonds de commerce, ne peut être accueillie si le cessionnaire n'établit pas le caractère intentionnel du comportement du cédant et le caractère déterminant du dol allégué, lesquels sont souverainement appréciés par les juges du fond' (Cass. Civ. 7 June 2011).

189   In the current version of art. 1304, the period is reduced to 5 years (law no. 685 of 3 January 1968).

190   If the cancellation of the contract is not sufficient to eliminate the damage: Cass. Civ., 14 November 1979, in Bull. Civ., I, no. 279, p. 226.

fraud would have had the choice between an action for nullity, and compensation for the tort suffered.[191]

8. How would we judge – under current Italian law – Nemorino and Dulcamara's story today, and on the basis of what categories?

According to art. 1439 of the Italian Civil Code, 'contract fraud is a cause for annulment of the contract when the deceptions used by one of the parties were such that, without them, the other party would not have agreed to the contract.'

The wording of art. 1439 is close to that of the *Code Civil*, since it regulates a purposeful fraudulent conduct, which is *decisive* for the conclusion of the contract. In addition, the reference to 'deception' becomes relevant not only to *statements* made by the party, but – more generally – to everything to be performed by him; the proof of 'deception' lies with the victim. The remedy looks similar: for the Italian Civil Code, contract fraud is a cause for annulment of the contract, and for the French Code Civil, as we have seen, the penalty is qualified *nullity*, but since the imprecision of the French Code is notorious on this subject, it is *relative* and not *absolute nullity*, which therefore can only be triggered by the person who suffered from the illicit conduct. Action, under both art. 1442 of the Civil Code and art. 1116 of the *Code Civil*, can be taken within five years from the time that the fraud was discovered. For our present purposes – and without going more fully into the various differences that characterize annullability and nullity of contracts – it appears that the consequences in the Italian system would be very similar to those deriving from the French Code. Following an action by Nemorino in court, the contract would be voided, and the goods exchanged would be subject to restitution.

Another element that should be noted is that, based on an established approach, contract fraud, under Italian law, also gives a right to compensation for damages: the two remedies, in particular, may act *cumulatively*, or *alternatively*, at the option of the victim of the fraud. Obviously, the two prospects produce different consequences. One part of the doctrine be-

---

191   In this sense A. DURANTON, *Cours*, cit., who stresses that the solution is shared by 'beaucoup d'interprètes, même la plupart'.

lieves, however, that compensation must be calculated differently depending on whether the claim is cumulative, or not, with that to obtain the annulment of the contract. In particular, in the case of a claim for damages, consideration must also be given to whether the author of the deception can refuse, under art. 1227, paragraph 2, to recognize the payment of damages which the victim would have avoided by annulling the contract.[192] It has been discussed whether it is possible to cause the annulment by what is called *dolus bonus*, namely the conduct consisting in general boasting or in the hyperbolical exaltation of the service offered, such as, essentially, to deceive a particularly gullible and naïve person. The preferred opinion now seems to be in the negative: it is observed that the provisions of art. 1439 do not envisage excusability among the requirements of error, nor does it attribute significance to a parameter of 'average foresight' in the assessment of the circumstances leading to the conclusion of the contract (the French system adopts the same approach). Of course, the consistency and the 'dangerousness' of the deception may prove to be significant for the annulment of the contract, but not so much in *subjective* terms (that is, the psychological state of the person deceived), as that of the concrete capacity to mislead the other party.

9. All three systems considered would, therefore, give Nemorino protection against the fraud of which he is the victim. The solutions, however, change. In terms of the *fate of the contract*, under the Austrian Code, in force at the time of the first performance of the opera in Milan, Nemorino could invoke the invalidity of the contract, the restitution of his sequin, but – at the same time – would have to undertake to offer an alternative to the return of the wine (already consumed). Based on the Napoleonic Code, with reference to the sources of the libretto, the solution would be the relative nullity of the contract, which could be invoked by Nemorino within a period of 10 years from discovery of the fraud. In this case, too, the problem of the return of the benefits of the contract would arise. Under the current Italian Civil Code, the remedy would be the annulment of the contract, to be exercised

---

192   See V. ROPPO, *Il contratto*, in *Trattato di diritto privato*, edited by G. Iudica and P. Zatti, II edition, Milan: Giuffrè, 2011, p. 759.

within five years from the date of discovery of the fraud. Again in this case, as we have seen, the restitution of the subject matter of the contract would arise (with the usual problem of an equivalent provision, due to the consumption of the contents of the bottle).

As to damages, the solutions are more variable. Under the Austrian *ABGB* system (as it stood at the time) and the Italian system, compensation and refunds may be combined; under the nineteenth-century French system, they could not. But there would arise the problem of assessing damages. In the end – albeit as a result of the vapours of the alcohol, instead of a miraculous love potion – Nemorino manages to win the beautiful Adina. Therefore, the result that Dulcamara promised is attained, though by means other than those claimed. An action for compensation – where permitted by the regulations applicable – would therefore, in all likelihood, not produce any useful result.

VII

Don Pasquale
(Gaetano Donizetti – Giovanni Ruffini)

How to scupper a sham marriage

1. The protagonist of *Don Pasquale* is a typical figure of the comic theatre tradition. The old man trying at all costs to get a wife is one of the archetypes from which the libretto of *Don Pasquale* stems, and of *opera buffa* as a genre.[193]

Don Pasquale closed Donizetti's career in this operatic genre. It shares many stylistic features with the foregoing work, *L'elisir d'amore*, including a deviation from the tendency of *opera buffa* to present fixed models. The figure of Don Pasquale, who is the victim of a true deception and mockery by the woman who turns out to be only his sham wife, proves to be tinged with markedly tragic elements, and in some respects with melancholy. The quest for marital harmony is represented as the pursuit of an impossible ideal, and the harsh reality – symbolized by the slap that Norina gives to the poor old man – is presented in all its starkness: old age, with its weight, destroys the dream of beauty and serenity that Don Pasquale had imagined for a moment he would be able to achieve.

The libretto is by Giovanni Ruffini and Donizetti himself. The paternity of the text – originally published anonymously – was definitively clarified only in the early twentieth century, and the story of its creation (impossible to summarize here) is almost worthy of a thriller.[194] The text is taken from an

---

193   See P. FABBRI, 'Una via donizettiana per l'opera comica', in *La Fenice prima dell'Opera*, no. 5, 2015, pp. 18 ff.

194   See the precise reconstruction by D. DAOLMI, 'Le interferenze di un musicista capriccioso', in *Teatro lirico di Cagliari. Stagione lirica e di balletto 2001: 'Don Pasquale'*. Cagliari: Scuola Sarda, 2002. The matter has been clarified by A. LAZZARI, Giovanni Ruffini, 'Gaetano Donizetti e il "Don Pasquale" (da documenti inediti)', in *La rassegna musicale*, XXXVI, vol. 205, 1915 (republished in D. DELLA PORTA [edited by], *Dentro Donizetti*, Bergamo: Bolis, 1983) and some years

earlier work of great success: the *dramma giocoso Ser Marcantonio* by Angelo Anelli (1761-1820), set to music by Stefano Pavesi (1779-1850), a prolific composer, almost forgotten today, the author of over 60 operas and very popular in his lifetime. *Ser Marcantonio* was presented for the first time at La Scala in Milan on 26 September 1810 and remained long in the repertoire.

Ser Marcantonio was, however, only the most direct source of *Don Pasquale*: in its turn, the libretto seems to have drawn on an earlier model, a comedy by Jean-Baptiste Rousseau entitled *L'hypocondre ou La femme qui ne parle point*.[195] This was a play written in 1733, but staged for the first time only in 1761 in Brussels, at the Théâtre de la Monnaie, when it was apparently an almost complete fiasco. Rousseau's comedy, which in turn revised an earlier English comedy by Ben Johnson dating from 1609 (*Epicoene, or The Silent Woman*), was also printed in a 'new edition' at Amsterdam in 1778, and some copies were on sale in Marseille, *chez Jean Mossy*,[196] hence it seems to have circulated quite widely.[197]

The history of *Don Pasquale* on the stage starts in France. The premiere was held at the Théâtre Italien in Paris on 3 January 1843 with an outstanding cast, including Giulia Grisi (Norina), Luigi Lablache (Don Pasquale), and Antonio Tamburini (Malatesta). The opera reached La Scala on 17 April. Ever since, Don Pasquale has been regularly presented in opera houses around the world.

---

later, G. RUFFINI, *I fratelli Ruffini: lettere di Giovanni e Agostino Ruffini alla madre dall'esilio francese e svizzero (1833-1835)*, edited by A. Codignola, Genoa: Società ligure di storia patria, 1925; F. WALKER, 'The Librettist of "Don Pasquale"', in *Monthly Musical Record*, LXXXVIII, 1958 pp. 219 ff.; J. ALLITT, 'Don Pasquale', in *The Donizetti Society Journal*, II, 1975, pp. 271 ff.; F. Bellotto, *Bibliografia*, in '*Don Pasquale*'. *Programma di sala del Teatro La Fenice. Stagione 2001-2002*, pp. 185-190.

195   In this sense, among others, P. FABBRI, *Una via*, cit., p. 19. Another source of *Don Pasquale*, often cited in the literature, is the farce by Giuseppe Foppa, *Diritto e rovescio*, performed in Venice for Ascension 1801, with music by Francesco Gardi. Paolo Fabbri, moreover, relates Foppa's text also to the model of Rousseau's comedy.

196   The text of the comedy can be found at the following address: https://books.google.it/books?id=rRWdxPqFmNMC&q=L_hypocondre_ou_la_femme_qui_ne_parle&dq=L_hypocondre_ou_la_femme_qui_ne_parle&hl=it&sa=X&ved=0ahUKEwiB7dr3osjLAhVF1xoKHQfeDIsQ6AEIJ-TAB. Information about the performance at the Théâtre de la Monnaie is available at the website www.carmen.demunt.be edited by the theatre itself, which gives further references to the sources.

197   P. FABBRI, *Una via*, cit., p. 19, considers, in particular, that Rousseau's comedy also served as the basis for other opera librettos, including *Diritto e rovescio* by Foppa-Gardi, cited above, and the 'melodramma buffo' by Carlo Defranceschi, *Angiolina, o sia Il matrimonio per sussurro*, set to music by Salieri for Vienna (1800).

2. The plot *of Don Pasquale* is, as mentioned above, that of a sham marriage foiled. Don Pasquale, described in the stage directions to the libretto as an 'elderly bachelor, one of the old school, thrifty, gullible and stubborn, at bottom a good man', is angry with his nephew Ernesto, the future heir to his wealth. Ernesto refuses to marry a noble and wealthy spinster, being in love with Norina, a charming widow, bourgeois but of modest means (in the stage direction she is described as a 'young widow, impulsive, kind, impatient of contradiction, but frank and affectionate'). So Don Pasquale decides to disinherit his nephew and get married himself. For this purpose he applies to Dr. Malatesta (described in the libretto as 'resourceful, witty, enterprising, a doctor and friend to Don Pasquale and a close friend of Ernesto's'). Don Pasquale asks Malatesta to find him a suitable wife. However, as a friend to Ernesto, Malatesta prefers to help the two young lovers. He proposes that Don Pasquale should marry his sister Sofronia, straight out of the convent. He asks Norina to impersonate Sofronia, so as to arrange a fake marriage, and then reduce Don Pasquale to despair, so persuading him to accept Ernesto's marriage plans. Meanwhile the latter, who is not aware of the scheme, is driven out of the house.

The scene that concerns us first here is the sham marriage, celebrated by Carlo, Malatesta's cousin, who comes on stage dressed as a notary. The scene is characterized, as in other cases (like *Così fan tutte*) by comic and grotesque elements: the garbled recollections of legal formulas, the et caeteras strewn through the texts read aloud, the notary's syllabic repetitions, who seems to spell out what he is writing.

With the notarial contract, Don Pasquale gives the girl half of his possessions (Act II.45).[198]

MALATESTA   Fra da una parte *et cetera*
                   Sofronia Malatesta,
                   domiciliata *et cetera*
                   con tutto quel che resta,
                   e d'altra parte *et cetera*

---

198   The text comes from the libretto in two languages published for the Parisian premiere at the Théâtre Italien: *DON PASQUALE | dramma buffo in tre atti | Musica del maestro Gaetano Donizetti | Decorazioni de SS.D. Ferri e Luigi Verardi | Parigi | Dai Torchj | 1842.*

Pasquale da Corneto
coi titoli e le formole
secondo il consueto,
entrambi qui presenti,
volenti e consenzienti,
un matrimonio in regola
a stringere si va.

DON PASQUALE *(al notaro)*
Avete messo?

NOTARO Ho messo.

DON PASQUALE Sta ben.
(Va alla sinistra del notaro)
Scrivete appresso.
(Come dettando)
Il qual prefato *et cetera*
di quanto egli possiede
in mobili ed immobili
dona tra i vivi e cede
a titolo gratuito
alla suddetta *et cetera*
sua moglie dilettissima
fin d'ora la metà.

NOTARO Sta scritto.

DON PASQUALE E intende ed ordina
che sia riconosciuta
in questa casa e fuori
padrona ampia assoluta,
e sia da tutti e singoli
di casa riverita,
servita ed obbedita
con zelo e fedeltà.

MALATESTA E NORINA *(a Don Pasquale)*
Rivela il vostro core
quest'atto di bontà.

NOTARO Steso è il contratto. Restano
le firme...

DON PASQUALE *(sottoscrivendo con vivacità)*
Ecco la mia.

MALATESTA *(conducendo Norina al tavolo con dolce violenza)*
Cara sorella, or via,

si tratta di segnar.

NOTARO   Non vedo i testimoni,
un solo non può star.

(Mentre Norina sta in atto di sottoscrivere, si sente la voce di Ernesto dalla porta d'ingresso. Norina lascia cader la penna)

ERNESTO   *(di dentro)* Indietro, mascalzoni,
indietro, io voglio entrar.

NORINA   Ernesto! Or veramente
mi viene da tremar!

MALATESTA   Ernesto! e non sa niente,
può tutto rovinar!

SCENA QUINTA

(Ernesto e detti. Ernesto senza badare agli altri va dritto a Don Pasquale)

ERNESTO   *(a Don Pasquale con vivacità)*
Pria di partir, signore,
vengo per dirvi addio,
e come a un malfattore
mi vien conteso entrar!

DON PASQUALE   *(a Ernesto)*
S'era in faccende: giunto
però voi siete in punto.
A fare il matrimonio
mancava un testimonio.
(volgendosi a Norina)
Or venga la sposina.

ERNESTO   *(vedendola, nel massimo stupore)*
(Che vedo? Oh ciel! Norina!
Mi sembra di sognar!)
(esplodendo)
Ma questo non può star.
Costei...

(Malatesta, che in questo frattempo si sarà interposto fra Don Pasquale e Ernesto, interrompe quest'ultimo)

MALATESTA   La sposa è quella.
(con intenzione marcata)
Sofronia, mia sorella.

ERNESTO   *(con sorpresa crescente)*
Sofronia! Sua sorella!

Comincio ad impazzar!

MALATESTA
(piano ad Ernesto)

Per carità, sta' zitto,
ci vuoi precipitar.
(piano a Don Pasquale)
Gli cuoce: compatitelo,
lo vo' capacitar.
(prende Ernesto in disparte)
Figliuol, non farmi scene,
è tutto per tuo bene.
Se vuoi Norina perdere
Non hai che a seguitar.
(Ernesto vorrebbe parlare)
Seconda la commedia,
sta' cheto e lascia far.
(Volgendosi alla comitiva)
Questo contratto adunque
si vada ad ultimar.

(Malatesta conduce a sottoscrivere prima Norina poi Ernesto, quest'ultimo metà per amore, metà per forza)

NOTARO
(riunendo le mani degli sposi)

Siete marito e moglie.

DON PASQUALE
Mi sento a liquefar.

NORINA E MALATESTA
(Va il bello a cominciar.)

(Appena segnato il contratto, Norina prende un contegno naturale, ardito senza impudenza e pieno di disinvoltura.)[199]

---

199   The English translation is based upon *Don Pasquale. Italian Text with an English Translation*, Boston: Oliver Ditson Company, 1888, available at https://archive.org/details/cu31924090833322, adapted to the version of the libretto used in the text.
MALATESTA Between, on one part – et cetera, Sophronia Malatesta, Residing at – et cetera; and all remainders over: and on the other part – et cetera, Pasquale of Corneto, with titles and formulas both of them being present, and willing and consenting, a marriage legal, valid, are going now to – cancel! /DON PASQUALE *(To the Notary)* Have you written? /NOTARY I have written / DON PASQUALE Very good! *(Goes to the left of the Notary)* You, then will write now *(As if dictating)*. The aforesaid Don et cetera. Of whatever he is possess'd moveables and immoveables – Gives – being of sound life – as his own and free act and gift, to the above named – et cetera, his beloved wife delectable, from this time, an equal half / NOTARY It is written /DON PASQUALE And he wills and orders that she shall farther be acknowledged in this house; and when not in it, the mistress wholly, absolute and by all, herself shall be, in the house, paid reverence due – served by all – by all obeyed with zeal and fidelity / MALATESTA and NOTARY *(To Don Pasquale)* In this you truly show your heart – this spontaneous act of bounty /NOTARY The contract's drawn: there but

Don Pasquale's troubles begin as soon as he signs the contract. At once Norina's attitude changes: she becomes arrogant, she swaggers about, and is wildly extravagant. She doubles all the servants' wages, sends for new carriages and horses, plans costly festivities, and orders clothes and jewels:

NORINA
> *(Al maggiordomo)*
> Di legni un paio sia
> stassera in scuderia,
> uno leggero e basso,
> in quello andremo a spasso,
> l'altro più greve e solido
> da viaggio servirà.
> Quanto ai cavalli poi,
> lascio la scelta a voi.
> Siano di razza inglese,
> e non si badi a spese.
> Otto da tiro: due
> da sella e basterà.

---

remain the signatures / DON PASQUALE (*Signing eagerly*) Here's mine! /MALATESTA (*Drawing Norina to the table with gentle compulsion*) Dearest sister, now come, thine; For thou must be the next to sign! /NOTARY I do not see the witnesses: one alone will not suffice (*While Norina is in the act of signing, the voice of Ernesto is heard from the outer door: Norina lets the pen fall*) / ERNESTO (*Within*) Back, villains! Back, I say! /NORINA (Ernesto, I really don't dissemble: in earnest I begin to tremble!) / SCENE V – Ernesto, without attending to the others, goes straight to Don Pasquale. ERNESTO (*To Don Pasquale, warmly*) Ere I finally take wing, I came here, sir, adieu to say: when, like some malefactor, they would from your doors drive me away / DON PASQUALE (*To Ernesto*) We were engaged – your coming, though, is nevertheless, most à propos: my happy marriage to complete, one witnes more, it seems, is meet (*turning to Norina*). Advance, my bride / ERNESTO (*seeing her, in the greatest amazement*) (What do I see? Great Heavens, Norina! It seems like some wild dream to me!) (*breaking out*) But I'm deceived – it cannot be. Who's this? (*The Doctor, who has by this time placed himself between Don Pasquale and Ernesto, interrupts the latter*) / MALATESTA The lady is the bride (*with marked significance*) Sophronia, sister dear, my pride! ERNESTO (*with increasing surprise*) Sophronia! She his sister – she! I feel that soon I mad shall be! /MALATESTA (*Aside, to Ernesto*) (For mercy's sake, be silent, pray! You'll ruin all, if more you say) (*aside to Don Pasquale*) He's wretched – pity on him take: I will persuade him to submit (*takes Ernesto aside*) My son, a scene, pray, do not make: all this is for your benefit. If you wish to loose Norina, you have only to proceed. (*Ernesto tries to speak*). Assist us in this comic scene – Peace let us manage – it will succeed (*turning round to the Servants*). This contract – all his folly past – we're going to conclude at last. (*The Doctor conducts, first Norina, to affix her signature; then, partly by persuasion and partly by force, Ernesto*) / NOTARY (*Joining the hands of the married couple*) You are husband, now, and wife / DON PASQUALE I feel I'm melting! /NORINA and MALATESTA The best part's going to commence! (*The contract has hardly been signed, when Norina resumes her natural manner: her self-possession and ease, without boldness*).

La casa è mal disposta,
la vo' rifar di posta,
sono anticaglie i mobili,
si denno rinnovar.
Vi son mill'altre cose
urgenti, imperiose,
un parrucchier da scegliere,
un sarto, un gioielliere,
ma questo con più comodo
domani si può far.

DON PASQUALE
(con rabbia concentrata)
Avete ancor finito?

NORINA
(seccamente)
No.
(Al maggiordomo)
Mi scordavo il meglio.
Farete che servito
sia per le quattro un pranzo
nel gran salon terreno.
Sarem cinquanta almeno,
fate le cose in regola,
non ci facciam burlar.
(D'un cenno congeda il maggiordomo che parte coi servi)

MALATESTA
(guardando Don Pasquale)
(Il cielo si rannuvola.)

ERNESTO
(Commincia a lampeggiar.)

NORINA
(volgendosi con calma a Don Pasquale)
Ecco finito.

DON PASQUALE
Grazie.
Chi paga?

NORINA
Oh bella! voi.

DON PASQUALE
A dirla qui fra noi
non pago mica.

NORINA
No?

DON PASQUALE
(riscaldato)
Sono o non son padrone?

NORINA
(con disprezzo)
Mi fate compassione.
(Con forza)
Padrone ov'io comando?

MALATESTA	*(interponendosi a Norina)*
	Sorella...
NORINA	*(a Don Pasquale con furia crescente)*
	Or or vi mando...
	Siete un villano, un tanghero...
DON PASQUALE	*(con dispetto)*
	È vero; v'ho sposato.
NORINA	*(come sopra)*
	Un pazzo temerario...
DOTTORE	*(a Don Pasquale che sbuffa)*
	Per carità, cognato.
NORINA	Che presto alla raggione
	rimettere saprò.

(Don Pasquale è fuori di sé, vorrebbe e non può parlare, la bile lo affoga)

DON PASQUALE	Son tradito, calpestato,
	son di riso a tutti oggetto.
	Quest'inferno anticipato
	non lo voglio sopportar.
	Dalla rabbia e dal dispetto
	sto vicino a soffocar.
NORINA	*(a Ernesto)*
	Or t'avvedi, core ingrato,
	che fu ingiusto il tuo sospetto.
	Solo amor m'ha consigliato
	questa parte a recitar.
	(Accennando a Don Pasquale)
	Don Pasquale, poveretto!
	è vicino ad affogar.[200]

---

200   NORINA (*To the Mayor-Dome*) Of carriages, mind, two at least this eve must in the co-ach-house be, one light and short, with it we shall stroll, the other more grave and solid, shall be for journeys used. As for the horses and the rest, I shall leave the choice to thee. Be they of English race, and no concerns for costs. Eight for carriages: two to ride and it's enough. The house most vilely is arranged – I'll alter it now. The furniture is antiquated – all must instantly be changed. There are thousands other things, urgent, imperious, a coiffeurs to choose, a taylor, a jeweller, but this with less haste tomorrow can be done /DON PASQUALE (*With concentrated rage*) Have you done, or have you not? /NORINA (*Snappishly*) No! The chief thing I'd forgot – Shall it then be served, lunch at four in the great hall below. We shall be fifty at least, do things as they should, let's not be laughed at (*She dismisses the Major-Domo by a gesture – he goes off with the Servants*). MALATESTA (*Looking at Don Pasquale*) (The sky is darkening) / ERNESTO (Lightning is approaching) /NORINA (*Turning calmly to Don Pasquale*) That's all / DON PASQUALE Thank you. Who pays? /NORINA Oh well! You / DON PASQUALE Here, between ourselves, I shall not

Norina, naturally, will have no truck with Don Pasquale. In fact, she actually leads him on to believe – even before thinking about the little matter of consummating the marriage – that she has a lover. Don Pasquale turns despairingly to Malatesta, who with Ernesto's help organizes a trap. The latter – unrecognized by Don Pasquale – will have to impersonate Norina's lover in a meeting in the woods, while Don Pasquale secretly watches.

After this scene, Don Pasquale announces to Ernesto that, to torment Sofronia and persuade her to leave, he will be able to marry Norina, and she will become the new mistress of the house. At this point, however, the plot hatched against the old man is revealed. Don Pasquale, happy to have got rid of his terrible wife, forgives everyone and celebrates Ernesto and Norina's union.

3. The story of *Don Pasquale* follows the same lines in Pavesi's *Ser Marcantonio*, but with a number of significant differences. In addition to a substantial dramatic reworking of the dramatic structure, necessary above all in *Don Pasquale* to adapt Anelli's story to the altered sensitivities of the nineteenth century,[201] it is the story of the fake marriage that unfolds differently. *Ser Marcantonio* represents not a marriage, but a betrothal. The agreement signed with the services of the (false) notary – impersonated by Tobia – is a mutual promise of marriage between Bettina and Marcantonio, with a provision for a penalty, against Marcantonio, in case of default. What follows is from Act I.XI:[202]

---

pay / NORINA No? DON PASQUALE (*Heated*) Am I master or not? /NORINA (*With contempt*) I pity you (*With energy*) Master where I command? /MALATESTA (*Interposing Norina*) Sister... / NORINA (*To Don Pasquale with growing rage*) Now, now I send you—You are a vilain, an old bumpkin / DON PASQUALE (*Bitterly*) It's true: I married you / NORINA (*As before*) A madman's rash... / MALATESTA (*To Don Pasquale, who is foaming*) Please, brother-in-law. NORINA Whom very shortly to his reason I know a way again to bring. (*Don Pasquale is enraged, he would like but cannot talk, rage suffocates him*) /DON PASQUALE I am betrayed, trod down and beat, a laughing-stock to all I meet: this Tartarus, before it's time, I'll not support. With mingled rage and spite, I am suffocating quit / NORINA (*To Ernesto*) Now you see, ungrateful heart, how unjust was your suspicion: love counselled thee to play this part. (*Points to Don Pasquale*) Don Pasquale, poor dear, is nearly suffocated quite!

201   See the observations by D. DAOLMI, *Le intereferenze*, cit.

202   The passages are taken from the libretto of the first Milanese performance: *SER MARCANTONIO* | *Dramma giocoso* | *per musica* | *in due atti* | *da rappresentarsi* | *nel* | *R.o Teatro alla Scala* | *l'autunno dell'anno 1810* | *Milano* | *Dalla Società Tipografica de' Classici Italiani*. The English courtesy translation is by the Author.

TOBIA	Ho steso già il contratto
	ne' modi più legali,
	s'hanno da far per patto
	stasera gli sponsali;
	e acciò lo sposo *etcetera*
	alla sua fé non manchi.
	Pagar promette, e s'obbliga
	ottantamila franchi,
	perché la sposa, *etcetera*,
	al caso, un altro coniuge
	si possa ritrovar.
TOBIA	Che dite?
BETTINA	Che dici?
MEDORO	Va benissimo,
	di meglio non può andar.
TOBIA	*(si mette a un tavolino a scrivere)*
	Or dica, signorina,
	il nome suo?
BETTINA	Bettina.
TOBIA	Il suo cognome?
BETTINA	Mascoli.
TOBIA	Mascoli?
BETTINA	Sì signor.
TOBIA	Lo sposo, già m'immagino,
	sarà quel giovinetto
	Pari d'età d'aspetto…
	proprio gli ha fatti amor.
MARCANTONIO	Lo sposo, ve lo replico,
	son io.
TOBIA	Misericordia!
	Voi sposo a lei? Scusatemi,
	creder no 'l posso ancor.
MARCANTONIO	(Io gli darei dell'asino,
	ma penso, ch'è un dottor.)
BETTINA, PASQUINO E MEDORO	(Ah! ah! Quest'è da ridere.
	Che faccia da impostor!)
TOBIA	Avanti: sottoscrivano
	gli sposi il lor contratto.
	I testimoni or vengano;

	bene. Il negozio è fatto.
	Or datevi la mano.
BETTINA E MARCANTONIO	Eccola... Oh che piacer!
MEDORO E TOBIA	Viva gli sposi.
MARCANTONIO	Nessun lo dée saper.
TOBIA	Quand'è così: fidatevi.
BETTINA E MEDORO	È un uom, che sa tacer.
TOBIA	Son uom, che sa tacer.[203]

The situation between Marcantonio and Bettina is revealed by the conversation between Marcantonio, Lisetta and Pasquino (Act II.2). It shows clearly that the two are not yet married, and the contract signed is a promise of marriage with a penalty of 80,000 francs:

LISETTA	E come fosse
	già vostra moglie a tutti noi comanda...
PASQUINO	E coll'idea di comparir signora,
	consultàti in mezz'ora
	ha cinque parrucchieri, e quattro sarti.
MARCANTONIO	E non vai, Marcantonio, ad impiccarti?
	Orsù, sposa sì fatta
	io non la voglio più.
PASQUINO	Come?... E vorreste
	gli ottantamille franchi
	dunque pagar?

---

203   TOBIA I have already written the contract in the utmost legal terms, tonight the bethrotal shall be agreed upon; and *etcetera* the bridegroom shall not breach his faith. He promises, and undertakes, to pay 80.000 francs, so that the bride, *etcetera*, if necessary, another groom may find / TOBIA What do you say? /BETTINA What do you say? / MEDORO It is fine, better than this it cannot be / TOBIA (*sits at a table in order to write*) Now tell me, lady, what is your name? BETTINA Bettina /TOBIA Your surname? /BETTINA Mascoli / TOBIA Mascoli? / BETTINA Yes, sir / TOBIA The groom, I imagine, is that young man over there... Same age and looks, love has truly made them / MARCANTONIO I repeat, I am the groom / TOBIA Heavens! You, her bridegroom? Sorry, I still can't believe it / MARCANTONIO (I should call him a donkey, but I think, he's a doctor) /BETTINA, PASQUINO, MEDORO (Ah! ah! This is something to laugh at! What an impostor!) /TOBIA Come now: the couple now sign the contract. Let the witnesses in; good. The contract is done. Now take your hands /BETTINA and MARCANTONIO Here it is... Oh what a pleasure! / MEDORO and TOBIA Cheers for the married! / MARCANTONIO Nobody must know it /TOBIA If this is so: trust me / BETTINA and MEDORO He is a man, who can be silent / TOBIA I am a man, who can be silent.

DON PASQUALE

MARCANTONIO	Questo è l'imbroglio: questo
	è quel siroppo, ch'io non so ingoiare.[204]

Again in Act II.5 the nature of the bond is stressed. Note, in particular, what Medoro says ('The old man intends to have no more weddings'), and what Tobia emphasizes ('You have to marry her, or pay up'), an expression that seems clearly reminiscent of *Le nozze di Figaro*:

TOBIA	Lisetta, ascolta.
	Tosto che viene il vecchio
	déi strillar quanto puoi: e tu, Dorina,
	fingendo un gran spavento
	cadrai su questa sedia in svenimento.
	(le presenta una sedia)
LISETTA	E perché questa scena?
MEDORO	Il vecchio intende
	di non far più le nozze,
	e insieme di non pagar quanto ha promesso.
TOBIA	Bisogna dunque adesso
	fargli un po' di timor. Poscia all'oscuro
	noi faremo in giardino
	un altro gioco, e te 'l dirà Pasquino.
	[omissis]
TOBIA	Orsù: sentite
	s'è ver, come voi dite, che Bettina
	abbia un qualche galante, assolvo il vecchio
	da qualunque promessa. Senza questo,
	non c'è scusa, o pretesto,
	dée sposarla, o pagar.[205]

204 LISETTA She commands us as if she were already your wife... / PASQUINO And by wanting to appear as a Lady she has already consulted, in half an hour, five coiffeurs, and four taylors / MARCANTONIO And don't you go, Marcantonio, to hang yourself? Come on, such a bride, I do not want here any more / PASQUINO How?... And you would therefore wish to pay 80.000 francs? /MARCANTONIO This is the trick: this is a syrup, I do not wish to take.

205 TOBIA Lisetta, listen to me. When the old man comes, you must shout as much as you can: and you, Dorina, feigning a fright, you shall fall on this chair, fainted *(he shows her a chair)* / LISETTA And why these scene? /MEDORO The old man does not wish to marry any more, and to not pay what he has promised / TOBIA We must now frighten him a bit. Then, at dark, we shall play in the garden another game, and Pasquino shall explain. *[omissis]* /TOBIA Come on: if, as you

Marcantonio tries to wriggle out of his promise, if possible without paying the penalty stipulated. The clandestine meeting between Bettina and her alleged lover could offer the solution:

MARCANTONIO	Povero Marcantonio!
	Questa faccenda come andrà a finire?
	Le ottantamille lire
	non le voglio pagar. Ma aver tal moglie
	io non voglio nemmen... Son imbrogliato.
PASQUINO	Padron... presto... Padron...
MARCANTONIO	Che cosa è stato?
PASQUINO	Bettina adesso al buio
	d'un qualche amante in traccia...
	se n'è andata in giardin...
MARCANTONIO	Buon pro le faccia.
	Questo è quel ch'io volea.
PASQUINO	Come?
MARCANTONIO	Non vedi,
	che così senza spesa
	mando per aria questo sposalizio?[206]

Events actually degenerate into a sham lawsuit, again reminiscent of *Le nozze di Figaro*. The issue of the alleged betrayal, and the fate of the promise of marriage, is addressed in the garden, with Pasquino in the guise of the judge. Marcantonio claims not to want to marry because of his betrothed's behaviour; others accuse him of inventing an excuse for not paying the penalty of 80,000 francs (Act II.10):

MARCANTONIO	Voi di qua, voi di là con quelle torce
	illuminate questo loco intorno,

---

say, it is true that Bettina has some other gallant, I absolve the old man from his promise. Without this, no excuse or pretext, he must marry her, or pay her.

206   MARCANTONIO Poor Marcantonio! How will this matter end? I do not want to pay 80,000 liras. But neither do I want such a wife... I am tricked. /PASQUINO Master... quick... Master /MARCANTONIO What is it? /PASQUINO Bettina now in the dark is in the garden... looking for some lover... /MARCANTONIO Good for her. This is what I wanted / PASQUINO What? /MARCANTONIO Don't you see, that in this way, with no expense I blow up this marriage?

da poterci veder come di giorno.
Qua il tavolino, e qua le sedie... oh... appunto.
Eccoli: signor giudice, e voi pure,
amici miei, sedete, ed ascoltate.
(vanno a sedere il giudice, e i vecchi)
Pria di tutto scusate, se a quest'ora
v'ho fatto incomodar. Ma qui si tratta
con un formal giudizio
di trarre un pover'uom dal precipizio.

PASQUINO   Dite senza preamboli.

MARCANTONIO   Sappiate,
che mi sono obbligato
di sposare una tal, che in apparenza
potea dirsi il model dell'innocenza.
Ora state a sentir. Mentre io l'aspetto
per far le nozze, con un suo galante
qui all'oscuro in giardin da solo a sola
ella se n' viene...

TOBIA   Ei mente per la gola.
Sappiate, signor giudice,
che il contratto di nozze è fatto in modo,
che, qualora egli manchi,
deve pagar ottantamille franchi:
ora, per non pagar, non ha riguardo,
con questa sua novella,
d'accusar quella tal, ch'è mia sorella.

MARCANTONIO   Ho in man le prove.

TOBIA   Son pretesti.

MARCANTONIO   Sciocco.

TOBIA   Bestia.

MARCANTONIO   Animal.

TOBIA   Per forza, o per amore,
o pagare, o sposarla...

PASQUINO   Asini: in faccia mia così si parla?
Orsù: state a sentir. Rompe ogni patto
una sposa infedel: abbia la pena
chi suo marito, e il suo dover maltratta.[207]

---

207   MARCANTONIO You, that way, you, the other way, with those lighted torches light up this

In the end, here, too, everything is settled, and Marcantonio – realizing the mockery against him – forgives all. The two pairs of young lovers can finally be united, and all agree on the moral:

TUTTI   Quest'è stata una buona lezione
         per un vecchio, che vuolsi ammogliar.[208]

4. The different structure of the libretto of *Ser Marcantonio*, compared to that of *Don Pasquale*, is evident in the simplification that the (actually rather complicated) story of the former underwent in *Don Pasquale*, through its adaptation by Ruffini and, as we know, Donizetti himself. The simplification also resulted in a reduction in the number of characters (the Anelli-Pavesi text interweaves the story of three couples); the plot is slimmed down (*Don Pasquale* lacks the trial scene, and many other passages are necessarily abridged, given the smaller number of characters); the plot is less complex (in particular the final section, with the discovery of the betrayal, and the revelation of the identity of the wife-fiancée is rather convoluted in *Ser Mancantonio*, given the need to resolve the question for the three couples involved).

At the same time, however, the simplification results in a less precise treatment of the legal situation found in *Don Pasquale* compared to the model. Malatesta says 'You are going to make a regular marriage'; the (bogus) notary states, at the end of his speech, 'You are husband and wife.' What is clearly lacking in *Don Pasquale* is the consummation of the marriage: but

---

place, so that it is like daylight. Here the table, here the chairs... oh.. right. Here they are: Judge, and you too, my friends, sit and listen (*the judge and the old people sit down*) First of all excuse me, if I disturbed you at this hour. But here with a formal judgment a poor man must be saved from a precipice /PASQUINO Speak without preambles / MARCANTONIO You should know, that I agreed to marry a girl, that apparently looked like the model of innocence. Now listen to me. While I wait for her to be married, with her lover here, in the dark, she comes / TOBIA He lies, surely. Judge, you should know that the marriage contract sets out that, if he refeuses, he must pay 80.000 francs: now, in order not to pay, he does not care, with this news, to accuse her, who is my sister / MARCANTONIO I have the proofs in my hand / TOBIA These are excuses / MARCANTONIO Silly/TOBIA Animal / TOBIA By force, or by love, to pay her or to marry her... / PASQUINO You donkeys: you talk to me like this? Come on: listen. An unfaithful wife breaks all promises: her husband bears the pain, and has the duty to mistreat her.
208   ALL This was a good lesson, for an old man who wants to marry.

this is an element that, on the basis of the legislation regulating marriage in the period, was not indispensable in order to attribute – at least temporarily – to Don Pasquale and Norina-Sofronia the status of husband and wife.[209] However, if Don Pasquale and Norina-Sofronia seem to be actually married, they would (though only fictitiously) be joined by a legal bond, indissoluble except by recourse to divorce. This point is, for obvious reasons of dynamic and theatrical effectiveness, omitted in *Don Pasquale*: the marital crisis is resolved simply by inducing Sofronia-Norina to abandon the marital home, in the light of the threat posed by the arrival of a new head of the family. Obviously, from a substantive standpoint, nothing has changed because the wedding was never held, and it was all a fiction; but the fact remains that, until the deception is discovered, Don Pasquale reasons as if he were actually married, and so do all the other characters. The legal categories should therefore have been adapted to the new situation created. It is in this respect that *Ser Marcantonio* is more accurate in representing the situation. While Anelli-Pavesi also make use of a (fake) law suit, to legally back up the question of the dissolution of the marriage vows, Donizetti neglects to go into details: the theatrical fiction enables him, however, to solve and overcome the legal niceties.

Now, if we assume that what emerges from the libretto of *Don Pasquale* is valid, the protagonist would be in a complicated situation. In this respect, it is appropriate to distinguish the patrimonial regime of the family (to be regarded in the light of the Napoleonic Code, given the place where the opera was first performed), from that of the marriage tie.

On the first point, the French Code of 1804 is unanimously regarded as assigning the wife a secondary position in the matrimonial relationship, subordinated to that of her husband. Significantly, the Napoleonic Code has traditionally been accused of sexism and a lack of concern for the position of women. Among the traits that characterize the approach adopted by the Code, we should at least number the following:

– the father of a child conceived in marriage was, by definition, the husband's;

---

209   In this sense M. EMANUELE, 'Fisiologia del matrimonio in musica: "Lolita" e "Don Pasquale"', in *'Don Pasquale'. Programma di sala del Teatro La Fenice. Stagione 2001-2002*, p. 49.

– the husband owed protection to his wife, and the wife owed obedience to her husband;

– with marriage, the woman passed from the protection of her parents to that of her husband;

– the woman had no right to administer the common goods, and could not dispose of her personal assets or manage them without her husband's permission, even in case of separation (until 1965);

– without her husband's permission, the woman could not practice a profession (until 1965);

– the woman could not perform legal acts (a prohibition partially repealed in 1938, and definitively in 1965).

The spouses had an obligation of mutual fidelity but not to the same extent (until 1975): a woman who committed adultery could be punished with imprisonment from three months to two years; a man, however, was liable to a fine, and only if he brought the concubine into the marital home.

Based on the above, Norina-Sofronia's 'patrimonial' vagaries could easily have been curbed by Don Pasquale as head of the family, endowed with the prerogatives granted by the Napoleonic Code.

As to divorce, its evolution in France can be divided into three phases. The first was the revolutionary period: from 1792–1793 a number of measures were adopted introducing divorce. In particular, the law of 8 May 1792 provided that divorce could be requested in three cases. Firstly if there was dementia, a Court sentence for a felony or heinous crime, commission of crimes, abuses or insults, degeneration of morals, abandonment of the conjugal home by one of the spouses, followed by evidence for at least five years that the spouse was dead, and emigration.

A second case was divorce by mutual consent, pronounced as a result of an irreconcilable disagreement between the spouses. The third case arose from incompatibility of character or rancour on the part of at least one of the parties. The law of 28 September 1792 established, in turn, that divorce might be pronounced in the case of a de facto separation lasting for six months between the spouses.

The framers of the Napoleonic Civil Code, and the Council of State – responsible for its re-reading – were divided on the issue of divorce. According to some (Jean-Étienne-Marie Portalis), divorce had to be considered as justified in the name of freedom of worship, while others (François Denis Tronchet and Jacques de Maleville) were decidedly against it. Napoleon himself was to play an important role in maintaining the institution, considering it a useful instrument to limit family conflicts. In this way, the French Code, approved in 1804, retained divorce, but limited it notably in the case of adultery by the husband: in the latter case a woman could file for divorce only if her husband had maintained his concubine in the conjugal home (art. 229). Divorce for 'incompatibility of character' was, on the other hand, limited: to obtain a divorce it was necessary that the life of the spouses together had become 'unbearable', and that there was a valid and urgent reason for their separation. This type of divorce was also restricted by the age of the spouses: the husband had to be over 25 years of age, the wife between 21 and 45 years of age; the marriage must have been celebrated at least two years before, and the dissolution of wedlock could not be requested after 20 years of marriage.

The third phase began with the Restoration. The *ultraroyalistes* were strongly against divorce: in 1815 Louis de Bonald (1754–1840), the author of a celebrated essay,[210] was the promoter of a law to abolish it, considering it a revolutionary degeneration. The Bonald law was passed on 8 May 1816.

Divorce was reintroduced in France only in 1884 (law 27 July 1884), on the initiative of Alfred Naquet. The debate over this law was particularly heated, and the text approved was the result of an inevitable compromise between the Catholics and the Left. Under the law of 1884 – destined to regulate the matter in France for nearly a century – divorce was only granted in the case of excessive behaviour, abuse, serious injury, or expressions that were wounding, defamatory, or rendered continuation of the marriage intolerable. It was therefore essential to provide proof of misconduct. The spouse who proved blameless could claim maintenance and custody of the children not yet of age. Divorce by mutual consent was not reintroduced, being only re-established with the 1975 reform (law no. 65-617 of 11 July 1975).

5. The situation we find in *Ser Marcantonio* is different, as we saw above. The question – which we have already examined in relation to *Le nozze di*

---

210   L. DE BONALD, *Du divorce considéré au XIXe siècle*, Paris: Le Clerc, 1801.

Figaro – is again the binding nature of a promise of marriage. Even in *Ser Marcantonio*, we witness a sort of degeneration, represented by the penalty that *Marcantonio* had undertaken to pay if he broke off the engagement. As we saw earlier in *Le nozze di Figaro*, the penalty would not have been binding on Marcantonio, because it contradicted to the principle of absolute freedom of wedlock. Hence the similarities between the two works in this respect are notable.

6. In the comedy by Jean-Baptiste Rousseau, *L'hypocondre ou La femme qui ne parle point*, the story is related to the other two by a sham marriage, but with no secondary variants. Firstly, the 'false spouse' is actually a man in drag (the brother of his beloved nephew, i.e. the counterpart of Ernesto). Secondly, the episode is represented, as in *Don Pasquale*, as a real marriage, from which the protagonist (old Morose, *baron hypocondre*) seeks to free himself by resorting to divorce (Act V.3). To this end, a consultation is held with bogus jurists who summarize the conditions for dissolving the marriage tie, under both canon and private law. The question is preceded by an analytical exposition of the rules of marriage, again under both canon and private law (in this case *droit coutumier*). The jurists enumerate cases which could lead to the dissolution of wedlock: an error of person; an error in the qualities of the person; bonds of kinship without a dispensation; lack of consent, including threats and fraud; impediment under canon law, resulting from a difference in worship (marriage between a baptized and unbaptized person); minority; adultery by the wife. To these conditions is added impotence on the part of the husband, which, if ascertained or declared by the person concerned, is a valid reason to dissolve the marriage, provided that the wife does not oppose it. Old Morose – eager to free himself from his shackles – declares he is unable to perform his conjugal duties, but the (fake) wife refuses to grant her consent to the dissolution of the marriage bond. The solution of the question, as in *Ser Marcantonio* and *Don Pasquale*, is entrusted to the discovery of the alleged infidelities of his (false) wife. On the whole, *L'hypocondre* presents, with considerable aplomb, themes that later emerge in *Ser Mancantonio* and *Don Pasquale*: the deception (Morose has married a man dressed up as a woman) is coloured by some intensely suggestive themes; the relationship between Morose and his pretended

wife is rocked by particularly violent outbursts; Lucinde, fiancé to Leandre (Morose's nephew) is represented as a consummate coquette, much airier in her behaviour than her future counterparts. This freedom also reflects the different historical setting of Rousseau's comedy, compared to the later works by Anelli and Ruffini. *L'hypocondre* dates from 1733, and displays the blasé spirit of the eighteenth century, which gave way in the nineteenth to the prudery and modesty of the nascent bourgeois age.

VIII

Rigoletto

(Giuseppe Verdi – Francesco Maria Piave)

Breach of an immoral contract

1. In Rigoletto (first performed at the Teatro La Fenice in Venice on 11 March 1851) private law issues are treated in relation to at least two points: first, they pertain to family law, bound up with the complicated, and somewhat obscure relationship between Rigoletto and his daughter Gilda; a second point relates to the contract concluded between Rigoletto and Sparafucile, by which the first hires the second to kill the Duke of Mantua.

In the first case, Piave's libretto, like the literary source from which it is taken (Victor Hugo's *Le roi s'amuse*), depicts a somewhat controversial father figure: not so much because of the protagonist's physical features and deformity, but because of Rigoletto's extremely jealous attitude to his daughter. He keeps Gilda segregated at home, almost 'buried alive', under the care of her vigilant guardian Giovanna. Rigoletto has issued strict instructions that the young woman is not to go out, except – rightly – to church. Gilda cannot form friendships; she does not even know who her mother was; she was orphaned at an early age, but the circumstances are unclear, and does not even know her own surname, as is evident in the duet with her father (Act I.9). Refusing to answer his daughter's questions, Rigoletto says curtly: 'What good would it do to tell you my surname?... It's useless! / I am your father and that should suffice...' We are, in short, very close to a case of maltreatment of a child (art. 572 of the Italian Penal Code). Although this side of the story would be worth developing in itself, here I mean to focus on the second of the points mentioned above: the relationship between Rigoletto and the assassin Sparafucile, which unfolds through a series of steps: namely, the two characters enter into an unlawful contract; the default by one of the parties (Sparafucile); and Rigoletto's terrible discovery of Sparafucile's default.

2. Rigoletto and Sparafucile first meet at night, in a dark lane (Act I.7: 'The deserted end of a cul-de-sac'). The scenes before their meeting were set in the ducal palace, with a fierce confrontation between Rigoletto and courtiers, including the Count of Monterone. Monterone, an old enemy of the Duke, publicly accuses him of having seduced his daughter: Rigoletto jeers at him and Monterone hurls curses in return, while the Duke orders his arrest. Rigoletto, terrified by his words, backs away. Monterone now hurls the famous curse[211] that will haunt Rigoletto until the drama's end. In the scene in question he broods, to himself, on its echo ('That old man cursed me!'). In the dark alley, outside the palace, Rigoletto encounters Sparafucile: in a few taut lines, the hired killer offers his services, which Rigoletto rejects for the time being.[212] The duet is characterized by a highly distinctive structure; on the one hand, a legato motif and on the other a structure resting on repeated notes, reminiscent of a dance movement, as if the music seeks to represent two different things at the same time, with a deliberately grotesque effect:[213]

RIGOLETTO	(Quel vecchio maledivami!)
SPARAFUCILE	Signor?...
RIGOLETTO	Va', non ho niente.
SPARAFUCILE	Né il chiesi... A voi presente un uom di spada sta.
RIGOLETTO	Un ladro?
SPARAFUCILE	Un uom che libera per poco da un rivale, e voi ne avete...

---

211   On the *motif* of the curse in *Rigoletto*, which returns in the central moments of the drama, and its dramatic function, see J. KERMAN, 'Verdi's Use of Recurring Themes', in H.S. POWERS (edited by), *Studies in Music History: Essays for Oliver Strunk*, Princeton: Princeton University Press, 1968, pp. 495 ff.

212   The text of the libretto quoted here is from the edition published for the premiere: *RIGOLETTO |Melodramma | di F. M. Piave | Musica | di Giuseppe Verdi | Da rappresentarsi | al Gran Teatro La Fenice | nella stagione | di Carnovale e Quadragesima | 1850-51 | Venezia | nella tipografia Gaspari*. The English translation is based upon the one by Dale Mc Adon, 1956, revised in 1989, available at www.murashev.com, amended in order to suit the version of the libretto used as a reference in the text.

213   See E. SALA, *The Sounds of Paris in Verdi's 'La Traviata'*, Cambridge: Cambridge University Press, 2013, p. 167.

RIGOLETTO	Quale?
SPARAFUCILE	La vostra donna è là.
RIGOLETTO	(Che sento!) E quanto spendere
	per un signor dovrei?
SPARAFUCILE	Prezzo maggior vorrei.
RIGOLETTO	Com'usasi pagar?
SPARAFUCILE	Una metà s'anticipa,
	Il resto si dà poi...
RIGOLETTO	(Dimonio!) E come puoi
	tanto securo oprar?
SPARAFUCILE	Soglio in cittade uccidere,
	oppure nel mio tetto.
	L'uomo di sera aspetto...
	una stoccata e muor.
RIGOLETTO	E come in casa?
SPARAFUCILE	È facile...
	m'aiuta mia sorella...
	Per le vie danza... è bella...
	chi voglio attira... e allor...
RIGOLETTO	Comprendo...
SPARAFUCILE	Senza strepito...
	(Mostra la spada)
	È questo il mio stromento.
	Vi serve?
RIGOLETTO	No... al momento...
SPARAFUCILE	Peggio per voi...
RIGOLETTO	Chi sa?...
SPARAFUCILE	*Sparafucil* mi nomino...
RIGOLETTO	Straniero?...
SPARAFUCILE	*(per andarsene)*
	Borgognone...
RIGOLETTO	E dove, all'occasione?...
SPARAFUCILE	Qui sempre a sera.
RIGOLETTO	Va'.

(Sparafucile parte)[214]

---

214   RIGOLETTO *(to himself)* The old man cursed me! /SPARAFUCILE Signor?... / RIGOLETTO Go – I have nothing / SPARAFUCILE And I asked for nothing. You see before you a swordsman / RIGOLETTO A robber? /SPARAFUCILE One who can rid you, for a small fee, of a rival, which you have. RIGOLETTO Who? /SPARAFUCILE Your woman lives there / RIGOLETTO

Sparafucile's services do, however, prove useful shortly after. Despite all Rigoletto's maniacal precautions, intended to keep his daughter away from all contact with the world and its temptations, Gilda has met the Duke and she has fallen in love. He passes himself off as a poor student (named Gaultier Maldé). The courtiers, in turn, believe that Gilda is Rigoletto's lover, and from vindictiveness mingled with jest, decide to kidnap her and carry her off to the ducal palace. There is no need to go into too much detail about what occurs on this occasion: for our purposes it is sufficient to focus on the scene in which Rigoletto wanders, tormented, into the Duke's palace, where, as he had guessed, his daughter is in the Duke's bedchamber. Leaving the chamber, she relates how she met someone she believed to be a penniless student. In Piave's libretto, whatever took place in the bedchamber is passed over in silence, obviously due to censorship, though it is not hard to imagine.

Rigoletto determines on revenge. He turns to Sparafucile, commissioning him to murder the Duke.

The contract between Rigoletto and Sparafucile is executed off stage, but we are made aware of it by the wording of the libretto, and we know the precise terms of the transaction: after the murder, Rigoletto himself will dispose of the corpse in the river. The price is twenty *scudi*, ten in advance and the balance on delivery (Act III.4):

RIGOLETTO   Venti scudi hai tu detto?... Eccone dieci;
             e dopo l'opra il resto.
             Ei qui rimane?

What's this! And how much would you charge me for a nobleman? / SPARAFUCILE I'd demand a higher price / RIGOLETTO How are you usually paid? / SPARAFUCILE Half in advance, the rest on completion / RIGOLETTO (The demon!) And how is it that you can work so safely? / SPARAFUCILE I either kill in the town or under my own roof. I wait for my man at night; one thrust and he dies / RIGOLETTO (to himself) And how do you work at home? / SPARAFUCILE It's simple. My sister helps me. She dances in the streets... she's pretty... she entices the victim, and then... / RIGOLETTO I understand / SPARAFUCILE Without a sound... /RIGOLETTO I understand. / SPARAFUCILE This is my instrument. (indicating his sword) Can it serve you? / RIGOLETTO No... not just now / SPARAFUCILE You'll regret it / RIGOLETTO Who knows? / SPARAFUCILE My name is Sparafucile / RIGOLETTO A foreigner? / SPARAFUCILE (as he leaves) Burgundian / RIGOLETTO And where, if the need should arise? / SPARAFUCILE Here, each night / RIGOLETTO Go! / SPARAFUCILE Sparafucile, Sparafucile. (He leaves.)

SPARAFUCILE	Sì.
RIGOLETTO	Alla mezza notte ritornerò.
SPARAFUCILE	Non cale. A gettarlo nel fiume basto io solo.
RIGOLETTO	No, no, il vo' far io stesso.
SPARAFUCILE	Sia!... Il suo nome?
RIGOLETTO	Vuoi saper anche il mio? Egli è *Delitto*, *Punizion* son io.

(Parte, il cielo si oscura e tuona)[215]

3. The contract between Rigoletto and Sparafucile is clearly for an illegal service (the commission of a murder). It is interesting to bring out the consequences of this fact, especially in the light of the subsequent events that unfold. The prospect, again, is of private law, not criminal law. Yet it is clear that the whole affair has a definitely criminal nature. Rigoletto is the instigator of a murder, Sparafucile its perpetrator. Both, in a criminal trial, would be held to account for their crimes.

As for the aspects that relate to private law, the framework of the preliminary question can again be established by taking into account the legislation applicable in the place where the opera was first performed, namely Venice in 1851. Austrian law is therefore applicable and, in particular, the 1811 Civil Code (*ABGB*). § 878 of the Austrian Code punishes illicit contracts with invalidity, stating that: 'One may conclude contracts of all the things that are in commerce. Whatever cannot be performed, whatever is absolutely impossible or illicit, cannot be the subject of a valid contract.' The validity of a contract, pursuant to art. 878, is affected both by cases of impossibility and of wrongfulness, that the doctrine considers assimilable:[216] but it is clear that contracts that violate criminal laws are not

---

215 RIGOLETTO Twenty *scudi* you said? Here are ten, and the rest when the work is finished. He is staying here? / SPARAFUCILE Yes / RIGOLETTO At midnight I shall return. / SPARAFUCILE No point: I can throw him in the river without help / RIGOLETTO No, no, I want to do it myself / SPARAFUCILE All right; his name? / RIGOLETTO Do you want to know mine as well? He is *Crime*, I am *Punishment*. (*He leaves; the sky darkens, lightning flashes.*)

216 So we read in G.A. CASTELLI (edited by), *Manuale del codice civile generale austriaco*, Milan: Visaj, 1839, *sub* § 878 *ABGB*: 'whatever is in opposition to the natural law *is legally impossible*, as is whatever infringes the penal laws' (my italics).

recognized as valid by private law.[217] § 878 *ABGB* opens up the prospect of the liability which may arise from inducing someone to enter into an invalid contract. If a void contract can give rise to no rights or obligations, the phase that preceded the contract, however, can: 'Whoever with such promises deceives another, or due to ignorance adversely affects him, or derives profit from the damage to him, is liable on this account.'

The pact between Rigoletto and Sparafucile, ultimately, has no legal value, not even on the level of liability. If we analyse the way Rigoletto comes to hire Sparafucile, it does not seem, in fact, that he was deceived by him, or that his act was covered by any of the cases referred to in § 878 *ABGB*. From Sparafucile's first appearance (Act I.7), Rigoletto is fully aware of the 'nature of the services' rendered by him and – as if words were not enough – the Burgundian also shows him his sword.

4. After the conclusion of the contract between Rigoletto and Sparafucile, things grow complicated. Maddalena – Sparafucile's sister – learns from her brother that he has been hired to kill the young man, who is already known to her.[218] She persuades Sparafucile to spare the young man, and invites him to kill Rigoletto instead (Act III.5). Sparafucile says he is prepared to replace the victim not with his counterpart in the negotiation, but with the first customer who comes to the inn before midnight (the time agreed with Rigoletto). Evidently Sparafucile remains true to his personal code of honour, which prevents him from killing the instigator of the crime he has undertaken to carry out, but he does not show the same sensibility more generally, in fulfilling his commitment to Rigoletto. Unseen, Gilda overhears the conversation:[219]

---

217 § 879 *ABGB* lists further specific cases of the nullity of contracts, which are added to the general cases regulated by art. 878.

218 Sparafucile only needs to tell Maddalena of the agreed price for the latter to fully grasp the situation: SPARAFUCILE *(piano a Maddalena)* (Son venti scudi d'oro.) [...] MADDALENA È amabile invero cotal giovinotto! | SPARAFUCILE Oh sì... venti scudi ne dà di prodotto... | MADDALENA Sol venti?... Son pochi!... Valeva di più. (SPARAFUCILE *[softly to Maddalena]* It means twenty gold *scudi* [...] Poor lad! He's so handsome! SPARAFUCILE Oh, yes... to the tune of twenty *scudi*. MADDALENA Only twenty!... That's not much! He was worth more.

219 The third act of the opera takes place on the banks of the Mincio, in the tavern where Maddalena (Sparafucile's sister, courted by the Duke) has made an appointment with the Duke himself. Rigoletto appears with his daughter and tells her to watch them flirting. Rigoletto

MADDALENA	Somiglia un Apollo quel giovine... io l'amo...
	ei m'ama... riposi... né più l'uccidiamo.
GILDA	*(ascoltando)*
	Oh cielo!
SPARAFUCILE	*(gettandole un sacco)*
	Rattoppa quel sacco...
MADDALENA	Perché?
SPARAFUCILE	Entr'esso il tuo Apollo, sgozzato da me,
	gettar dovrò al fiume...
GILDA	L'inferno qui vedo!
MADDALENA	Eppure il danaro salvarti scommetto,
	serbandolo in vita.
SPARAFUCILE	Difficile il credo.
MADDALENA	M'ascolta... anzi facil ti svelo un progetto.
	De' scudi già dieci dal gobbo ne avesti;
	venire cogl'altri più tardi il vedrai...
	Uccidilo, e venti allora ne avrai,
	così tutto il prezzo goder si potrà.
SPARAFUCILE	Uccider quel gobbo!... Che diavol dicesti!
	Un ladro son forse? Son forse un bandito?...
	Qual altro cliente da me fu tradito?...
	Mi paga quest'uomo... fedele m'avrà.
GILDA	Che sento!... Mio padre!...
MADDALENA	Ah, grazia per esso.
SPARAFUCILE	È duopo ch'ei muoia...
MADDALENA	*(va per salire)*
	Fuggire il fo adesso...
GILDA	Oh buona figliola!
SPARAFUCILE	*(trattenendola)*
	Gli scudi perdiamo.

---

promises to avenge Gilda, and tells her to travel to Verona, where he will join her the day after: 'RIGOLETTO *(to Gilda)* Taci, il piangere non vale; / ch'ei mentiva or sei secura... / Taci, e mia sarà la cura / la vendetta d'affrettar. / Pronta fia, sarà fatale, / io saprollo fulminar. | RIGOLETTO M'odi, ritorna a casa... / Oro prendi, un destriero, / una veste viril che t'apprestai, / e per Verona parti... / Sarovvi io pur doman... | GILDA Or venite... | RIGOLETTO Impossibil. | GILDA Tremo. | RIGOLETTO Va!' (RIGOLETTO *[to Gilda]* You are now convinced he was lying. Hush, and leave it up to me to hasten our revenge. It will be quick, it will be deadly, I know how to deal with him. Listen to me, go home. Take some money and a horse, put on the men's clothes I provided, then leave at once for Verona. I shall meet you there tomorrow. GILDA Come with me now / RIGOLETTO It's impossible /GILDA I'm afraid. RIGOLETTO Go!).

MADDALENA	È ver!...
SPARAFUCILE	Lascia fare...
MADDALENA	Salvarlo dobbiamo.
SPARAFUCILE	Se pria ch'abbia il mezzo la notte toccato
	alcuno qui giunga, per esso morrà.
MADDALENA	È buia la notte, il ciel troppo irato,
	nessuno a quest'ora da qui passerà.[220]

It is at this point that Gilda forms the insane plan to take the Duke's place, sacrificing herself for him:

GILDA	Oh qual tentazione!... Morir per l'ingrato!...
	Morire!... E mio padre?... Oh cielo, pietà!

(Battono le 11 ½)[221]

The pact between Rigoletto and Sparafucile requires that the corpse should be returned to Rigoletto in a sack and thrown in the Mincio river. Rigoletto is convinced he has received the Duke's corpse, but he soon learns the truth (Act III.9):

RIGOLETTO	Egli è là!... morto!... Oh sì!... vorrei vederlo!
	Ma che importa!... è ben desso!... Ecco i suoi sproni!...

---

220   MADDALENA He's an Apollo, that young man; I love him, he loves me... let him be... let's spare him / GILDA *(listening)* Dear God! /SPARAFUCILE *(throwing her a sack)* Mend this sack! / MADDALENA Why? /SPARAFUCILE Because your Apollo, when I've cut his throat, will wear it when I throw him in the river / GILDA I see hell itself! /MADDALENA But I reckon I can save you the money and save his life as well / SPARAFUCILE Difficult, I think. MADDALENA Listen... my plan is simple. You've had ten *scudi* from the hunchback; he's coming later with the rest... Kill him, and the twenty... SPARAFUCILE Kill the hunchback? What the devil do you mean? Am I a thief? Am I a bandit? What client of mine has ever been cheated? This man pays me, and I shall deliver / MADDALENA Ah, have mercy on him! /SPARAFUCILE He must die / MADDALENA *(she runs towards the stairs)* I'll see he escapes in time /GILDA Oh, merciful girl! /SPARAFUCILE *(holding her back)* We'd lose the money / MADDALENA That's true! /SPARAFUCILE Don't interfere / MADDALENA We must save him / SPARAFUCILE If someone else comes here before midnight, they shall die in his place / MADDALENA The night is dark, the weather too stormy; no one will pass by here at this late hour.
221   GILDA Oh, what a temptation! To die for the ingrate? To die! And my father?... Oh, Heaven, have mercy! *(A distant clock chimes half-past eleven.)*

Ora mi guarda, o mondo!...
quest'è un buffone, ed un potente è questo!...
Ei sta sotto a' miei piedi!... È desso! È desso!...
è giunta alfin la tua vendetta, o duolo!...
Sia l'onda a lui sepolcro,
un sacco il suo lenzuolo!...
(Fa per trascinare il sacco verso la sponda, quando è sorpreso
dalla lontana voce del Duca, che nel fondo attraversa la scena)
Qual voce!... Illusion notturna è questa!...
(Trasalendo)
No!... No!... Egli è desso!... È desso!...
Maledizione!
(Verso la casa)
        Olà... dimon bandito?...
Chi è mai, chi è qui in sua vece?...
(Taglia il sacco)
Io tremo... è umano corpo!...
(Lampeggia)

He realizes the truth on opening the sack, discovering that, instead of the Duke, the victim is Gilda (Act III.10):

RIGOLETTO   Mia figlia!... Dio!... Mia figlia!...

The few words, spoken between Rigoletto and his dying daughter, separate the horrifying discovery of Gilda's death from the finale. The work ends with Rigoletto recalling the curse hurled at him by Monterone:

RIGOLETTO   Gilda! Mia Gilda!... è morta!...
        Ah la maledizione!![222]

---

222   RIGOLETTO He's in there!... Dead! Oh, but I must see him! But what's the use?... It's him all right! I can feel his spurs! Now look upon me, Oh world! Here is a buffoon, and this is a mighty prince! He lies at my feet! It's him! Oh joy! At last you are avenged, Oh grief! Let the river be his tomb, a sack his winding sheet! *(He is about to drag the sack towards the river, when he hears, to his amazement, the voice of the Duke in the distance)* / RIGOLETTO His voice!... This is a trick of the darkness! *(drawing back in terror)* No!... No! This is he!... *(shouting towards the house)* Damnation! Hola!... You devil of a bandit! *(He cuts open the sack.)* Who can this be, here in his stead? *(lightning)* I tremble... It's a human body! My daughter!... Oh God!... My daughter!

5. Piave and Verdi took the story of Rigoletto from Victor Hugo's *Le roi s'amuse* (1832). The latter text elicited a violent reaction on the part of the censorship after its first performance in Paris (22 November 1832, at the the Comédie Française).

In general, the relationship between *Rigoletto* and Hugo's play is very close: this was, moreover, Verdi's intention, made clear in the instructions he gave Piave, in which he recommended the librettist to follow the structure of the original step by step.[223] The opera's fidelity to the original is therefore marked, including the events that interest us here, notwithstanding the need – which increasingly characterized Verdi's relations with his librettists – to abridge and condense the action of the originals.[224] In Hugo's play, at the start of Act II (II.1), Triboulet (the counterpart of Rigoletto) meets Saltabadil (the counterpart of Sparafucile) in the 'recoin le plus désert du cul-de-sac Bussy'. Their dialogue is very close, in both structure and content, to that between Rigoletto and Sparafucile. Then (in Act IV.3), Triboulet gives Saltabadil twenty gold *écus*, as a down payment: the contract is concluded offstage. The terms of the stipulation are the same: ten *écus* down and ten as settlement. The body is then to be thrown in the river (in this case the Seine).[225]

Ah, no, it cannot be! My daughter? My Gilda?... Oh, my daughter.

223 See Verdi's letter of 3 June 1850 addressed to Piave: 'I received yours of 14 May. At last!!!... Do not treat either the division of the scene or the sack as an obstacle. Stick to the French and you won't go wrong. As for the title, if we can't keep *Roi s'amuse*, which would be fine... the title will have to be *La Maledizione di Vallier*, or *La Maledizione* for short. The whole subject is in that curse, which also becomes the moral. An unhappy father who weeps for his daughter's lost honour is mocked by a court jester, whom the father curses, and this curse takes hold of the fool in a terrifying way – it strikes me as moral and great, great in the highest degree. Mind you, La Vallier should appear (as in the French) no more than twice and say very few emphatic prophetic words' (the letter is quoted by M. LAVAGETTO, *Un caso di censura. Il 'Rigoletto'*, Milan: Il Formichiere, 1979, p. 27).

224 This point, and in general the 'brevity' of Verdi's librettos, is rightly stressed in M. LAVAGETTO, *ibid.*, pp. 34 ff.; IDEM, *Quei più modesti romanzi. Il libretto nel melodramma di Verdi*, Turin: Garzanti, 1979, pp. 19 ff.

225 This is the text in Hugo' play: SALTABADIL N'en prenez pas la peine. / Je puis jeter tout seul un cadavre à la Seine. | TRIBOULET Non, je veux l'y jeter moi-même. | SALTABADIL À votre gré. / Tout cousu dans un sac je vous le livrerai. | TRIBOULET *(lui donnant l'argent)* Bien. À minuit! J'aurai le reste de la somme. | SALTABADIL Tout sera fait. Comment nommez-vous ce jeune homme? | TRIBOULET Son nom? Veux-tu savoir le mien également? / Il s'appelle le crime, et moi le châtiment!

Further close similarities include:
- Saltabadil tells his sister (Maguelonne) of the wicked pact;[226]
- Maguelonne persuades Saltabadil to save the king;[227]
- The decision to kill the first comer who arrives before midnight, instead of the original victim;[228]
- The payment of the balance due (Act V.1), and the tragic discovery of the finale.

The relationship between the original and Piave's libretto has been the subject of analysis and investigations in several respects, including the attempt to identify the process by which Hugo's controversial text was adapted to the morality, sensibility and above all the censorship of the context in which *Rigoletto* was developed. In this respect, the original story was the subject of adaptations and adjustments already by Verdi and Piave, even before the actual acts of censorship. They omitted or concealed some 'awkward' references: for instance, the most overtly 'political' passages (but ones that were also dramatically less effective in Hugo's text), or those that clearly revealed the consummation of the sexual intercourse between Gilda and the Duke. The relations between *Rigoletto* and the censorship, however, remained controversial and led to a series of mutilations and adaptations of the original, some made in various later remakes.[229]

---

226   MAGUELONNE Ce jeune homme est charmant! | SALTABADIL Je crois bien. / Il met vingt écus d'or dans ma poche. | MAGUELONNE Combien? | SALTABADIL Vingt écus. | MAGUELONNE Il valait plus que cela.

227   MAGUELONNE Tuer un beau garçon qui n'est pas du commun, / pour un méchant bossu fait comme un S! | SALTABADIL En somme, / J'ai reçu d'un bossu pour tuer un bel homme, / cela m'est fort égal, dix écus tout d'abord; / J'en aurai dix de plus en livrant l'homme mort. / Livrons. C'est clair. | MAGUELONNE Tu peux tuer le petit homme / quand il va repasser avec toute la somme. / Cela revient au même. | BLANCHE Ô mon père! | MAGUELONNE Est-ce dit? | SALTABADIL *(regardant Maguelonne en face)* Hein! pour qui me prends-tu, ma sœur? suis-je un bandit? / Suis-je un voleur? Tuer un client qui me paie!

228   The decision is taken after Maguelonne suggests Saltabadil should replace the corpse with a bundle (a point absent from *Rigoletto*): SALTABADIL Voyons. L'autre à minuit viendra me retrouver. / Si d'ici là quelqu'un, un voyageur, n'importe, / vient nous demander gîte et frappe à notre porte, / Je le prends, je le tue, et puis, au lieu du tien, / Je le mets dans le sac. L'autre n'y verra rien. / Il jouira toujours autant dans la nuit close, / Pourvu qu'il jette à l'eau quelqu'un ou quelque chose. / C'est tout ce que je puis faire pour toi. | MAGUELONNE Merci. / Mais qui diable veux-tu qui passe par ici?

229   For an analysis of the 'reconstruction' of Rigoletto, following the actions of the censorship and the need to tone down the text to suit the settings where it would be performed (Rome,

6. As can be seen, relations between Rigoletto and Sparafucile pass through several stages: the negotiations and the conclusion of the contract (off stage); the payment of an advance on the full price; Sparafucile's breach of contract (to which he is induced by a third person); the payment of the balance; the discovery of Sparafucile's default. If the contract between Rigoletto and Sparafucile had been valid, Rigoletto could have sued Sparafucile, applying at the very least for damages.

In this case, however, the contract is not valid: in fact it is null, or rather an 'immoral' contract. The 'normal' result of the declaration of nullity of a contract, in the legal systems examined here, would be restitution. In the case of a void contract, the law seeks to restore the parties to the original situation, as if the contract had never existed, had never been entered into. Starting from the tradition of Roman law, the rule of restitution would instead be excluded for items exchanged or services rendered under contracts that are repugnant to conscience (or, as art. 2035 of the Civil Code now rules, to 'morality').[230] This solution was, first of all, expressly accepted by the Austrian Code of 1811. § 1174, in fact, states: 'When someone has knowingly taken something in exchange for the performance of an act that is impossible or illegal, restitution cannot be made. Whether it is subject to confiscation is determined by political laws. However, application may be made for restitution in the case of a consideration presented with the purpose of preventing an illegal act to the person who was to commit it.' Note, as we have already seen, that the Austrian Code equates impossibility and illegality: they are, of course, quite distinct cases and in other systems considered here they are treated differently. The *impossibility* of a service or an object is one thing; its *illegality* is another. Moreover, even

---

Naples), see M. LAVAGETTO, *Un caso*, cit., pp. 77 ff., who rightly speaks of 'variations entailed by the blatant violation of one or more articles of the code, written or unwritten, on the basis of which we have seen the institutional censorship or prior censorship functioning; and "discretionary" variants entrusted to the sensibility of the individual (whether poets or censors), and "derived variants", which are the result of a kind of structural inertia, complying with those minimum requirements of coherence that no text (even the least compact and most disrupted) can completely disregard.'

230   The rule, intended to prevent unethical contracts or those for an immoral purpose, derived from the Roman principle that *nemo ex suo delicto meliorem suam conditionem facere potest*: it was retained by intermediate law, and applied, for example, in the Italian Civil Code of 1865 (but formally set out only later in the 1942 Code, under art. 2035), in the Swiss Code (art. 66 C.O.), in § 817 of the German Civil Code, and in (as quoted in the text) § 1174 *ABGB*.

within the sphere of illegality, different situations can be distinguished: a contract may be unlawful because contrary to a provision of imperative law, or because it is inconsistent with provisions that provide for criminal penalties, or because it is connoted by particular negativity on the plane of morality and the conscience. These distinctions, however, do not emerge clearly from § 1174 *ABGB*. But, for our purposes, the differences evoked above are irrelevant: it seems evident that the contract between Rigoletto and Sparafucile would be among those covered by § 1174.

The solution to Rigoletto's problem, according to the Austrian Civil Code – in force in Venice on the evening of the first performance, 11 March 1851 – would, therefore, be the crystallization of the situation created. In terms of private law, no recognition could be given to an unlawful agreement, but the return of the twenty *scudi* would also be strictly excluded.

7. The rule of restitution – which generally governs the consequences of a declaration of a void contract – is disapplied under art. 2035 of the Civil Code in force in Italy for contracts contrary to 'morality'. According to art. 2035, 'one who has executed a service for a purpose that also on his part constitutes indecency cannot reclaim the sum he paid'. In this case, unlike the Austrian Civil Code, the forfeiture of the service is limited to certain contracts only: those that are contrary to the concept of 'morality'.

The rule – introduced into Italian legislation with the Civil Code of 1942[231] – is derived, also in this case, from the tradition of Roman law.[232] For some time, however, its effective application has been debated, since the notion of 'morality' is problematic to identify and reconstruct.

At first, after the promulgation of the 1942 Civil Code, in jurisprudence there was uncertainty about the actual scope of art. 2035, since the question was whether the rule should apply only to *immoral* contracts, or also

---

231   No provision similar to that of art. 2035 of the Civil Code in force was present in the 1865 Civil Code. The latter, along the lines of the French model of the Napoleonic Code, was not intended to codify the rule deriving from the principle *nemo auditur propriam turpitudinem allegans*, though that principle – referring to 'immoral' contracts – was consistently applied by the Courts. The applicability of the rule to purely fraudulent contracts, as well as those that were immoral, remained controversial. See. G. TERLIZZI, *Il contratto immorale tra regole giuridiche e regole sociali*, Naples: ESI, 2012, p. 114.

232   See D. MAFFEIS, *Contratti illeciti o immorali e restituzioni*, Milan: Giuffrè, 1999, pp. 77, ff.

to contacts that are, more generally, illegal, because, for instance, in contrast with criminal law.[233] The system has subsequently been stabilized in the sense that, for both the prevailing doctrine and case law, only the illegality of a contract arising from its immorality leads to the application of art. 2035 c.c., and prevents, therefore, the return of payments already performed.[234] The orientation of the more recent case law tends, therefore, to the application of the rule of art. 2035 c.c. in borderline cases, which are not to be confused with the judgment of mere illegality of the contract, but that require the subsistence of actual immorality. Hence, also under current Italian law, Rigoletto would be unable to obtain restitution of the sum paid to Sparafucile, as their contract would be considered *immoral*.

Now, if this is the solution that, without great difficulty, arises from the application of the law on restitution for illegal contracts, one can actually wonder whether it is an efficient solution in terms of concrete results. In this regard, it can be observed that art. 2035 c.c. – sanctioning immoral contracts by deleting them from the world of law, to the point that the judge should not even deal with them, in order to impose, at least, restitution – produces a contradictory effect. The rule ends up by crystallizing the situation created by the immoral contract, with the result, if one side of the contract has been performed, that it favours one of the parties against the other. Naturally, the one who is disadvantaged is the one who has performed under the contract, and the one benefited is the one who has received it.[235] The latter is not only enriched as a result of having received the godds or services based on an immoral contract, which is repugnant to Law, but he is not required to fulfil the contract, nor are there instruments to force him to do so.[236] By applying art. 2035 c.c. to Rigoletto, Sparafucile is enriched at the expense of the poor jester. He not only fails (consciously)

233   *Ibid.*, pp. 100 ff.
234   The position was clarified after a celebrated contribution by W. BIGIAVI, 'Ripetibilità del sovrapprezzo pagato al mercato nero', critical note on Cass., 29 April 1946, in *Diritto e Giurisprudenza*, in 1946, I, p. 280. Subsequently, the position consolidated as defined by Cass. 7 June 1956, no. 1953 Cass. 16 April 1957, no. 1294.
235   A well-known position is taken up on this point by P. RESCIGNO, 'In pari causa turpitudinis', in *Rivista di diritto civile*, 1966, I, pp. 1 ff.
236   D. MAFFEIS, *Contratti illeciti*, cit., p. 91, offers a more 'secular' judgment, in the sense that he considers the debate, in the end, irrelevant, being the result of a specific legislative decision.

to fulfil the contract, he not only appropriates the ten crowns as a down payment, he not only receives the balance of the payment agreed, but he is not required to restore the sum received. The rule laid down by 2035 c.c., so radical in sanctioning the immorality of the contract, ends up by itself being an immoral rule, because it leaves the benefit in the hands of the party who gained it illegally, without allowing the judge to choose among a range of situations which, in each case, might deserve a different solution.[237]

8. The situation in the French legal system – to which, for our purposes, we can refer Hugo's text, as the original of *Rigoletto* – is not perfectly identical to Austrian or Italian law.

In France, under the *Ancien Régime,* the rule of restitution was applied in the case of indecent or immoral contracts (*nemo auditur*), even though, at times, its scope was not clear: this situation arose to a great degree from the difficulty of singling out a clear distinction between different types of 'illegal' contracts, and the different treatment to be accorded to each type. The rule of restitution, despite its roots in France, was not consolidated in the 1804 Napoleonic Code, for historical reasons that have been widely investigated and which we cannot go into here. The result was a situation of uncertainty that saw doctrine and jurisprudence differ on its persistence in the French system, with conflicts that were even raised in front of the Court of Cassation.[238]

---

237   On a different plane from that dealt with in the text, one might also assume the existence of an action for damages, which Rigoletto could bring against Sparafucile, also constituting himself as civil party in a hypothetical criminal trial. This is, however, one of the many aspects of the action that cannot be explored here, for obvious reasons of space.

238   Until 1913, the dispute concerned the Civil Chamber of the Cour de Cassation and the then existing Chambre des Requêtes: while the Civil Chamber held that a merely unlawful contract was not an obstacle to reclaiming a restitution, the Chambre des Requêtes refused to grant restitution both in the case of simply unlawful contracts, and in immoral contracts. The conflict between the two chambers was then smoothed over, following a decision in 1913 (Ch. Req., 6 Jan. 1913, in *Dalloz*, 1014, I, p. 13), after which the Chambre des Requêtes no longer rejected restitution. The Chambre des Requêtes was suppressed by the law of 22 July 1947: it had the function of filtering the appeals that were to be judged by the Civil Chamber of the French Court of Cassation. When it was obvious that the appeal would be dismissed by the Civil Chamber, the Chambre des Requêtes would reject the application; on the contrary, if the application appear justified, it admitted the appeal. Over time, the Chambre des Requêtes had acquired independence and autonomy of judgment, and consequently considerable importance in French case law, becoming a full-blown civil chamber, which carefully examined appeals, virtually duplicating the Civil Chamber. For this

Since the 1950s, French case law has always tended to recognize restitution in the case of void contracts, rejecting it only in a *limited* number of *exceptional* situations. Some proposals for the legislative reform of the French Civil Code were even made to expressly exclude the principle of restitution under an immoral contract, in order to resolve any doubts about the matter.[239] Among the contracts being discussed, with regard to their re-inclusion in the number of the 'immoral' contracts, one could not, however, qualify the contract whose object is the performance of murder, as in the case of Rigoletto and Sparafucile. Such a contract seems clearly likely to remain among those to which, even in the light of a jurisprudential trend in France tending increasingly to narrow the scope of the rule of non-restitution, the latter would continue to apply. Hence, even in France Rigoletto would not find protection, although within a different legislative framework.

9. In conclusion: the story of Rigoletto, like that of *Le roi s'amuse*, rests (as Verdi himself said) on two axes. The first is the series of vicissitudes which arise from the 'light character of the libertine Duke'.[240] The second is the curse: 'the whole subject is that curse',[241] stated Verdi himself. The curse that Monterone hurls at Rigoletto in Act I resurfaces at various points of the drama until the tremendous finale. The curse is not, however, only the one tinged with supernatural elements, but is also that of the evil contract, to which the law refuses to offer any recognition or protection, ignoring it completely. At the same time, the practical effect is to crystallize its consequences, so that Sparafucile emerges from the story advantaged and clearly a winner on all fronts.

---

reason the 1947 law suppressed it.
239   This was the proposal by the Commission de Réforme du Code Civil (1946-1947), which was ultimately dismissed. The reasons for this proposal mainly resided in the difficulty of distinguishing between simply illegal contracts and immoral contracts and in the asserted 'immorality' of a rule that prevents restitution, for reasons similar to those mentioned in the text.
240   Letter from Giuseppe Verdi to Antonio Somma, Sant'Agata, 22 April 1853, in S. RICCIARDI (edited by), *Corrispondenza Verdi-Somma*, Parma: Istituto nazionale di studi verdiani, 2003, pp. 41-42.
241   Letter from Verdi to Piave, Cremona, June 3, 1850, in F. ABBIATI, *Giuseppe Verdi*, 4 vols., Milan: Ricordi, 1959, pp. 63-64.

IX

La traviata

(Giuseppe Verdi – Francesco Maria Piave)

Power of attorney to sell and gifts

1. Giuseppe Verdi's *La traviata*, the setting of a libretto by Francesco Maria Piave, was inspired, as is well known, by two works by Alexandre Dumas, *fils*, inspired in their turn by the life of Alphonsine Plessis/Marie Duplessis.[242] They are the novel *La dame aux Camélias* (1848), and the eponymous play, staged at the Théâtre du Vaudeville in Paris on 2 February 1852, in the form of a *pièce mêlée de chant*.[243]

It seems, though the question is debated,[244] that Verdi attended one of the earliest performances of Dumas' play and drew inspiration for his work from it, although less directly than a certain tradition has sometimes suggested. After being in Paris in February-March 1852,[245] it was only in September of that year that he wrote to his friend, the publisher Léon Escudier, asking him to send him ('right away') a copy of Dumas' play. By mid-October, Francesco Maria Piave had already prepared the structure of the libretto: the so-called *selva*, i.e. a sketch or outline of the libretto itself.

La traviata was staged for the first time at La Fenice in Venice on 6 March 1853. The first night was not very successful, as is well known, but the epi-

---

242   As noted by E. SALA, The *Sounds of Paris in Verdi's La Traviata*, Cambridge: Cambridge University Press, 2013, p. 6, 'the myth of the lady of the camellias does not start with Marguerite Gautier and Violetta Valery but with Alphonsine Plessis/Marie Duplessis (whose life is already, in a way, mythical).' More recently, on the life of Marie Duplessis, see the volume by J. KAVANAGH, *The Lady of the Camellias. Life and Legend of Marie Duplessis*, New York: Knopf, 2013.

243   The most comprehensive analysis of *vaudeville*, in its musical component, is by E. SALA, *The Sounds of Paris*, cit., pp. 113 ff.

244   See F. DELLA SETA, 'La traviata, dal dramma alla musica', in *La Fenice prima dell'Opera*, 2004-2005, no. 1, pp. 9 ff.

245   On Verdi's stays in Paris in the years before the composition of *La Traviata*, see E. Sala, *The Sounds of Paris*, cit., pp. 16 ff.

sode – probably less serious than has traditionally been related[246] – proved untypical, since *La traviata* has always been one of the best known and most popular works in the whole operatic repertoire, and is definitely one of the summit's of Verdi's achievement. The story of the Lady of the Camellias (Marie, Marguerite, Violetta, and others, depending on the context), has inspired countless adaptations and repetitions in the theatre and the cinema, and continues to inspire writers, musicians and artists of different disciplines. The echoes of the Lady continue to reverberate through different fields and spheres, and are found in more evident forms in references, quotations and artistic evocations[247] in various forms: in short, it is, perhaps – as has been said – the most important female myth of the bourgeois age.[248] *La traviata* condenses the story of Violetta Valéry and Alfredo Germont's tormented love[249] into three, dramatically compact acts, which develop tautly, a trait typical of Verdi's finest operas. The plot is universally known and there is no need here to retell or seek to summarize it. Rather, what is important for our purposes is to observe that – in a text that reveals and explores the values and hypocrisies of bourgeois society, and compares them with the subversive power of passion and love – the theme of *money* and patrimonial relations has equally great importance. Both the literary sources of *La traviata* and the opera itself lay great stress on money. It is, of course, money that guides the life of the protagonist, who has made prostitution her occupation. It is also money, together with a concern for the family's 'good name', that impels Alfredo's father to make his destructive incursion into the relationship between his son and Violetta, leading to their traumatic separation. It is money that is the two lovers' constant concern. Violetta is chronically in search of money; Alfredo intends to divest

---

246   See F. DELLA SETA, *La traviata*, cit., pp. 12 ff.
247   For an interesting analysis of the echoes of *La Traviata* in the cinema, see M. MARICA, 'Violetta Superstar', in *La Fenice prima dell'Opera*, cit., pp. 35 ff., in which the author examines three films for the purpose: *Pretty Woman* (director Gary Marshall, 1990), *Harem Suarée* (Ferzan Özpetek, 1999) and *Moulin Rouge* (Baz Luhrmann, 2001).
248   So, in the wake of others, E. SALA, *The Sounds of Paris*, cit., p. 61.
249   I have not found sources for the reasons which led Piave and Verdi to change the names in the French original: probably, they were purely phonetic-musical. E. SALA, *The Sounds of Paris*, cit., p. 15, cites a coincidence, perhaps a source, for the name Violetta: in the *Dialogues of Courtesans* by Lucians of Samosata (second century AD), one of the courtesans has a name that literally means 'violet'.

himself of his assets to benefit Violetta. It is cash that – in the famous scene in Act III – Alfredo flings at Violetta, denouncing her (supposed) betrayal. Financial matters, in short, pervade the narrative, in Dumas' two texts and Verdi's masterpiece.[250]

In particular, in the context of the story that forms the link between Violetta (Marguerite, in Dumas' texts) and Alfredo (Armand, in Dumas' texts), two events occur of a purely patrimonial character on the dramatic and the narrative plane. They are of central importance, being crucial to the development of the narrative. They are developed with a somewhat different scope and content in the three texts retrieved, namely the 1848 novel, the 1852 play, and Verdi's opera, but are still present in all three, namely:

– Violetta/Marguerite's decision to sell her goods, both to pay off her debts and keep herself and Alfredo/Armand;

– Alfredo/Armand's related decision (unperformed) to give Violetta/Marguerite his possessions; this decision develops in part as a response to his beloved's.

In Verdi's opera the two events are juxtaposed and both narrated in Act II. They are, moreover, extremely condensed compared to the sources in Dumas. The first is presented at the beginning of Act II. The setting, as indicated in the libretto, is in a 'country house near Paris': this is the place where Violetta and Alfredo have retired, to fulfil their relationship in intimacy far from the worldliness and gossip of the capital. The latter point is well described by Alfredo in the cantabile in Scene I, 'De' miei bollenti spiriti', followed by the cabaletta 'Oh mio rimorso!... Oh infamia!...'[251]

ALFREDO   Lunge da lei per me non v'ha diletto!...
               (deponendo il fucile)
               Volaron già tre lune

---

250   Dumas' novel begins, moreover, with the scene of the auction of Marguerite's goods; an episode that reflects the auction held in February 1847 in the apartment of the most celebrated courtesan in Paris, causing a stir in the press and comments of the day (see E. SALA, *The Sounds of Paris*, cit., pp. 63 ff.).

251   The text comes from the libretto of the first performance in Venice: LA TRAVIATA | *Libretto* | *di Francesco Maria Piave* | *Musica* | *di Giuseppe Verdi* | *espressamente composta* | *pel Gran Teatro La Fenice* | *da rappresentarsi* | *nella stagione di Carnovale e Quadragesima* | *1852-53.* | *Venezia* |*Coi tipi di Teresa Gattei.*

dacché la mia Violetta
agi per me lasciò, dovizie, amori,
e le pompose feste
ove, agli omaggi avvezza,
vedea schiavo ciascun di sua bellezza...
Ed or contenta in questi ameni luoghi
solo esiste per me... qui presso a lei
io rinascer mi sento,
e dal soffio d'amor rigenerato
scordo ne' gaudii suoi tutto il passato.
 De' miei bollenti spiriti
 il giovanile ardore
 ella temprò col placido
 sorriso dell'amore!
 Dal dì che disse: Vivere
 io voglio a te fedel,
 dell'universo immemore
 mi credo quasi in ciel.[252]

The scene ends, pervaded by Alfredo's happiness, expressed in an aria which actually depicts a rather artless character, with traits of adolescence. Alfredo fails to understand the situation he is in, nor does he realize how serious their plight is.

Then Alfredo's ingenuousness is shattered in an instant, as Scene II gives way to a direct encounter with Annina, in which he learns that Violetta has been seeking to sell her goods for the upkeep of both of them. It is a crucial moment in the action, because this information leads to his immediate departure for Paris, in order (as we learn in Scene 5) to turn all his property over to Violetta, so leaving the field open to the arrival of Germont *père* and

---

252 The English courtesy translation of the libretto is taken from the version available on the website: http://www.murashev.com: ALFREDO *(putting down his shotgun)* I have no joy in life when she is far away! Three months have passed since Violetta gave up for me a life of ease, luxury, love affairs and the pomp of society, where, surrounded by adoration, she enslaved all with her beauty. Now, happy in this quiet country home, she has forgotten everything for me. And here, near her, I feel like a man reborn; invigorated by the pulse of love, I have forgotten the past in the joy of being with her. The violent fire of my youthful spirits was tempered by the quiet smile of her love! Ever since the day when she said: 'I want to live only for you' I seem to live in heaven, unmindful of the world.

the latter's dramatic confrontation with Violetta. If Alfredo had not hurried to Paris but taken part in the encounter between his father and Violetta, things may have turned out quite differently (Act II.2):

ALFREDO	Annina, donde vieni?
ANNINA	Da Parigi.
ALFREDO	Chi tel commise?
ANNINA	Fu la mia signora.
ALFREDO	Perché?
ANNINA	Per alienar cavalli, cocchi, e quanto ancor possiede...
ALFREDO	Che mai sento!
ANNINA	Lo spendìo è grande a viver qui solinghi...
ALFREDO	E tacevi?
ANNINA	Mi fu il silenzio imposto.
ALFREDO	Imposto!... e v'abbisognan?...
ANNINA	Mille luigi.
ALFREDO	Or vanne... andrò a Parigi... Questo colloquio ignori la signora... Il tutto valgo a riparare ancora.
	(parte)[253]

After an exchange between Annina and Violetta, in the course of which Violetta asks about Alfredo's whereabouts, Violetta receives a letter from Flora inviting her to an evening party with him. Violetta has no intention of accepting the invitation ('in vain she will await me...') (Act II.4). The transition to the next scene, the encounter between Violetta and Germont *père* – is rapid. It takes just four words, spoken by Giuseppe ('A gentleman is here'):

VIOLETTA	(legge la lettera) Ah! ah!... scopriva Flora il mio ritiro!...

---

253   ALFREDO Annina, where have you come from? /ANNINA From Paris/ALFREDO Who sent you? /ANNINA My mistress/ALFREDO Why? / ANNINA To take the horses, the carriages, and whatever else is hers / ALFREDO What is this! /ANNINA It is very expensive, living here all alone/ ALFREDO What are you hiding from me? /ANNINA I was sworn to silence/ALFREDO Sworn! Tell me, how much is needed? / ANNINA A thousand louis / ALFREDO Go now – I shall go to Paris. Madam must know nothing of our talk. I can still take care of everything. (he leaves).

	E m'invita a danzar per questa sera!...
	Invan m'aspetterà...
	(getta il foglio sul tavolino e siede.)
GIUSEPPE	Giunse un signore...
VIOLETTA	(Ah! sarà lui che attendo...)
	(accenna a Giuseppe d'introdurlo)
GERMONT	Madamigella Valéry?...
VIOLETTA	Son io.
GERMONT	D'Alfredo il padre in me vedete!
VIOLETTA	*(sorpresa gli accenna di sedere)*
	Voi!
GERMONT	*(sedendo)*
	Sì, dell'incauto che a rovina corre
	ammaliato da voi.
VIOLETTA	*(alzandosi risentita)*
	Donna son io, signore, ed in mia casa
	ch'io vi lasci assentite
	più per voi che per me.
	(per uscire.)
GERMONT	(Quai modi!) Pure...
VIOLETTA	*(torna a sedere)*
	Tratto in error voi foste...
GERMONT	De' suoi beni
	egli dono vuol farvi...
VIOLETTA	Non l'osò finora...
	Rifiuterei.
GERMONT	*(guardandosi intorno)*
	Pur tanto lusso...
VIOLETTA	A tutti
	è mistero quest'atto... A voi nol sia...
	(gli dà le carte)
GERMONT	*(dopo averle scorse coll'occhio)*
	D'ogni avere pensate di spogliarvi?...
	Ah il passato perché, perché v'accusa?...
VIOLETTA	Più non esiste... or amo Alfredo, e Dio
	lo cancellò col pentimento mio.[254]

---

[254] VIOLETTA *(Reading the letter)* Aha! Flora has found my hideaway! She has invited me to a dance this evening! She'll wait for me in vain / GIUSEPPE A gentleman to see you / VIOLETTA It must be the man I'm expecting. *(She gestures for Giuseppe to admit him)* /GERMONT Mademoiselle

It is worth observing the rapidity of the transition in this scene from Alfredo's discovery of the sale Violetta's assets to the communication of Germont *père* in which he informs Violetta of his son's intention of giving her his belongings ('De' suoi beni egli dono vuol farvi'). If Alfredo made his decision just a few moments before his father's arrival, following the discovery of the sale of Violetta's assets, it is hardly clear how Germont *père* could have received this information so soon. It is, evidently, an awkward effect of the compression of events in Piave's libretto compared to Dumas' novel and play. In the latter, as we will see, the sequence of events is inflected in a different way (and there are also significant differences between the novel and the play).

2. What undoubtedly passes unnoticed in the condensed structure of Piave's libretto is an episode with precise legal implications, which can be identified as follows.[255] First, the conversation between Alfredo and Annina (Act II.2) reveals a sale of assets, through a special commission Violetta has entrusted to Annina. Annina claims to have travelled to Paris on behalf of, and on instructions from, Violetta ('ALFREDO Who sent you? | ANNINA My mistress').

The next scene (Act II.3) opens with Violetta who enters 'with various papers in her hands', speaking with Annina: there is no reference to the fact that Violetta was in Paris with Annina. So it has to be inferred that Annina went alone to Paris, to sell the goods on Violetta's behalf. Hence we have

---

Valéry? /VIOLETTA Yes /GERMONT I am Alfredo's father! VIOLETTA *(Surprised, she offers him a chair.)* /You! GERMONT Yes, father of this reckless lad, who is rushing to his ruin because of you / VIOLETTA *(rising, with resentment)* I, sir, am a woman and in my own home. Now please excuse me, more for your sake than for mine. *(She is on the point of going out)* /GERMONT (What spirit!) And yet – /VIOLETTA You have been badly advised /GERMONT He wants to give you all his possessions / VIOLETTA So far, he hasn't dared – I should refuse /GERMONT *(looking about him)* Such luxury – / VIOLETTA This paper is a secret from everyone. But it shall not be from you. *(She gives him the paper)* / GERMONT *(after looking at them briefly)* Heavens! What is this! You wish to sell everything you own? Ah, why does your past accuse you so? /VIOLETTA The past does not exist – I love Alfredo now; God wiped out my past with my repentance.

255   In the relation between Violetta and Alfredo one can read, in addition to those mentioned in the text, further significant aspects relevant to private law: consider, for example, the theme of the consequences of cohabitation *more uxorio* between the couple (on this subject, for an overview of the state of the question in Italy, see P. LOVATI, R. RIGON, *La coppia e la famiglia di fatto dopo la riforma della filiazione*, Turin: Giappichelli, 2014).

here, naturally, a relationship of agency: Annina has sold the goods on behalf of Violetta.

As already mentioned, the premiere of *La traviata* took place in Venice in 1853. At the time, those who attended the performance could read about this matter in the 1811 Austrian Civil Code (*ABGB*), in force in the Lombard-Venetian Kingdom. In the *ABGB*, a power of attorney is defined by § 1002, on the basis of which 'a power of attorney is the term for a contract by which one person undertakes to act on behalf of another, performing business committed to him.' The wording makes it clear that, in the framework of the power of attorney, as regulated by the Austrian Code, the power to act in another's name is an essential element of the relationship. The deal – in this case the sale of Violetta's assets – was therefore concluded for and on behalf of the latter.

Little is known about how the power of attorney in question was structured. First, we do not know if Annina had a written power of attorney or not, since (under § 1005 *ABGB*) 'the power of attorney may be given in spoken or in written form.' It is, however, to be assumed that the power of attorney was written, because in practice – in the case of the sale of movable property, unless of a modest amount – the purchasers would almost certainly have required proof of Annina's agency. It is interesting, in this respect, to observe that § 1005 itself is careful to specify that 'power of attorney is also the name of the document that is issued by the principal to the agent'. Within the structure of the Austrian Code, therefore, a power of attorney is both the agreement between principal and agent, and the relevant document.

It is not clear, secondly, whether Annina has received compensation for her work: art. 1004 *ABGB* requires, in this regard, an explicit agreement, unless the remuneration is not to be inferred 'tacitly taking into consideration the condition of the agent'. Hence the final paragraph of § 1004 *ABGB* would apply, which stipulates that 'with the exception of this case, the power of attorney is a gratuitous contract'.

Thirdly, since it is a power of attorney for the sale of goods, it would have to be special. The distinction between the two categories is made in § 1008 *ABGB*, according to which:

'A special power of attorney is required in the following circumstances:

- whether the things are to be sold in another person's name, or received in return for payment;
- to conclude contracts for a mortgage or bailment;
- to demand money or the equivalent of it;
- to initiate legal proceedings, or to request, accept or submit oaths;
- to conduct transactions.'

Finally, as regards the effects of the power of attorney granted by Violetta, § 1009 provides that the agent 'is required [...] to transfer to the beneficiary all the profits that arise from the proxy.' So Annina would have had to consign to Violetta the sums received, or at least documentation for them. From the few, brief words between Alfredo and Violetta, it is not clear whether Annina incurred expenses, if only for travelling to Paris: if she had, Violetta would have been obliged to reimburse or anticipate them, but only if Annina had authorized them (§ 1014 ABGB). If, moreover, Annina had suffered any injury during her trip to Paris, Violetta would have had to accept liability, since 'if the agent in executing the power of attorney suffers any injury due to unforeseeable circumstances, and if he is acting gratuitously, he may ask for a sum corresponding to the remuneration that would have been due to his work calculated at the maximum estimated value, if the power of attorney had been granted for a consideration.'

If, however, Annina had exceeded the limits of the power of attorney (for example, by selling a good that Violetta had not specified was to be alienated), Violetta would be obliged in this respect only if she had approved the deal, or had in any case derived an advantage from it (§ 1016 ABGB). It should also be observed that Piave is somewhat inconsistent in the account he gives of the sale by power of attorney. In the confrontation between Annina and Alfredo, the sale seems to have taken place. However, in the subsequent conversation between Germont *père* and Violetta, things look differently:

GERMONT   *(dopo averle scorse coll'occhio)*
                 D'ogni avere pensate di spogliarvi?...
                 Ah il passato perché, perché v'accusa!...

For the sake of consistency, Germont should, rather, say 'You have already stripped yourself of all your belongings?' Perhaps, however, Germont's expression should not be understood in the technical sense, closely reflecting a moment of particular emotivity in his confrontation with Violetta.

3. The second legal issue that arises in the context of the scenes from *La traviata* evoked above is Alfredo's donation to Violetta. In Piave's libretto this is again treated very briefly, as compared to Dumas' novel and play (see below). The question is condensed into a single sentence uttered by Germont's father, who turns to Violetta and says, 'He means to give you all his possessions.' To which Violetta replies, 'So far, he hasn't dared to – I would refuse.' Germont concludes, in turn, with a mixture of irony and concern, looking around: 'Yet such luxury...'
It appears clear that Alfredo has in mind the idea of a true *donation*: at least, so Germont tells Violetta. In the Austrian Civil Code of 1811, donation is governed by art. 938 and following. Its general features are clearly identified: a donation is, first of all, a contract (§ 938), and to take full effect it requires a written instrument, accompanied by the delivery of the asset. In particular: 'The act of a donor does not arise from a contract of donation made only verbally, and without the effective transfer of the good. This right must be based on a written document' (§ 943 *ABGB*).
The contractual nature of the donation makes it necessary, for it to become effective, the acceptance of the donee. Hence, Violetta's statement that she intends to 'refuse' Alfredo's donation. This point should at least have reassured Germont *père* of the effective protection of the family's assets: Violetta, in these few words, confirms she is a fully emancipated woman, accustomed to look after herself, and – to avoid touching her partner's property – ready to sell her own property. However, as we all know, Germont *père* has not called on Violetta over a purely financial matter, but to persuade her to break off her relationship with Alfredo, protecting the family's name and his daughter's future, both 'blackened' by the scandal they have attracted. Piave's libretto does not make clear the nature of the donation: Germont merely speaks of 'goods'. The point is noteworthy because, both in the novel and the drama, this aspect is developed fairly fully, as we shall see.

4. Before shedding some light, necessarily very briefly, on the main ways Piave's libretto deviates from Dumas' two texts, with regard to the two is-

sues we are analysing, it seems appropriate to consider them in relation, firstly, to the French Civil Code (legislation relevant to the literary sources of the libretto) and then the Italian Civil Code in force today.

As for the French Civil Code, the solutions are substantially similar to those provided by the Austrian Code. With reference to the question of Annina, art. 1984 of the *Code Civil* confirms – for the purposes that interest us here – the same approach we have already seen, stating that: 'Le mandat ou procuration est un acte par lequel une personne donne à une autre le pouvoir de faire quelque chose pour le mandant et en son nom.' Hence under the *Code Civil*, the power of attorney presupposes the power to act in another's name ('en son nom'). As to the form, the power of attorney is not subject to particular or solemn forms, subject to the limits that arise – in the case of a verbal power of attorney – from the possible recourse to testimonial evidence. In particular, art. 1985 states that 'Le mandat peut être donné ou par acte public, ou par écrit sous seign privé, même par lettre. Il peut aussi être donné verbalement; mais la preuve testimoniale n'en est reçue que conformément au titre des contrats ou des obligations conventionnelles en général.'

Hence, also according to the Civil Code, Annina would probably have to execute the power of attorney gratuitously, although on this point art. 1986 provides, as a general rule, that the power of attorney is gratuitous, unless otherwise agreed to the contrary (art. 1986: 'Le mandat est gratuit, s'il n'y a convention contraire'). The question of the general or special nature of the power of attorney does not entail significant differences between the Austrian and French Codes. Art. 1987 of the *Code Civil*, firstly, establishes a distinction between a special power of attorney (conferred in relation to a single transaction, or a specific business alone), and a general power of attorney given in relation to all the principal's affairs. It then establishes that 's'il s'agit d'aliéner ou hypothéquer, ou de quelque autre acte de propriété, le mandat doit être exprès.' Also in France, finally, Annina would have been entitled to reimbursement of the expenses incurred (art. 1999: 'Le mandant doit rembourser au mandataire les avances et frais que celui-ci a faits pour l'exécution du mandat et lui payer ses salaires lorsqu'il en a été promis').

As to Alfredo's donation, art. 894 of the *Code Civil* states that 'la donation entre vifs est un acte par lequel le donateur se dépouille actuellement et irrévocablement de la chose donnée, en faveur du donataire qui l'accepte.' Again in this case, acceptance by the donee is a condition for the effectiveness of the donation.

5. Unlike the Austrian Code and the Napoleonic Code, the 1942 Italian Civil Code distinguishes between agency (*mandato*) and power of attorney (*procura*). The general notion of power of attorney (art. 1703 c.c.), by which 'the power of attorney is a contract by which one party undertakes to carry out one or more legal acts on behalf of the other', gives rise to the two forms of the power of attorney with representation (art. 1705) and power of attorney without representation (art. 1706). The difference between these two forms is reflected, in particular, on the effects of the power of attorney in the relation between principal and agent, and in that between the agent and third parties. In the case of power of attorney without representation, the agent acquires the rights and obligations arising from acts executed with third parties, and the latter have no other relation with the principal. The scheme safeguards the right of the principal, however, to exercise credit rights (art. 1705) arising from the execution of the power of attorney, unless this would prejudice the rights attributed to the agent by Art. 1706 and following of the Civil Code. In the power of attorney without representation, the principal may, instead, claim movable property purchased by the agent, subject to the rights acquired by third parties as a result of the possession of good faith. If the things purchased are registered real estate or movable property, the agent is obliged to retransfer them to the principal. The distinction between power of attorney with or without representation – which is unmatched in the other two systems used as benchmarks – is reflected in the distinction between *mandato* (agency) and *procura* (power of attorney). Under Italian Civil Code, the *procura* is the legal deed, addressed to third parties, by which a subject grants the power to perform legal acts on his behalf and in his interests to another person; the effects of these legal acts will be directly imputed to the principal himself. The term *procura* also signifies the document by which it is possible to prove the existence of the legal power of attorney, according to the same assimilation that is seen to operate in the Austrian system with regard to the power of attorney. *Mandato* and *procura*, therefore, are distinct under the Civil Code in force, and

pursuant to art. 1392 c.c., the *procura* has no effect if it is not given in the same forms as prescribed for the contract that the principal has to conclude, unlike the provisions of art. 1986 of the *Code Civil* and § 1004 *ABGB*.

As to the remuneration of the agent, art. 1709 c.c. establishes that agency is presumed to be performed for a consideration. The measure of consideration, if not established by the parties, is determined on the basis of professional fees or practices and, failing that, by the Court. Moreover, art. 1720 of the Civil Code stipulates that the principal must reimburse any sums anticipated by the agent, with statutory interest from the date on which the payments were made: the heading of the article makes it clear that the reference to sums anticipated includes expenses.

In the approach adopted by the Italian Civil Code, particular rules concern the *contratto di commissione*, which is a subspecies of the *mandato* without representation: this is the contract by which a person, called the *committente* (or principal), grants a power of attorney without representation to another subject, called the *commissionario*, to buy or sell assets on his behalf in return for a commission. The *commissione* is governed by arts. 1731-1736 c.c.: the contract is characterized by the fact of offering the *commissionario* the right to acquire for himself the things he has been commissioned to sell, or to supply what he had been commissioned to buy, on condition that the object of the *commissione* are securities, currencies or commodities having an *official market price*.[256]

The brief remarks set out above clearly reveal the apparent difference in Annina's position if we apply the Italian Civil Code: first, her relationship to Violetta and to third parties would differ depending on whether the power of attorney was conferred with or without representation. If Annina had acted according to the schemes of the Napoleonic Code or the Austrian Code, the power of attorney would have to be considered as with representation, and – applying the Italian scheme – Annina could have received from Violetta either a power of attorney (*mandato*) with representation or

---

256   Another difference lies in the aggrement of the so-called 'star del credere': based on the specific agreement or custom of the place in which the deal is concluded, the agent is responsible to the principal for the fulfilment of the obligations assumed by the third party in the deal. In this case, the agent is entitled to special remuneration.

a *procura* for the sale of the goods. Annina would – probably – be remuner-
ated for its job, unless gratuitousness had been an express condition of the
contract, and she would have the right to receive expenses and statutory interest. Finally, if the goods subject to sale had been securities, currencies or
commodities with an official price, her relationship with Violetta could possibly be framed as a commission, and therefore Annina could have bought
for herself the goods Violetta wished to sell and (perhaps) also make a profit.
Finally, examining the situation of Alfredo, according to the Italian Civil
Code in force, his position corresponds to that reconstructed in relation to
the Austrian and French Codes: under art. 769 of the Civil Code, a donation
is a contract, and the consent of the donee is essential for its completion.

6. We have already noted the fact that *La traviata* presents deviations from
Alexandre Dumas' novel. Given that there are also significant deviations
between Dumas' play and the novel, it follows inevitably that Piave's libretto deviates from both, with differences that have been extensively studied.
With specific reference to the two situations here under examination (the
sale of the assets of the protagonist, and the donation by Alfredo), the principal distinctions can be identified as follows. In comparison, in the first
place, to the novel, the deviations are particularly marked, both with regard
to the sale of the assets of the protagonist (called Marguerite in the novel),
and about the circumstances in which Armand/Alfredo becomes aware
of it. In the novel, Armand, suspicious at the disappearance of certain of
Marguerite's assets (a carriage and a cashmere shawl), rummages in the
drawers of his beloved and notices the absence of jewels and diamonds.
He calls on their friend Prudence in Paris and learns the truth: Marguerite
has had to sell some of her assets to pay off her creditors, and pawn others:
so, unlike Piave's libretto, part of the goods have been pledged for a loan
of money, and the legal framework changes. Marguerite has practically
been reduced to poverty, but she still has debts for at least thirty thousand
francs. In Dumas' novel, it is Prudence who has sold Marguerite's goods,
as emerges from the conversation with Armand (Chapter XVIII):

'Come,' said I, without beating about the bush, 'tell me frankly. Where are Marguerite's horses?'

'Sold.'

'And the shawl?'

' Sold.'

'And the diamonds?'

'Pawned.'

'And who has sold and pawned all them?'

'I.'

'Why did you not tell me?'

'Because Marguerite made me promise not to.'

'And why did you not ask me for money?'

'Because she wouldn't let me.'

'And where has this money gone?'

'In payments.'

'Is she much in debt?'

'Thirty thousand francs or thereabouts.'[257]

Prudence tries to open Armand's eyes, reminding him that:

'By the side of that ideal life, there is a material life, and the purest resolutions are held to earth by threads which seem slight enough, but which are of iron, not easily to be broken. If Marguerite has not been unfaithful to you twenty times, it is because she has an exceptional nature. It is not my fault for not advising her to, for I couldn't bear to see the poor girl stripping herself of everything. She wouldn't; she replied that she loved you, and she wouldn't be unfaithful to you for anything in the world. All that is very pretty, very poetical, but one can't pay one's creditors in that coin, and now she can't free herself from debt, unless she can raise thirty thousand francs.'

Armand responds by saying he will obtain the sum by raising a loan, and will give it to Prudence to cover Marguerite's outstanding debts. So, in the novel, Armand's decision is not just the result of an emotional reaction in the face of the discovery of what Marguerite has done, but is also motivated by the desire to raise the money to pay off her remaining debts. Of this there remains no trace in Piave's libretto.

In Chapter XIX the matter is raised between them, and Marguerite expresses the question in this way:

---

257   The English text is taken from A. DUMAS *fils*, *The Lady of the Camellias*, English translation by E. Gosse, London: Signet Press, 2004, Ch. XVIII.

'I wanted ... to arrange everything without telling you, pay all my debts, and take a new flat. In October we should have been back in Paris, and all would have come out; but since Prudence has told you all, you will have to agree beforehand, instead of agreeing afterward. Do you love me enough for that?'

7. In the novel, also Armand's gift also takes a particular form, not described in *La traviata*. We learn that Armand had received an annuity from his mother, and it is this income that Armand plans to allocate to Violetta (Chapter XIX):

'That very moment I settled what my future was going to be. I calculated what money I had, and determined to make over to Marguerite the income my mother had left me, which seemed to me barely sufficient to recompense her for the sacrifice I accepted.
Then there would remain to me the five thousand francs my father allowed me yearly, and which was enough to live upon whatever might happen.
I did not tell Marguerite what I had resolved to do, for I was convinced she would refuse my gift.
My mother had left me a sum of sixty thousand francs, which was put out on mortgage on a house I had never even seen. All I knew was that each quarter-day an old friend of our family, who was also my father's lawyer, handed me seven hundred and fifty francs'.

In the novel, Armand then goes to the notary to complete the formalities. His father, learning of Armand's intentions from the notary, speaks to him harshly (Chapter XX):

'I came here to prevent your ruining yourself for this girl. When your mother died she left you enough to live honourably, but not enough to squander it on your mistresses.'

8. In the play, staged at the Théâtre du Vaudeville on 2 February 1852, the events that concern us here undergo further changes that in part resemble Piave's text more closely, though the latter is still at a considerable distance from its source.
The question of the sale of Violetta goods is raised, as in the novel, by the disappearance of the horses and (also, in this case) the carriage, and the

cashmere shawl, so arousing Armand's suspicions. In the play, however, diamonds are included among these goods (and not, as in the novel, jewellery in general). Armand seeks an explanation from Prudence, to whom Marguerite had given them (so, unlike the scene in the novel, Armand has no need to rummage in Marguerite's drawers). Here is Act III.1:

ARMAND	Ah! you here, Prudence! It's well—I wished to speak to you. Two weeks since, as I arrived here on my daily visit to dear Marguerite, you were about leaving, and in Marguerite's carriage.
PRUDENCE	Exactly.
ARMAND	Since then neither carriage nor horses have returned. A week since, on leaving, you complained of cold, and Marguerite lent you a cashmere shawl, which I do not think you have returned. Yesterday I saw her place in your hands bracelets and diamonds—to be reset, she said. Where are the horses, the carriage, the bracelets, and the diamonds?
PRUDENCE	Must I tell you?
ARMAND	I entreat you.
PRUDENCE	The horses have taken themselves and the carriage back to the man from whom they came, for they were not paid for.
ARMAND	The diamonds—
PRUDENCE	Pledged. Perhaps you would like to see the duplicates?
ARMAND	Why did you not tell me?
PRUDENCE	Marguerite forbade me.
ARMAND	And why these sales?
PRUDENCE	To obtain money, to be sure. Oh, I suppose you imagine it is quite enough to marry, and live a pastoral and ethereal life... [258]

At the end of the conversation with Prudence, Armand comes to his decision:

---

258   Adapted from the English translation, A. DUMAS *fils*, *The Lady of the Camellias*, London: Thomas Hailes Lacy, 1905.

ARMAND	What sum would be necessary for—
PRUDENCE	Thirty thousand francs at least.
ARMAND	Obtain a fortnight's grace from the creditors, and I will pay all.
PRUDENCE	You will embroil yourself with your father, and infringe on your future fortune.
ARMAND	I had prepared for this. I knew that Marguerite had creditors, and had written tomy lawyer's that I wished to dispose of a small estate left me by my mother,[259] and have just received his answer. The deed is quite prepared, and presently I shall return to Paris in order to sign it. In the meantime, pray be careful that Marguerite knows nothing of what I am about to do.
PRUDENCE	But the papers that I bring—
ARMAND	When I am gone, give them to her as if nothing had occurred, for she must be ignorant of our conversation.

If, on the development of the play, the fate of Armand's inheritance follows the lines of the novel (namely, the attempted assignment of the annuity in favour of Marguerite), there are some further points of difference with regard to Marguerite. During her interview with Armand's father, Marguerite indicates further bills of sale of goods in favour of an 'homme d'affaire', whose trade is to sell paintings, furniture, and luxury goods in general, and exhibits a deed prepared for the purpose.[260] She addresses M. Duval, Armand's father, in the following words (Act III.4):

MARGUERITE	I will tell you what I would have preferred to keep silent about. But, because above all I want the esteem of Armand's father, I will speak. Since I met your son, because my love does not even resemble for an instant everything that was given this name around me, I have pledged and sold my cashmere shawls, diamonds, carriages; and when a little while ago,

---

259   In the original French: 'une délégation du bien que je tiens de ma mère'.
260   Reference to a 'businessman' is also made by Violetta in *La traviata*, just before the arrival of Germont.

	they told me someone was asking for me, I thought I was receiving a financial intermediary,[261] whom I would sell all the furniture, the pictures, the curtains, and the rest of the luxury that reproaches me. Finally, if you doubt my words, look here. I was not expecting you, sir, so you can hardly believe that this bill of sale was prepared for you, and if you doubt it, read this deed. *(She hands him the deed of sale that Prudence gave her.)*
DUVAL	*(reading paper with astonishment)* A disposal of all your property with the requirement that the purchaser should pay your debts—the surplus to be returned to you. Could I have been mistaken?

It is obvious that this additional element of the episode concerning Marguerite's property complicates the picture, resulting in a sale of movable goods, to which is added a power of attorney to pay third party creditors, using the proceeds.

Finally, in the play, there is one last brief episode that is significant on the patrimonial plane. Marguerite gives Nanine power of attorney (*mandato/procura*) to sell a bracelet, as she has just lent two hundred francs to Prudence, who had come to claim it for 'the gifts to be made' (Act V.5):

NANINE *(returning)*	Did she come asking for money again?
MARGUERITE	Yes.
NANINE	And you gave it to her?
MARGUERITE	The sum is so little, and she was in such great need, she said. We need it, too, though. There are gifts to be made. Take this bracelet they sent me, go and sell it and come back later.

Perhaps I am hazarding too much, but this last, brief exchange may have given Piave the model on which to build his own way of interpreting the story of the sale of Marguerite's goods that, as we have seen, in *La traviata* turns on the power of attorney Violetta gave Annina. And since there is

---

261   In the original French: 'un homme d'affaires'.

no trace in Verdi's masterpiece of the other issues referred to in Dumas' novel, it may be a plausible conjecture.

In short, *La traviata* is certainly about love and death, but it is also about money, loans, donations, financial transactions, and debts to be paid off. To Violetta and Alfredo, love therefore also has a very prosaic dimension: the dimension of money, which guides and inspires many of their actions, with a determinism that the myth of romantic love struggles to acknowledge.

X

Das Rheingold
(Richard Wagner)

Contracts are binding[262]

1. In the massive architecture of Wagner's *Ring* cycle, *Das Rheingold*, as is well known, is the backstory (or more correctly the prologue[263]) to the whole narrative, which unfolds through the three following days and operas (*Die Walküre*, *Siegfried* and *Götterdämmerung*). The function of *Das Rheingold* is, however, not just to introduce the audience of the *Ring* to the complex world of the three works that follow, their mythology, symbolism, and the themes that develop in them: *Das Rheingold* embodies the profound reasons justifying the whole narrative destined to lead to the final downfall of the gods.

The *Ring* cycle can, and has been, explored from countless points of view. Wagner's Tetralogy continues to prove one of the most fertile grounds in the whole history of musical theatre: a unique phenomenon in the European cultural panorama, stimulated by the presence and interweaving in Wagner's masterpiece of mythological, philosophical, political, psychological and social themes, and the various perspectives from which it is therefore possible to investigate the edifice raised by Wagner's achievement.

Here, far from attempting a complete reconstruction of such a complex edifice, I would like to present some ideas as a way of imagining a reading

---

262   A version of this paper has already been published in the volume *Studi in onore di Giovanni Iudica*, Milan: EGEA, 2014, pp. 37-62.
263   The subtitle of *Das Rheingold* is *Vorabend zu dem Bühnenfestspiel 'Der Ring des Nibelungen'*. The opera was composed by Richard Wagner between 1853 and 1854 and performed for the first time on 22 September at the Nationaltheater in Munich in 1869. The libretto is taken from the text published in the edition of the Teatro alla Scala for the Bicentenary Edition of the *Ring*, in 2013. The English text is taken from the website http://www.rwagner.net/libretti/rheingold/e-rhein-s1.html, with some personal corrections by the Author.

of *Das Rheingold* (and therefore of the motifs underlying the whole Wagnerian Tetralogy), in a perspective close to private law, and contract law in particular. Without any pretension to a complete treatment, or a rereading of the whole Wagnerian Universe, I would like to bring out some aspects of it that would *enable* – with a view to a possible, future development of these ideas, which can be extended to the other operas in the *Ring* – an analysis of the complex Wagnerian construct from the side of law, and specifically private law, and of the profound economic and social changes in the age of the work's composition. Some similar ideas have already been offered by a German author.[264]

2. In one of the central passages of *Das Rheingold*, at the culmination of the close-knit dialogue between the gods and giants, the giant Fasolt addresses the following words to Wotan:

FASOLT
Lichtsohn du,
leicht gefügter!
hör' und hüte dich:
Verträgen halte Treu'!
Was du bist,
bist du nur durch Verträge;
bedungen ist,
wohl bedacht deine Macht.
Bist weiser du
als witzig wir sind,
bandest uns Freie
zum Frieden du:
all deinem Wissen fluch' ich,
fliehe weit deinen Frieden,
weisst du nicht offen,
ehrlich und frei

FASOLT
Son of light,
easily swayed,
hearken and beware:
hold firm to your bond!
What you are,
you are only by contracts:
limited
and well defined is your power.
You have more wisdom
than we have wits;
you bound us, who were free,
to keep peace:
I will curse all your wisdom
and flee from your peace
if openly,
honourably and freely

---

264   See E.E. WIESER, 'Der Ring des Nibelungen im Licht des Zivilrechts', in H. Avenarius, H. Engelhardt, H. Heussner, F. von Zerzschwitz (edited by), *Festschrift für Erwin Stein zum 80 Geburtstag*, Bad Homburg: Verlag Gehlen, 1983, pp. 383 ff.

Verträgen zu wahren die Treu'! –	you do not know to keep faith in your bond!
Ein dummer Riese	A simple giant
rät dir das:	thus counsels you:
du Weiser, wiss' es von ihm!	wise one, weigh his words!

Fasolt's words, as we have seen, are set in the context of the dispute that takes place on stage between Fasolt, his brother Faffner, and Wotan. It starts from a clear case of *breach of contract*. The giants had agreed to build a wonderful, new dwelling place of the gods for a price. The price agreed was Freia the goddess, the sister of Fricka, Wotan's wife. Freia has a key function in the economy of the gods, since she grows the fruit from which the gods themselves draw their nourishment and strength. It is, therefore, a heavy price for the gods to pay. If they lose Freia, they will probably be doomed to waste away and ultimately disappear. Wotan, however, entices the giants, convincing them to embark on the immense work of building Valhalla, promising them a particularly desirable reward.[265]

The work is now complete and the two giants are rightly demanding the price, urging Wotan to *respect the pact* ('Verträgen halte Treu!'). They remind him that his power is based solely and exclusively on contracts ('Was du bist, / bist du nur durch Verträge').

On the level of the social hierarchy around which the ring turns (and, in general, the Nordic mythology from which Wagner drew his inspiration), the giants certainly occupy a lower position than the gods: they cannot aspire to the attain the heights of those who (Wotan in particular) are supposed to be the guardians of order and equilibrium in the universe. Rather the giants represent brute, primal force, far from the refined world of the gods, and are subject to them. How then can a clumsy giant can even *permit himself* to call to order Wotan, the supreme deity of the German pantheon, the personification of sacredness, religion and the Germanic mythologies? And then, what do contracts (*Verträge*) have to do with the

---

265   Hence it is likely that the giants were enticed by the idea of receiving Freia in exchange for their work, as this compensation would allow them to weaken the race of the gods and take advantage of them, so enabling them to establish a new, social order.

gods? The mere fact that a jurist, in approaching the world of the Wagnerian Tetralogy, can raise these questions is itself a topic of interest, which is worth remarking. Perhaps the *Ring* lends itself, among other approaches, to a reading from the perspective of contract law.

3. We will take the events in the order they happen. After the dwarf Alberich steals the gold from the Rhine maidens – an episode that occupies the whole first scene of *Rheingold* – we quickly enter into the theme that concerns us here. The action now takes place near Valhalla. In the opening scene, Fricka and Wotan slumber: Fricka awakes with a start and, in turn rouses Wotan: 'Erwache, Mann, und erwäge!' ('Wotan, husband! awake and observe!'). The observation she urges on her husband touches on the essential point that concerns us, the contract between Wotan and the giants, which Wotan has entered into rather thoughtlessly – trusting to his position of strength – by requiring the giants to build the dwelling place of the gods in exchange for Freia. The image of the castle dwelling of the gods, now complete, stirs Fricka's anguish and her desire to protect her sister, as well as the whole race of the gods.

The contract is sufficiently clear. It is, essentially, a procurement contract, or rather a mixed contract, related to a procurement contract, for which the price is not in money, but in kind. Wotan has consented to the contract, but it is clear he had no intention, from the outset, of respecting its provisions.

WOTAN
[*omissis*]
 und Freia, die gute,
 geb' ich nicht auf;
 nie sann dies ernstlich mein Sinn.

WOTAN
[*omissis*]
 And I will not yield
 our good Freia:
 in truth, I never had any such intention

Hence Wotan entered into the contract at the very least in bad faith, perhaps led into it on the advice of Loge, who had acted as his legal consultant (and also as fixer) in negotiations with the giants. In his original intention not to fulfil the contract, he already betrays the profound contradiction that moves the universe and the order established by the gods, now fated to perish.[266] From the point of view of the giants, however, there is no backing out of the bargain: the work is done, and the contractor must be paid. The giants claim the price:

FASOLT

Bedungen ist,
was tauglich uns dünkt:
gemahnt es dich so matt?
Freia, die Holde,
Holda, die Freie,
vertragen ist's,
sie tragen wir heim.

FASOLT

We asked what
seemed to us fair;
is your memory so weak?
Freia the fair,
Holda the free,
it was agreed
we should take home.

Pressed by the giants to fulfil his side of the bargain, Wotan reveals his real plan: he has no intention of surrendering Freia to the giants.

It is at this juncture that the key phrase appears, addressed by Fasolt to Wotan, as the giant urges the absolute need to respect the terms of the contract. In enjoining him to fulfil the agreement, Fasolt reminds Wotan that respecting a contract is of paramount importance, not only in terms of their bilateral relationship, but because Wotan's very existence is derived from contracts: ('Was bist du, / bist du nur durch Verträge; / bedungen ist, / wohl bedacht deine Macht' / 'What you are, / you are only by contracts; / limited, / and well defined is your power').

Any breach of this contract is, therefore, not just a matter that concerns the rights and obligations of both parties, but one on which depends the very credibility of the gods, and of Wotan in particular. Though Wotan is the greatest deity in the Wagnerian pantheon only 'durch Verträge,' meaning only through and by virtue of the contracts he has entered into, and obviously respected (so

---

266   This is not the place the question the reasons for which Wotan deliberately concluded a contract with the clear intention of not fulfilling it: the reasons, in other words, why Wotan himself decided to enter into a collision course with the order that he himself is, and should protect. This question is one of the principal issues of the whole philosophy underlying the Tetralogy, and can not be summed up in a few lines. Here, however, we are not concerned with the *motives* that ultimately actuate Wotan, but rather with his decisions and the consequences they have on the plane of a possible 'legal' interpretation of the Tetralogy.

far), it is clear that *the contract* is the foundation of society and the social order represented in *Das Rheingold*, and from this point on of the whole Tetralogy. Certainly, it can almost be taken for granted that the reference to a 'contract' can be understood here in various, and perhaps many highly articulated acceptations. And these acceptations have given rise to different readings of the whole architecture of the Tetralogy viewed in perspectives that are quite different from the one evoked here. The first, and most immediate, is the attempt to understand the 'contract' Fafner mentions as a kind of 'social contract', with the consequence of legitimizing one of the most classic readings of the whole *Ring* in a perspective of struggle or social conflict, one which fits perfectly into the risings that characterized Europe and Germany in the nineteenth century.

But if we confine ourselves to the most immediate textual elements, it is at the same time clear that Wotan and Fasolt's dispute is centred, in the first place, on the contract (*Vertrag*) that binds them directly and specifically to the construction of the magnificent new residence of the gods.

The validity of the contract, which Fafner affirms peremptorily, is therefore, above all, the value to be assigned to the fulfilment of a negotiated agreement, *in a society that accords it a fundamental value.*

The legal order, which the giants are now demanding should be respected, justifies Wotan's own power, and recognition of his representative 'social' position, in the historical context in which Wagner's sensibility developed: a reality, and a historico-social environment, clearly imbued with economic values and relationships.

It is the contract that then becomes, first of all, the driving force behind the whole affair, and the breach of contract leads, in the subsequent development of the *Ring*, to the downfall of the gods themselves. The non-fulfilment of the contract executed by Wotan with the giants is – as Fasolt's words stress – a very serious act, since it questions the rules that sustain the society willed by the gods themselves, and constitute its *raison d'être*. The giants demand compliance with the contract, both as – legitimately – claiming the promised service, and because breach of contract would undermine the very basis of the order of Wagner's legendary universe.

4. As we have already seen, Wotan does not intend to respect the agree-

ment. He blames Loge (who arrives belatedly at the scene of the dispute),
actually accusing him of having created a 'tangled web':

WOTAN
Endlich Loge!
Eiltest du so,
den du geschlossen,
den schlimmen Handel zu schlichten?

WOTAN
Loge at last!
Is this how you hasten
to set to rights
the tangled web you spun?

Loge reminds him, however, the way things stand. It was not Loge who
entered into the contract with the giants, but Wotan himself:

LOGE
Wie? Welchen Handel
hätt' ich geschlossen?
Wohl was mit den Riesen
dort im Rate du dangst?
In Tiefen und Höhen
treibt mich mein Hang:
Haus und Herd
behagt mir nicht.
Donner und Froh,
die denken an Dach und Fach,
wollen sie frei'n,
ein Haus muss sie erfreu'n.
Ein stolzer Saal,
ein starkes Schloss,
danach stand Wotans Wunsch.
Haus und Hof,
Saal und Schloss,
die selige Burg,
sie steht nun fest gebaut.
Das Prachtgemäuer
prüft' ich selbst,
ob alles fest,
forscht' ich genau:
Fasolt und Fafner
fand ich bewährt:
kein Stein wankt in Gestemm'.

LOGE
What? What bargain
did I conclude?
That which you contracted
with the giants in council?
My whim takes me
to depths and heights:
house and hearth
delight me not.
Donner and Froh,
they are dreaming of food and shelter!
When they want to wed,
a house would gladden them.
A stately home,
a stronghold,
this was Wotan's wish.
House and court,
hall and keep,
the glorious fortress
now firmly stands;
its proud walls
I myself tested;
I made sure
that all was solid;
I found Fasolt and Fafner
reliable:
not a stone but was firm in its place.

Nicht müssig war ich,	I was not idle,
wie mancher hier;	as were many here:
der lügt, wer lässig mich schilt!	he lies who rebukes me as lazy!

Wotan replies that Loge has actually promised him to 'redeem' Freia; but Loge, with some rather twisted arguments, justifies his action. It was, says Loge, not an obligation to redeem Freia, but a commitment to think about 'how to free her'; a subtle argument, not without a touch of irony in the *ésprit de finesse* displayed by the pseudo-jurist Loge:

LOGE

LOGE

Mit höchster Sorge	To consider
drauf zu sinnen,	with the utmost care
wie es zu lösen,	how to release her
das hab' ich gelobt.	that I promised.
Doch, dass ich fände,	But that I could find
was nie sich fügt,	what never existed
was nie gelingt, –	and never could succeed,
wie liess sich das wohl geloben?	how could that ever be promised?

The situation seems at this point to have reached an impasse. But as Loge relates the tale of the events that led to the theft of the Rhine gold, a way out seems to emerge. Not only has the theft of the Rhine gold made immense wealth available – certainly sufficient to remunerate the service rendered by the giants – but the gold, if forged into a ring, could grant its possessor the power to conquer the world:

LOGE

LOGE

Ein Tand ist's	It is a toy
in des Wassers Tiefe,	in the depths of the water,
lachenden Kindern zur Lust,	to give pleasure to laughing children;
doch ward es zum runden	but if it were fashioned
Reife geschmiedet,	into a round ring
hilft es zur höchsten Macht,	it would bestow supreme power
gewinnt dem Manne die Welt.	and win its master the world.

In this way, Loge devises the solution that should enable to find a way out of the dilemma in which they find themselves. They could steal the gold from Alberich, and offer it to the giants in lieu of Freia. The substitution, however, should only concern the gold, and not the ring forged by Alberich that – in Wotan's words – gives 'power and treasures beyond measure' to its possessor. This is made immediately evident by Wotan's reflections in the context of the development of the action, which leads him to take the decision to propose substituting the gold, now in Alberich's possession, for Freia.

WOTAN *(sinnend)*
 Von des Rheines Gold
 hört' ich raunen:
 Beute-Runen
berge sein roter Glanz;
 Macht und Schätze
schüf' ohne Mass ein Reif

WOTAN *(meditating)*
 I have heard talk
 of the Rhine's gold:
 its glittering glow hides
runes of riches;
 a ring would give unbounded
power and wealth.

The only way to get hold of the gold (and the ring) is by theft. Loge is naturally well aware of this, and he almost goes so far as to maintain the legitimacy of such an act perpetrated against one who, in turn, is a thief:

LOGE
        Durch Raub!
 Was ein Dieb stahl,
 das stiehlst du dem Dieb;
ward leichter ein Eigen erlangt?
Doch mit arger Wehr
 wahrt sich Alberich;
 klug und fein
 musst du verfahren,
ziehst den Räuber du zu Recht,
 um des Rheines Töchtern,
 den roten Tand,
(Mit Wärme)
das Gold wiederzugeben;
denn darum flehen sie dich.

LOGE
        By theft!
 What a thief stole,
 you steal from the thief:
could possessions be more easily acquired?
But Alberich guards himself
 with guile;
 you must act
 shrewdly and subtly
to bring the thief to justice
 and to return
 to the Rhinemaidens the gold,
(With warmth)
their shining toy;
for that is what they beg of you.

The giants, after consultation, accept the proposal, though they do not seem fully persuaded of it. It is Fafner who breaks the deadlock:

FAFNER
Glaub' mir, mehr als Freia
frommt das gleissende Gold:
auch ew'ge Jugend erjagt,
wer durch Goldes Zauber sie zwingt.
(Fasolts Gebärde deutet an, dass er sich
wider Willen überredet fühlt. Fafner tritt
mit Fasolt wieder an Wotan heran)
  Hör', Wotan,
  der Harrenden Wort!
Freia bleib' euch in Frieden;
  leicht'ren Lohn
  fand ich zur Lösung:
uns rauhen Riesen genügt
des Niblungen rotes Gold.

FAFNER
Belive me, that glittering gold
is worth more that Freia:
for eternal youth he gains
who commands it by gold's magic
(Fasolt's gestures show that he is reluctantly
coming round. Fafner comes
forward to Wotan again with Fastolt)
  Hear, Wotan,
  what we have at last to say!
Freia may stay with you in peace;
  an easier fee
  I've found in settlement:
we rough giants would be satisfied
with the Niblung's shining gold.

What occurs at this juncture is a complex phenomenon. Firstly, the nova-tion of the object of the contract (Freia/gold) seems reducible to the scheme of *datio in solutum*. However, the structure of this substitute payment suf-fers from a number of critical points:
– first of all, the item he has offered to substitute is not *materially* in Wotan's disposal;
– the item he has offered to substitute is not even *legally* at Wotan's dispos-al, as it does not belong to him;
– the original price (Freia) is replaced by a promise of procuring the new item. In this expectation, the giants provisionally 'hold' the original price (Freia) as collateral (*'Pfand'*) for the exact fulfillment of the contract, as novated;[267]

---

267   The attempt of the gods to prevent Freia's abduction fails, as they are losing their strength, not having yet fed on the goddess's apples, 'LOGE Jetzt fand ich's: hört, was fehlt euch! / Von Freias Frucht / genoss et ihr heute noch nicht. / Die Goldenen Äpfel / in ihrem Garten / sie euch machten tüchtig und jung / asst ihr sie jeden Tag. / Des Gartens Pflegerin / ist nun ver pfändet; / An den Asten darbt / dorrt und das Obst, / bald fällt es herab faul. -- / Mich Kummert's minder; / An mir ja kargte / Freia von je, / knausernd die köstliche Frucht: / denn nur halb so echt / Bin wie ich, Herrliche, ihr! / Doch ihr alles setztet / auf das jüngende Obst: / wussten das wohl die

– the guarantee is a pledge, with an agreement for forfeiture: the giants specify that, if Wotan does not return with the promised gold by evening, they will keep Freia for good.[268] In saying this, the giants do not win Wotan's consent, but in reality hold Freia (against her will, and against the will of the gods): they, therefore, likewise break the schemes of contract law;
– the giants, besides, are also in bad faith: they know very well that the gold is not Wotan's, and thus agree to conclude an invalid contract.[269] At the moment when they are given the gold, the act will contradict the *nemo dat* rule (*nemo dat quod non habet*) for fungible movable goods.
From these facts, dense with meaning, and critical on the plane of the law of contract, the following events unfold.

4. Wotan and Loge travel to the kingdom of the Nibelungs and, with a series of deceptions, they manage to steal Alberich's gold and the ring that he has forged, together with the magic helmet. The appropriation of the gold is clearly an act committed by Wotan contrary to law, with the fact that Alberich, in turn, had stolen it from the Rhine maidens being irrelevant. This new infraction of the legal order by Wotan prompts Alberich's famous curse, fated to fall on the ring and those who possess it:[270]

Riesen; / Auf euer Leben / legten sie's an: / sorgt nun, wie ihr das wahrt! / Ohne die Äpfel, / alt und grau, / greis und Gramlich, / welkend zum Spott aller Welt, / erstirbt der Götter Stamm. ('LOGE I have it: hear what it is you lack! / Of Freia's fruit / you have not yet eaten today: / the golden apples / in her garden / make you hearty and young / when you eat them every day. / She who tended the garden / is now a hostage; / on the branches the fruit fades and withers; / soon it will decay and fall. / It irks me less; / to me Freia / has always been ungenerous, / niggardly with the precious fruit: / for I am only half as godlike / as you glorious ones! / But you staked all / on the youth-giving fruit: / this the giants knew well; / your life / they laid against it: / now take care to defend it. / Without the apples, / old and grey, / hoary and haggard, / withered, the scorn of all the world, / the race of gods will die.').

268 'FAFNER Fort von hier / sie six entführt! / Bis Abend - achtet's wohl! - / Pflegen wir sie als Pfand; / Wir wieder kehren; / Doch wir kommen, / bereit und liegt nicht als Lösung / das Rheingold licht und rot -fasolt Zu End ,Frist ist dann die, / Freia verfallen! / folge für immer sie uns! ('FAFNER Let her be carried / far from here! / Till evening – pay due heed – / we will hold her as hostage: / we shall return; / but when we come, / if as ransom the bright gleaming Rhinegold / is not lying ready – / she is kidnapped!)

269 'FAFNER Schwer baute / sich dort die Burg; / Leicht wird dir's / list'ger mit Gewalt / (was im Neidspiel uns nie Gelang) / den Niblungen fest zu Fahn. ('FAFNER The castle there / was hard to build: / it will be easy for you, /with cunning craft / (which we in quarrels could never command), / to fetter the Niblung firmly.')

270 The curse of Alberich is twofold: the first against love (and its 'force of renewal'); the second

---

ALBERICH *(sich erhebend)*	ALBERICH *(rising)*
Bin ich nun frei?	Am I free now?
(Wütend lachend)	*(With angry laughter)*
Wirklich frei? –	Truly free?
So grüss' euch denn	Then thus I give you
meiner Freiheit erster Gruss! –	my freedom's first greeting!
Wie durch Fluch er mir geriet,	Since by curse it came to me,
verflucht sei dieser Ring!	accursed be this ring!
Gab sein Gold	Since its gold gave me
mir Macht ohne Mass,	measureless might,
nun zeug' sein Zauber	now may its magic bring
Tod dem, der ihn trägt!	death to whoever wears it!
Kein Froher soll	It shall gladden
seiner sich freun,	no happy man;
keinem Glücklichen lache	its bright gleam shall light
sein lichter Glanz!	on no one lucky!
Wer ihn besitzt,	Whoever possesses it
den sehre die Sorge,	shall be consumed with care,
und wer ihn nicht hat,	and whoever has it not
den nage der Neid!	be gnawed with envy!
Jeder giere	Each shall itch
nach seinem Gut,	to possess it,
doch keiner geniesse	but none in it
mit Nutzen sein!	shall find pleasure!
Ohne Wucher hüt' ihn sein Herr;	Its owner shall guard it profitlessly, for
doch den Würger zieh' er ihm zu!	through it he shall meet his executioner!
Dem Tode verfallen,	Forfeit to death,
fessle den Feigen die Furcht:	faint with fear shall he be fettered;
solang er lebt,	the length of his life
sterb' er lechzend dahin,	he shall long to die,
des Ringes Herr	the ring's master
als des Ringes Knecht:	to the ring a slave,
bis in meiner Hand	until again I hold in my hands
den geraubten wieder ich halte! –	what was stolen!
So segnet	Thus,

---

against the greed and arrogance of the gods. On the basis of Alberich's curse, the Tetralogy can also be seen as the story of the epilogue of a world based on greed, of which revolutionary Europe in the mid-nineteenth century was, in Wagner's view, a sort of reflection.

in höchster Not	in direst distress,
der Nibelung seinen Ring!	the Niblung blesseshis ring!
Behalt' ihn nun,	Keep it now,
(Lachend)	*(Laughing)*
hüte ihn wohl:	guard it well;
(Grimmig)	*(Grimly)*
meinem Fluch fliehest du nicht!	my curse you cannot escape!
(Er verschwindet schnell in der Kluft.)	*(He disappears rapidly into the cleft)*

On returning to the giants, it is now time for Wotan to fulfill the contract. The giants ask for as much gold as will cover the whole person of Freia. The reference to the pledge/Freia now reappears:

FAFNER	FAFNER
Gepflanzt sind die Pfähle	These poles we've planted
nach Pfandes Mass;	to the measure of the pledge:
gehäuft nun füll' es der Hort!	now fill the space full with the hoard.

The fulfillment, however, in accordance with the good rules of the law of contracts, must be *exact*: all the spaces, all the voids must be filled with the gold. Only then will the pledge be restored, and the contract can be said to have been complied with:

FAFNER	FAFNER
Nicht so leicht	Not so light
und locker gefügt!	and loosely packed!
(Er drückt mit roher Kraft die Geschmeide dicht zusammen)	*(He presses together the gold with rough force)*
Fest und dicht	Fill the measure
füll' er das Mass.	firm and close!
(Er beugt sich, um nach Lücken zu spähen)	*(He bends to peer at the spaces)*
Hier lug' ich noch durch:	I can still see through it here:
verstopft mir die Lücken!	stop up these chinks!

After claiming the helmet – useful to fill a first hole that still appears through the pile of gold covering Freia – there remains a tiny chink. The only way to fill it is with the gold ring, and the giants demand it. Loge intervenes, but to no avail:

LOGE

Nimmersatte!
seht ihr denn nicht,
ganz schwand uns das Gold?

FAFNER

Mitnichten, Freund!
An Wotans Finger
glänzt von Gold noch ein Ring:
den gebt, die Ritze zu füllen!

WOTAN

Wie! Diesen Ring?

LOGE

Lasst euch raten!
den Rheintöchtern
gehört dies Gold;
ihnen gibt Wotan es wieder.

WOTAN

Was schwatztest du da?
Was schwer ich mir erbeutet,
ohne Bangen wahr' ich's für mich!

LOGE

Schlimm dann steht's
um mein Versprechen,
das ich den Klagenden gab!

LOGE

Ever insatiable!
Can't you see
that all the gold has gone?

FAFNER

By no means, friend.
On Wotan's finger
still glints a ring of gold:
give it here to fill the crack!

WOTAN

What! This ring?

LOGE

Listen to me!
This gold belongs
to the Rhinemaidens:
Wotan will give it back to them.

WOTAN

What idle chatter is this?
What I won with such difficulty
without a qualm I'll keep for myself.

LOGE

Then it goes badly
with the promise
I gave the lamenting maidens.

Notice how Loge makes clear to the giants their bad faith (and therefore the fact that what is taking place is a case that breaks the rule of *nemo dat*): the gold – Loge notes – actually belongs to the Rhine maidens, and it is to the latter that the ring should be returned (Loge is clearly lying, because neither of them have any intention of doing so). It should also be noted that, at this juncture, Wotan again tries to free himself from the terms negotiated with the giants. He has no intention of parting with the ring, and actually seizes on the reference that Loge makes to 'his promise' to declare:

WOTAN

Dein Versprechen bindet mich nicht;
als Beute bleibt mir der Reif.

WOTAN

Your promise does not bind me:
the ring remains with me as booty.

Wotan's stubbornness is overcome only after the intervention – almost a kind of *deus ex machina* – of Erda, who urges him to get rid of the ring, since it is designed to lead to 'dark destruction':

ERDA *(die Hand mahnend gegen Wotan ausstrekkend)*
Weiche, Wotan! Weiche!
Flieh' des Ringes Fluch!
  Rettungslos
  dunklem Verderben
weiht dich sein Gewinn.

ERDA *((holding out her hand in admonition to Wotan)*
Yield, Wotan, yield!
Escape from the ring's curse.
  To dark destruction
  irredeemably
its possession dooms you.

In a reading that brings out the aspects comprised in this analysis, the end of the Gods is already marked by the 'breaking' of the contract by Wotan, and his repetition of unlawful conducts.

5. The curse of the ring soon falls on the giants themselves. It is true that they have rightly claimed the exact fulfillment of the contract on the part of Wotan and, to that end, the ring was none other than the last piece of gold needed in order for the contract to be performed *exactly*. However, as we have seen, the giants were not in good faith, as they were well aware that the gold did not belong to Wotan and that to recover it he would have to commit a theft. The giants have therefore also broken the legal order and the rules of contracts.

They have knowingly received, in recompense for their work, a good that belongs neither to the gods nor Wotan, and whose ownership or lawful possession they are, therefore, unable to legally claim.

If, then, it is true that the giants likewise violate the rules of private law, the ring's curse has every reason to unfold its effects on them, as if to emphasize the impossibility, for the established order to tolerate violations of the juridical order. Among the giants, the violation, however, degenerates into crime. Fafner and Fasolt each claims for himself exclusive possession of the ring, and Fafner slays Fasolt:

FASOLT *(stürzt sich auf Fafner,*	FASOLT *(flings himself on Fafner, who*
der immerzu eingesackt hat)	*continues stuffing gold in the sack)*
Zurück! Du Frecher!	Back, over-bold one!
Mein ist der Ring;	Mine is the ring:
mir blieb er für Freias Blick!	for it I gave up Freia's gaze.
(Er greift hastig nach dem Reif;	*(He hastily snatches the ring and they*
sie ringen)	*wrestle together)*
FAFNER	FAFNER
Fort mit der Faust!	Take your hands away!
Der Ring ist mein!	The ring is mine!
(Fasolt entreisst Fafner den Ring)	*(Fasolt snatches the ring from Fafner)*
FASOLT	FASOLT
Ich halt' ihn, mir gehört er!	I hold it: it belongs to me.
FAFNER *(mit seinem Pfahle ausholend)*	FAFNER *(brandishing the club)*
Halt' ihn fest, dass er nicht fall'!	Hold it fast in case it falls!
(Er streckt Fasolt mit einem Streiche zu	*(He fells Fasolt to the ground with*
Boden: dem Sterbenden entreisst er dann	*one blow, then quickly wrests*
hastig den Ring)	*the ring from him as he dies)*
Nun blinzle nach Freias Blick!	Now blink at Freia's gaze:
An den Reif rührst du nicht mehr!	the ring you will not touch again!
(Er steckt den Ring in den Sack und rafft	*(Fafner puts the ring into the sack*
dann gemächlich den Hort vollends ein.	*and then begins stowing away*
Alle Götter stehen entsetzt: feierliches	*the whole pile)*
Schweigen)	

Only now does Wotan realize the consequences of his actions, and the significance of Erda's admonition. Loge, however, seeks to reassure him, but in vain:

WOTAN *(erschüttert)*	WOTAN *(shocked)*
Furchtbar nun	Terrible now
erfind' ich des Fluches Kraft!	I find the curse's power.
LOGE	LOGE
Was gleicht, Wotan,	What can equal
wohl deinem Glücke?	your luck, Wotan?
Viel erwarb dir	Great your gain
des Ringes Gewinn;	when you won the ring;
dass er nun dir genommen,	still more it profits you

nützt dir noch mehr:	now that it is taken;
deine Feinde – sieh!	for see, your foes
fällen sich selbst	fell each other
um das Gold, das du vergabst.	for the gold that you gave up.
WOTAN	WOTAN
Wie doch Bangen mich bindet!	Yet how anxiety weighs upon me!
Sorg' und Furcht	Dread and fear
fesseln den Sinn:	fetter my mind;
wie sie zu enden,	how to end it
lehre mich Erda:	Erda must teach me:
zu ihr muss ich hinab!	I must go down to her.

Wotan therefore wishes to descend into the depths of the earth to Erda, to seek a better understanding of the fate that awaits him and the whole race of the gods. The journey to Erda, however, never takes place. Wotan is invited by Fricka to go to Valhalla, for the moment forgetting their anxieties. While Loge mocks the illusion of eternity that the gods still seem to have, he hears in the background the wailing of the Rhine Maidens, lamenting the loss of the gold and with it the downfall of the established order:

DIE DREI RHEINTÖCHTER *(in der Tiefe des Tales, unsichtbar)*	THE THREE RHEINMAIDENS *(from the depths of the valley unseen)*
Rheingold! Rheingold!	Rhinegold! Rhinegold!
Reines Gold!	Purest gold!
wie lauter und hell	How clear and bright
leuchtest hold du uns!	you once shone on us!
Um dich, du klares,	For your lustre
wir nun klagen:	we now lament!
gebt uns das Gold!	Give us the gold!
O gebt uns das reine zurück!	O give us its glory again!

Loge then speaks vainly and somewhat vacuously, bidding the Rhine-maidens bask in the gods' new splendour. The pacts have been broken, the law infringed, and what appears a sign of splendour conceals false-hoods:

LOGE *(in das Tal hinabrufend)*	LOGE *(giving voice to the valley)*
Ihr da im Wasser!	You there in the water,
Was weint ihr herauf?	why wail to us?
Hört, was Wotan euch wünscht!	Hear what Wotan wills for you.
Glänzt nicht mehr	No more gleams
euch Mädchen das Gold,	the gold on you maidens:
in der Götter neuem Glanze	henceforth bask in bliss
sonnt euch selig fortan!	in the gods' new radiance!
(Die Götter lachen und beschreiten	*(The gods laugh as they*
mit dem Folgenden die Brücke)	*pass over the bridge)*
DIE DREI RHEINTÖCHTER	THE THREE RHEINMAIDENS
Rheingold! Rheingold!	Rhinegold! Rhinegold!
Reines Gold!	Purest gold!
O leuchtete noch	If but your bright gleam
in der Tiefe dein laut'rer Tand!	still glittered in the deep!
Traulich und treu	Now only in the depths is there
ist's nur in der Tiefe:	tenderness and truth:
falsch und feig	false and faint-hearted
ist, was dort oben sich freut!	are those who revel above!

6. Very different readings of *Das Rheingold* and, in general, the whole Wagnerian Tetralogy are possible. In legal terms, the most immediate perspective, and one that already been investigated, is the one that springs from criminal law. It is all too easy to find in the complex plot of the *Ring* – as in many works in the history of opera, which turns out continuous panoplies of heinous crimes – a long series of violations that are criminally relevant. Already in *Das Rheingold* we have borne witnesses, in order, to theft, kidnapping, theft again, and finally murder. And, in the subsequent episodes of the *Ring*, the list of offences is enriched: incest, burglary, again murder, and much else.[271]

In this brief analysis we have shown that, above all in the *Rheingold*, particular stress is laid on the contract, the rules governing it, and the consequences of their violation.

---

271   On this subject, a reference is required to the volume, whose content is partly parodistic and satirical, by E. von PIDDE (pseudonym), titled *Richard Wagners 'Ring des Nibelungen' im Lichte des deutschen Strafrechts*, Munich: Ullstein, 2003.

This hardly seems to be coincidental. The composition of *Das Rheingold* straddles the years 1853–1854, hence we are in the nineteenth century, in the great age of codification, and a period of profound, far-reaching social and economic changes. Germany itself was on the point of undertaking the task of codifying its private law, which would lead to the *Bürgerliches Gesetzbuch* of 1896 (coming into force on 1 January 1900). That codification, however – an outstanding example of refined legal systematization – looked more towards the past, not the future: a future that, within a few years, with the outbreak of the Great War, would see the disappearance forever of the old world order.

The structure of the *Ring* reflects this sensibility. In *Das Rheingold* one can grasp the spirit of an age that looked to the systematization of the law of contract and obligations, as an essential component of the construction of the social and civil order. The monument of the *BGB*, in this respect, was the fulfilment not only of an immense work of systematization of private law in general, but also the reflection of the sensibility of an age, some of whose traits, as well as the symptoms of its own crisis, can already be sensed in the prologue to Wagner's Tetralogy. The downfall of the gods stems, in the universe of the *Ring*, from the violation of a contract, committed by the greatest authority representative of the social order: Wotan. Everything then inevitably ends with the twilight of the gods, and the beginning of a new age.

The breach of contract signifies that Wotan enters into contradiction with himself, and with the (legal) order he represents and embodies: the denial of the foundations on which rests the representative universe of the gods. The fact that the imbalance originated from a failure to fulfil a contract reveals therefore the profound changes in the socio-economic structures underpinning Wagner's work and thought in the nineteenth century.

XI

Gianni Schicchi

(Giacomo Puccini – Joachim Forzano)

A medieval fake testament

1. Together with *Il Tabarro* and *Suor Angelica*, *Gianni Schicchi* forms part of what is known as Giacomo Puccini's *Triptych*: three one-act works to librettos by Giovacchino Forzano, composed beginning in 1904.[272] In Puccini's intentions, the three were meant always to be performed together. But because *Gianni Schicchi* proved remarkably successful, it soon began to make its way on its own and is now often represented independently, or in combination with other operas not by Puccini. *Gianni Schicchi* closes the Triptych with laughter (somewhat macabre, to tell the truth), following the very different atmospheres of the other two works that comprise it: a conclusion, however, in which Puccini engaged with the comic tradition, revisiting models, in some respects, that actually seem to draw on certain eighteenth-century schemes (in particular, the integration of the arias into the dramatic fabric[273]), though absorbing the more recent achievements of European musical theatre (Strauss, Stravinsky).

Originally conceived for the opera house in Rome, *Gianni Schicchi* actually had its premiere at the Metropolitan Opera House in New York on 14 December 1918, together with the two other works in the *Triptych*.[274] The libretto has two literary sources: an episode of Dante's *Divina Commedia*, and a one-act play entitled *Le testament du Père Leleu* by Roger Martin du

---

272   A comprehensive bibliography on the other two operas in the *Triptych* is available online on the website of the Centro Studi Giacomo Puccini, at http://www.puccini.it/index.php?Ead=249.

273   The observation is by M. GIRARDI, 'Puccini, Giacomo', in *The New Grove Dictionary of Music and Musicians*, edited by S. Sadie and J. Tyrrell, London: Macmillan, 2001, vol. 20, pp. 566-580.

274   Due to the outbreak of World War I (so G. D'ERRICO, *Genesi, drammaturgia e analisi tematica del 'Gianni Schicchi' di G. Puccini*, Rome: Universitalia, 2009, pp. 3 ff., which also contains a brief account of the success – though not triumphant – of the premiere).

Gard (first performed in Paris at the Théâtre du Vieux Colombier, 5 February 1914).

As to the *Divina Commedia*, it provided not so much a true antecedent of the libretto as a quotation: Dante meets Gianni Schicchi in Hell, in the circle of the counterfeiters (Canto XXX, ll. 3233 and 4245), to which he has been condemned for falsification of person, having deceitfully taken the place of Buoso Donati the Elder.[275] The incident, widely recounted by the commentators, with variations, has a basic structure that remains constant in the different versions. Gianni Schicchi was well known for his skill at mimicking people. When the wealthy Buoso died, Schicchi's friend Simone Donati (Buoso's nephew) asked him to sneak into the bed of the deceased. Then, calling a notary, he dictated a will in favour of Donati – save for a precious cow which he left to himself – which was duly ratified.[276] Apart from the few references in the *Divina Commedia*, Forzano could also draw on the *Commento* on Dante's poem by an anonymous Florentine of the fourteenth century printed between 1866 and 1874. This reveals many details of the story which appear used in the libretto.[277]

In Puccini's opera, *Gianni Schicchi* is summoned urgently by a relation of Buoso Donati, who has just died, to help them deal with a rather awkward situation: the deceased has bequeathed all his estate to a monastery without leaving anything to his relatives. Gianni Schicchi, initially reluctant, is brought round by the pleading of his daughter Lauretta (in the celebrated romanza 'O mio babbino caro'). She is in love with Rinuccio, Buoso Donati's young nephew. Gianni Schicchi devises an ingenious plan: since no one yet knows of Buoso's death (except, of course, his family), he has his body moved to another room, slips into his bed and dictates his last will

---

275   *Divina Commedia*, Inferno: 'E l'aretin che rimase, mi disse: "Quel folletto è Gianni Schicchi e va rabbioso altrui così conciando"' (Canto XXX, ll. 32-33); 'Questa a peccar con esso così venne, falsificando sé in altrui forma, come l'altro che là sen va, sostenne, per guadagnar la donna de la torma, falsificare in sé Buoso Donati, testando e dando al testamento norma' (Canto XXX, ll. 43-45).

276   For further information about the figure of Gianni Schicchi in the *Commedia*, see the entry 'Gianni Schicchi' edited by G. VARANINI, in *Enciclopedia Dantesca*, Rome, Treccani, 1970, available online at the following address: http://www.treccani.it/enciclopedia/gianni-schicchi_(Enciclopedia-Dantesca)/.

277   ANONIMO, *Commento alla Divina Commedia d'Anonimo fiorentino del secolo XIV*, edited by P. Fanfani, Bologna: Gaetano Romagnoli, 1866–1874.

to the notary. Actually, Schicchi dictates to the Notary a testament quite different from what his relatives were expecting, for he says he wishes to leave his most valuable property to his 'dear, affectionate friend... Gianni Schicchi', having first reminded the relatives that the law punishes whoever falsifies a wills by cutting off his right hand and sending him into exile together with his accomplices.

The relatives obviously protest vociferously, but Schicchi continues to harp on the subject of exile, and then has Buoso's relatives ejected from the house, which now belongs to him. Lauretta and Rinuccio celebrate their love, while Gianni Schicchi rejoices in his own craftiness.

2. After the opening scene, in which all the relatives gather in Buoso's house to mourn his passing, they begin to hunt for his testament. Buoso was wealthy, and his relatives are expecting to inherit substantial riches. They search high and low, and Rinuccio (Buoso's nephew) finds it. The young man takes advantage of this opportunity to extract consent to marry Lauretta, Gianni Schicchi's daughter, whom the Buoso family look down on as being too bourgeois. The relatives' curiosity and haste to read the contents of the testament prevent the matter from being thrashed out properly. They feel it is more urgent to read the document. The relatives are on tenterhooks. The libretto takes the action forward rapidly, with a wealth of details and stage directions, showing the care taken by the authors to build up the scene:

RINUCCIO   Salvàti!
                    (Legge sul rotolo di pergamena)
                    'Testamento di Buoso Donati.'
(Tutti accorrono con le mani protese per prendere il testamento. Ma Rinuccio mette il rotolo di pergamena nella sinistra, protende la destra come per fermare lo slancio dei parenti e, mentre tutti sono in un'ansia spasmodica.)
                    Zia, l'ho trovato io!...
                    Come compenso, dimmi...
                    Ah! dimmi, se lo zio
                    – povero zio! – m'avesse
                    lasciato bene bene,
                    se tra poco si fosse tutti ricchi...

	in un giorno di festa come questo,
	mi daresti il consenso di sposare
	la Lauretta figliola dello Schicchi?
	Mi sembrerà più dolce il mio redaggio...
	potrei sposarla per Calendimaggio!
TUTTI *tranne* ZITA	– Ma sì!
	– Ma sì!
	– C'è tempo a riparlarne!
	– Qua, presto il testamento!
	– Non lo vedi
	che si sta con le spine sotto i piedi?
RINUCCIO	Zia!...
ZITA	Se tutto andrà come si spera,
	sposa chi vuoi, magari... la versiera![278]

One of those who is most concerned about Buoso's will is Rinuccio, who hopes it will allow him to marry Lauretta. So he asks if Gianni Schicchi can be present with his daughter, in the expectation that his hopes will be fulfilled:

RINUCCIO	Ah! lo zio mi voleva tanto bene,
	m'avrà lasciato con le tasche piene!
	(a Gherardino che torna ora in scena)
	Corri da Gianni Schicchi,
	digli che venga qui con la Lauretta:

---

278   The passages from the Italian libretto are taken from that of the premiere at the Metropolitan: *GIANNI SCHICCHI |Giacomo Puccini | Price 35 Cents | G. Ricordi & Company | 14 East 43rd Street | New York | Copyright 1918. by Ricordi & Company.* The English translation of the Libretto is based upon the one by E. PETRI, Ricordi & Company, 1918, available at https://archive.org/details/GianniSchicchi, with some amendments to suit the version of the libretto used as a reference in the text.
RINUCCIO We're saved! (Reading from a roll of parchment): 'The last will of Buoso Donati.' *(All rush towards him with outstretched hands to grab the will, but Rinuccio, holding the parchment tightly in his left hand, raises his right to stop the avalanche of relatives who, burning with impatience, cannot keep still)* /AUNT 'tis I who found the will!... As a recompense, tell me... Ah, tell me if Uncle Buoso – poor Uncle! Has made me legatee; If we find all of us suddenly rich, On this joyous occasion Would you consent that I should marry Lauretta, Schicchi's fair daughter? That thought would make me happier on this day. And I could make her mine the first of May! /ALL (EXCEPT THE OLD WOMAN) All right! here's time to talk it over! Come, come, show us the will! What do you fear? We're all on pins and needles waiting here! / RINUCCIO Aunt! /THE OLD WOMAN If in that will there be no hitch I leave you free to wed even a witch!

c'è Rinuccio di Buoso che l'aspetta!
(Gli dà due monete)
A te, due popolini:
comprati i confortini!
(Gherardino corre via.)[279]

Excitement surrounds the opening and reading of the will. There is a general atmosphere of expectancy, but also hypocrisy at the memory of the deceased, with everyone naturally thinking only of what they hope to inherit. The wait is punctuated by comments and conjectures about the estate. Each thinks of his own advantage and what Buoso might have left him.

ZITA	'Ai miei cugini Zita e Simone!'
SIMONE	Povero Buoso!
ZITA	Povero Buoso!
SIMONE	*(in un impeto di riconoscenza accende anche le tre candele del candelabro spento)* Tutta la cera tu devi avere! Insino in fondo si deve struggere! Sì! godi, godi! Povero Buoso!
TUTTI	*(mormorano)* Povero Buoso! – Se m'avesse lasciato questa casa! – E i mulini di Signa! –Poi la mula! Se m'avesse lasciato...
ZITA	Zitti! È aperto!

---

279   RINUCCIO Uncle Buoso who cared so much for me, No doubt has left me there enough for three! (*to Gherardino who comes ba*ck): Run, run to Gianni Schicchi Tell him to come right over with his girl As' Rinuccio's poor head is in a whirl! (*Giving him two coins*): These pennies will be handy For you to buy some candy! (*Gherardino rushes out*)

A un tratto i visi si cominciano a rannuvolare... arrivano ad una espressione tragica...
finché Zita si lascia cadere seduta sullo sgabello davanti alla scrivania. Simone è il primo
del gruppo impietrito, che si muove, si volta, si vede davanti le tre candele testé accese, vi
soffia su e le spegne; cala le sarge del letto completamente; spegne poi tutte i candelabri.
Gli altri parenti lentamente vanno ciascuno a cercare una sedia e vi seggono. Sono come
impietriti con gli occhi sbarrati, fissi; chi qua, chi là.

SIMONE   Dunque era vero! Noi vedremo i frati
                             ingrassare alla barba dei Donati!

LA CIESCA   Tutti quei bei fiorini accumulati
                             finire nelle tonache dei frati!...[280]

Only Gianni Schicchi can recoup the situation. Rinuccio is convinced but, given the setting, he has a hard time convincing the relatives of his idea. They quickly organize the impersonation, and everyone prepares to receive the notary. Gianni Schicchi, however, launches his warning:

GIANNI   Prima un avvertimento!
                             O messeri, giudizio!
                             Voi lo sapete il bando?
                             'Per chi sostituisce
                             sé stesso in luogo d'altri
                             in testamenti e lasciti,
                             per lui e per i complici
                             c'è il taglio della mano e poi l'esilio!'
                             Ricordatelo bene! Se fossimo scoperti:

---

280   THE OLD WOMAN 'To my dear cousins Zita and Simone!' / SIMONE Dear, dearest Buoso!
/ THE OLD WOMAN Dear, dearest Buoso! / SIMONE (*In an impulse of gratitude lights the three candles on the candelabrum*) All these three candles will burn for thee! Melting 'till ended inside the lee! Rest thou in peace dear, dearest Buoso! / ALL (*whispering*) Dear, dearest Buoso! – I hope he has bequeathed me this house! – The old saw-mills of Signa! – And then his mule! – I hope he has bequeathed... / THE OLD WOMAN Hush! it's open! (*Suddenly, a cloud overshadows all faces... until they take a tragic look... till the old woman fairly drops on the stool placed in front of the desk. Simone is the first of the petrified group to move; he turns around and seeing the three candles, he had lighted a few moments before, blows on them and puts them out; he drops the bed curtains completely, then he puts all the candles out. Slowly, the other relatives move towards different chairs and sit down. There they stay, like graven images, eyes wide open and staring straight ahead*) / SIMONE So it was true! The convent and the priest will fatten on the wealth of that old beast! All the good florins made by theft and lurch are now to fill the coffers of the church!

la vedete Firenze?
(accennando la torre di Arnolfo che appare al di là del terrazzo)
Addio, Firenze, addio, cielo divino,
io ti saluto con questo moncherino,
e vo randagio come un ghibellino!...

TUTTI
(soggiogati, impauriti, ripetono)
Addio, Firenze, addio, cielo divino,
io ti saluto con questo moncherino,
e vo randagio come un ghibellino!...

(Si bussa. Gianni schizza a letto; i parenti rendono la stanza semioscura; mettono una candela accesa sul tavolo dove il notaio deve scrivere; buttano un mucchio di roba sul letto; aprono.)[281]

The arrival of the public notary, Messer Amantio, marks the start of the declaration of the testamentary dispositions. Pinellino and Guccio (respectively, a shoemaker and a dyer) act as witnesses:

MESSER AMANTIO, PINELLINO, GUCCIO
(I tre mestamente)
Messer Buoso, buon giorno!

GIANNI
Oh! siete qui?
Grazie, messere Amantio!
O Pinellino calzolaio, grazie!
Grazie, Guccio tintore, troppo buoni
di venirmi a servir da testimoni!

PINELLINO
(commosso, fra sé e sé)
Povero Buoso!
io l'ho sempre calzato...
vederlo in quello stato...

---

281   GIANNI First, you must heed my warning! My dear friends, do be careful! And keep in mind this law! 'Whoever substitutes Himself in place of others wo falsify a will shall loose, with his accomplices, one hand, and all will have to leave the State.' Soho do keep well in mind! In case we are found out Do you see there our Florence? *(pointing to Amolfo's tower which is plainly visible through the open window)*: Florence, farewell, farewell, city of charm! I wave good-bye with this poor, handless arm! My fate is now to beg from farm to farm! / ALL *(subjugated, frightened, in repetition)* Florence, farewell, farewell, city of charm! I wave good-bye with this poor, handless arm! My fate is now to beg from farm to farm! *(A knock is heard at the door. Gianni jumps into the bed, the relatives' close the shutters so as to darken the room and place a candle on the table at which the notary is to sit to write out the will. They throw all sorts of things in a heap on the bed and then open the door).*

	vien da piangere!
GIANNI	Il testamento avrei voluto scriverlo
	con la scrittura mia,
	me lo impedisce la paralisia...
	perciò volli un notaio,
	solemne et leale...
	(In questo tempo il notaio ha preso dalla sua cassetta
	le pergamene, i bolli, ecc. e mette tutto sul tavolo)
MESSER AMANTIO	Oh! messer Buoso, grazie!
	Dunque tu soffri di paralisia?
	(Gianni allunga in alto le mani agitandole tremolanti.
	Gesto di compassione di tutti; voci: "Povero Buoso!")
	Oh! poveretto! Basta! I testi videro,
	testes viderunt!
	Possiamo incominciare... Ma... i parenti?...
GIANNI	Che restino presenti![282]

The dictating of the will is rendered very effectively in the libretto and stage directions, with some broadly comic elements, with legal Latin and clichés drawn from tradition. At first Gianni appears to have fallen in with the wishes of Buoso's relatives, as everyone expects, but then the atmosphere changes rapidly. Gianni's intentions become clear, but beyond protesting, Buoso's relatives – mindful of Gianni's warning – have to swallow the bitter pill.

MESSER AMANTIO	Dunque incomincio:
	'In Dei nomini, anno D.N.J.C. ab eius salutifera
	incarnatione millesimo ducentesimo nonagesimo nono,
	die prima Septembris, indictione undecima, ego notaro

---

282   MASTERS AMANTIO, PINELLINO, GUCCIO THE THREE *(sadly)* Master Buoso, good day! /GIANNI Oh! are you here? Thank you, Master Amantio! Pinellino, the shoemaker, thank you! Thank you, Guccio, the dyer, you are too good to come and act as witnesses for me! /PINELLINO *(very much moved, aside)* Poor Master Buoso! I have served him for years and the state he appears to be in, makes me cry! / GIANNI It was my firm intention to write out my own will with my hand but paralysis forbids me!... understand. Therefore I want a notary. *Solemne et leale...* (*In the meantime the notary has taken from his box parchments, seals, etc., disposing them all on the table*) /MASTER AMANTIO Thank you, good Master Buoso! Are you sure it's paralysis that ails you? (*Gianni raises his trembling hands from under the covert. A movement of general pity. Several are heard to mutter: 'Poor Buoso'*) Oh! that will do! both witnesses have seen! *Testes viderunt!* Let's begin! Do you want these folks to hear? / GIANNI Yes, yes, they can stay here!

	Amantio di Nicolao, civis Florentiae, per voluntatem Buosi Donati scribo hoc testamentum...'
GIANNI	*(con intenzione, scandendo ogni parola)*
	'Annulans, revocans
	et irritans omne aliud testamentum!'
I PARENTI	– Che previdenza!
	– Che previdenza!
MESSER AMANTIO	Un preambolo: dimmi, i funerali,
	– il più tardi possibile –
	li vuoi ricchi? fastosi? dispendiosi?
GIANNI	No, no, pochi quattrini!
	Non si spendano più di due fiorini!
I PARENTI	– Oh! che modestia!
	– Oh! che modestia!
	– Povero zio! che animo!
	– Che cuore! ...
	Gli torna a onore!
GIANNI	Lascio ai fratri minori
	e all'Opera di Santa Reparata...
	(I parenti, leggermente turbati, si alzano lentamente)
	... cinque lire!
I PARENTI	*(tranquillizzati)*
	– Bravo!
	– Bravo!
	– Bisogna
	sempre pensare alla beneficenza!
MESSER AMANTIO	Non ti sembrano un po' poco?...
GIANNI	Chi crepa e lascia molto
	alle congreghe e ai frati
	fa dire a chi rimane:
	eran quattrin rubati!
I PARENTI	– Che massime!
	– Che mente!
	– Che saggezza!
MESSER AMANTIO	Che lucidezza!
GIANNI	I fiorini in contanti
	li lascio in parti eguali fra i parenti.
I PARENTI	– Oh! Grazie, zio!
	– Grazie, grazie, cugino!
GIANNI	Lascio a Simone i beni di Fucecchio.

SIMONE	Grazie!
GIANNI	Alla Zita i poderi di Figline.
ZITA	Grazie.
GIANNI	A Betto i campi a Prato.
BETTO	Grazie, cognato!
GIANNI	A Nella ed a Gherardo i beni d'Empoli.
NELLA e GHERARDO	Grazie, grazie!
GIANNI	Alla Ciesca ed a Marco i beni a Quìntole!
LA CIESCA, MARCO	Grazie!
TUTTI	*(fra i denti)*
	(Or siamo alla mula,
	alla casa ed a' mulini.)
GIANNI	Lascio la mula mia,
	quella che costa 300 fiorini,
	ch'è la migliore mula di Toscana...
	al mio devoto amico... Gianni Schicchi.
TUTTI I PARENTI	*scattando*
	Come?! Come!?
	– Com'è?...
MESSER AMANTIO	*'Mulam relinquit eius amico devoto Joanni Schicchi.'*
TUTTI	Ma...
SIMONE	Cosa vuoi che gl'importi
	a Gianni Schicchi
	di quella mula?...
GIANNI	Tienti bono, Simone!
	Lo so io quel che vuole Gianni Schicchi!
	Lascio la casa di Firenze al mio
	caro devoto affezionato amico
	Gianni Schicchi!
I PARENTI	*(erompono)*
	– Ah! Questo no!
	– Un accidente
	a Gianni Schicchi!
	– A quel furfante!
	– Ci ribelliamo!
	– Ci ribelliamo!
	– Si, sì, piuttosto...
	– Ci ribelliamo!
	– Ci...ri...be...Ah!
	– Ah! Ah! Ah! Ah!...
GIANNI	Addio, Firenze...

	Addio, cielo divino...
	Io ti saluto...
	(A questa vocina si calmano fremendo)
MESSER AMANTIO	Non si disturbi
	del testatore
	la volontà!
GIANNI	Messer Amantio, io lascio a chi mi pare!
	Ho in mente un testamento e sarà quello,
	se gridano, sto calmo... e canterello!...
GUCCIO, PINELLINO	Oh! Che uomo! Che uomo!
GIANNI	*(continuando a testare)*
	E i mulini di Signa?...
I PARENTI	I mulini di Signa?...
GIANNI	I mulini di Signa (addio, Firenze!)
	li lascio al caro (addio, cielo divino!)
	affezionato amico... Gianni Schicchi!
	(Ti saluto con questo mancherino!...)
	Ecco fatto!
	(i testi ed il notaio sono un po' sorpresi)
	Zita, di vostra borsa
	date 100 fiorini al buon notaio!
	e 20 ai testimoni!
MESSER AMANTIO,	*(Non son più sorpresi)*
PINELLINO e GUCCIO	O messer Buoso! Grazie!
	(Fanno per avviarsi verso il letto)
GIANNI	*(arrestandoli con un gesto della mano tremolante)*
	Niente saluti. Niente... Andate, andate...
	Siamo forti!...

MESSER AMANTIO, PINELLINO, GUCCIO

(commossi, avviandosi verso la porta)

    – Ah! che uomo!...

               – Che uomo!

                    – Che peccato!

      – Che perdita!...

             – Che perdita!...

(ai parenti)

                – Coraggio![283]

---

283   MASTER AMANTIO Then I'll commence! In Dei nomini, anno D. N. J. C, ab eius saluti-
fera incarnatione millesimo, duecentesimo nonagesimo nono, die prima septembris indictione

Then Gianni expels all the relatives from the house, so paving the way to Lauretta and Rinuccio's marriage:

Appena usciti il notaio e i testi, i parenti restano un istante in ascolto finché i tre si sono allontanati, quindi tutti – tranne Rinuccio che è corso a raggiungere Lauretta sul terrazzino – a voce soffocata da prima, poi urlando feroci contro Gianni:

---

undecima, ego notaro Amantio di Nicolao, civis Florentiae, per voluntatem Buosi Donati scribe hoc testamentum... / GIANNI (*with intention and emphasising each word*) Annullans, revocans et irritans aliud testamentum! / THE RELATIVES Wonderful foresight! – Wonderful foresight! MASTER AMANTIO First of all, do tell me: about your funeral (I hope as late as possible) Must it be grand? Expensive? Impressive? /GIANNI I haven't that kind of pride! Two florins you may spend at the outside! / THE RELATIVES Oh! what modesty! Oh! what modesty! Wonderful man! What soul! – Generous heart! He's good and smart! / GIANNI I leave to the monastery and the order of Santa Reparata (*The relatives, somewhat worried, slowly get up*) Say... five liras! / THE RELATIVES (*now easy in their minds*) Splendid! Splendid! – Tis fair to keep in mind our duty towards the poor! / MASTER ANTONIO Methinks it's a small sum! / GIANNI Who leaves a lot of money for poverty's relief will make the people say "He must have been a thief!" What principles! – What mind! – What great wisdom! Wonderful keenness! /GIANNI All bonds and cash in hand I leave in equal shares to my relations! THE RELATIVES Oh! Thank you, uncle! – Thank you! I Thank you, dear cousin! / GIANNI To Simone the farm lands of Fucecchio / SIMONE Thank you! /GIANNI And to Zita my corn fields of Figline! / THE OLD WOMAN Thank you! /GIANNI To Betto, Prato's meadows / BETTO Thank you! Thank you! / GIANNI To Nella and to Gherardo, Empoli's lands / NELLA AND GHERARDO Thank you! Thank you! / GIANNI To Ciesca and to Marco all in Quintole / CIESCA AND MARIO Thank you! / ALL (*with clenched teeth*) Now we get to the mule, to the house and to the saw mills / GIANNI I leave my own young mule, For which I paid three hundred florins and which is the best mule of Tuscany... To my devoted friend... Gianni Schicchi. THE RELATIVES (*all jumping up at once*): What's that? What's that? – What's that? /MASTRO ANTONIO Mulam relinquit eius amico devoto Joanni Schicchi. / ALL But... / SIMONE What use do you suppose could be that mule to Gianni Schicchi? / GIANNI Do please keep quiet, Simone! I know what things likes best our Gianni Schicchi! I leave my house in Florence to my dear most affectionate and devoted friend, Gianni Schicchi! / THE RELATIVES (*in an outburst of rage*) -That is too much! -Not on your life! – To Gianni Schicchi! – That cursed rascal! -We all rebel! – We all rebel! – Rather we would – We... all... re... Ah!... – Ah! Ah! Ah! / GIANNI Farewell, Florence... farewell divine sky... I salute you (*upon hearing this, they calm down*) / MASTRO ANTONIO Don't you disturb the final will of Master Buoso / GIANNI Master Amantio, I leave to those I wish! That is my will and such it must If they yell I will sing / GUCCIO AND PINELLINO What a wonderful man! / GIANNI (*continuing his dictation*): And the saw mills of Signa / THE RELATIVES Yes, the saw mills of Signa? / GIANNI And the saw mills of Signa (farewell, Florence) Go to my dear (farewell, city of charm) And most devoted friend... Gianni Schicchi! (I wave good-bye with this poor, handless arm!). And that is all! (*The witnesses and the notary seem rather surprised*) Zita, from your own purse You'll give one hundred florins to the notary And twenty to the witnesses! / AMANTIO, PINELLINO, GUCCIO (*no longer surprised*) Master Buoso! Thank you! (*They move towards the bed*) / GIANNI (*stopping them with a wave of his trembling hand*) Kind friends! No farewells! Please be going! Let's be brave! AMANTIO, PINELLINO, GUCCIO (*moves, walking towards the door*) – Ah! What a man!... – What a man! – What a pity! – What a loss!... – What a loss!... (*to the relatives*) – Be brave!

I PARENTI	– Ladro! Ladro! Furfante!
	– Traditore! Birbante!
	– Iniquo! Ladro! Ladro!
	Si slanciano contro Gianni che, ritto sul letto,
	si difende come può; gli riducono la camicia in brandelli
GIANNI	Gente taccagna! Senza la dote
	non do il nipote!
	non do il nipote!...
	Ora la dote c'è!
	ora la dote c'è!...
	(afferrando il bastone di Buoso, che è a capo del letto,
	dispensa colpi...)
	Vi caccio via!
	È casa mia!
	È casa mia!
TUTTI	– Saccheggia! Saccheggia!
	– Bottino! Bottino!
	– La roba d'argento!...
	– Le pezze di tela!...
	– Saccheggio! Saccheggio!
	– Bottino! Bottino!
	– Ah! Ah! Ah!...

(I parenti corrono qua e là rincorsi da Gianni. Rubano. Gherardo e Nella salgono a destra e ne tornano carichi con Gherardino carico. Gianni tenta di difendere la roba. Tutti mano a mano che son carichi, si affollano alla porta, scendono le scale. Gianni li rincorre. La scena resta vuota.)

RINUCCIO	*(Dal fondo apre di dentro le impannate del finestrone;*
	appare Firenze inondata dal sole; i due innamorati restano
	sul terrazzo)
	Lauretta, mia Lauretta!
	Staremo sempre qui!
	Guarda! Firenze è d'oro!
	Fiesole è bella!
LAURETTA	Là mi giurasti amore!
RINUCCIO	Ti chiesi un bacio!
LAURETTA	Il primo bacio!
RINUCCIO	Tremante e bianca
	volgesti il viso...
A DUE	Firenze da lontano

ci parve il Paradiso...

(Si abbracciano e restano nel fondo abbracciati.)[284]

3. The story of *Gianni Schicchi* is set in Florence in 1299,[285] and the point at issue is clearly the institution of the will and testament.

In modern legal systems, wills have long been subject to detailed regulation, and the matter represented in Puccini's opera lends itself to being examined and resolved on the basis of specific provisions. First, those concerning the form and content of the will; then the rules pertaining to its validity, invalidation, the rights of the heirs, and other matters. The will drafted in *Gianni Schicchi* is, in particular, a public testament which, in the Italian Civil Code, is now regulated by art. 603: a public testament is that received by a notary in the presence of two witnesses.[286] The testator, in the presence of witnesses, declares his will to the notary, who personally sets

---

284   (*As soon as the notary and his witnesses have gone out, the relatives at first remain 'quiet a moment listening to the vanishing footsteps of the three men. Then, all, with the exception of Rinuccio, who has rushed out to join Lauretta on the terrace*) THE RELATIVES Robber! Robber! Vile scoundrel! Traitor! Traitor! Cheap counsel! Imposter! Robber! Robber! (*They all rush in a mass towards Gianni, who, standing on the bed, defends himself as best he can. They tear his night-gown to shreds*) / GIANNI You miserly lot! Without a good dowry I won't consent! I won't consent! There is a dowry now! There is a dowry now! (*Grabbing Buoso's stick hanging from a bed post, he wields it around with wonderful effect*): Get out, ye swine! This house is mine! This house is mine! / ALL – Let's rummage! Yes, let's pillage! – Let's grab all we can! – The fine silverware! – Silk, velvets and linen! – Let's rummage! Come, let's pillage! – Let's grab all we can! Ah! ah! ah! (*The relatives run around here and there pursued by Gianni. They steal all that comes under their hands. Gherardo and Nella go up stairs and come back laden with loot. Gianni does all he can to prevent the relatives from carrying away too much. All, as they have their arms full crowd around the door and rush downstairs. Gianni runs after them. The stage remains empty.*) / RINUCCIO (*way up stage, opens the large window. Florence appears, bathed in glorious sunshine. The two lovers remain on the terrace*): Lauretta, my dear Lauretta! This house will be our own! Behold our radiant Florence! Fiesole is beautiful! / LAURETTA There you promised love eternal! /RINUCCIO I begged a kiss! / LAURETTA Yes, my first kiss! / RINUCCIO All white and trembling you turned your face... and Florence in the valley, looked like a Paradise! (*They embrace and remain upstage clasped in each other's arms*).
285   As indicated in Forzano's libretto. E. RESCIGNO, *Dizionario pucciniano*, Milan: Ricordi, 2004, p. 162, believes that the date is not correct, because Gianni Schicchi actually died, at the latest, in February-March 1280.
286   In fact, on the issue of witnesses, there is an old debate: some hold that the presence of the two witnesses is not indispensable when the testator dictates the document to the notary; they would be required only when the testament is *read* and shown to the witnesses. From this thesis there follows the legitimacy of a will written without witnesses and only with the notary, and only later shown to the witnesses (see G. BRANCA, 'Dei testamenti ordinari', in *Commentario Scialoja-Branca*, Bologna: Zanichelli, 1986, pp. 116 ff.).

it down in writing, then reads the will to the testator in the presence of the witnesses. Each of these formalities has to be mentioned in the will.

The will must indicate the place, date and time when it was subscribed, and be signed by the testator, the witnesses and the notary. If the testator is unable to sign, or can do so only with great difficulty, he must declare the cause, and the notary must specify this statement before reading the document.

Pursuant to art. 606 of the Civil Code, a public testament is null if it lacks the signature of the notary or the testator: for any other defect of form, the will can be annulled by the testator. The action for annulment is barred after a period of five years from the day the testamentary dispositions were made.

Save as stated above, a public testament will be granted probate until an action for fraud is brought. The latter is the case (regulated by art. 221 and following of the Code of Civil Procedure), which has the purpose of depriving a public deed of its intrinsic ability to 'stand', i.e. to serve as proof of acts or relations, so aiming, through the judicial sentence, to achieve the result of completely stripping the document of its value, eliminating not only its own effects, but also any further effects ascribed to it by law (see, *ex multis*, the judgments of the Court of Cassation, Cass. no. 8362/2000; Cass. no. 18323/2007).

A public testament is, essentially, difficult to invalidate. Certainly, in the case of *Gianni Schicchi*, there is an underlying problem: the testator's identity has not been ascertained with due care by the notary, who trusts, essentially, to contingent circumstances. This exposes the testament to a clear risk (or rather certainty) that it could be challenged as a forgery, with the result of restoring full effect to the previous will, drafted by the real Buoso with his own hand.

Another element worth mentioning in relation to the legislation affecting a public testament, is the function of the notary. The notary's role as a public official, who guarantees against errors, confusions and inaccuracies, cannot, however, mean that the notary replaces the testator, or influences his decisions. A notary is, nonetheless, permitted to offer suggestions, warnings, and explanations that do not influence the deceased's will, as was stated some time ago by the Court of Cassation (Cass. 13 April 1960, in

Foro it., rep. 1960, under the entry *Testamento*, no. 28). The fake notary in *Gianni Schicchi* does not seem, however, to go beyond this limit, except – perhaps – when he observes the 'smallness' of the sum the testator intends to leave the friars and the Opera of Santa Reparata.

4. The origins of the legislation concerning testaments are ancient, dating back to Roman law. It was, however, in the Middle Ages, in which *Gianni Schicchi* is set, that the institution underwent major changes, while retaining some of its original features intact.

In Roman society, the testament was recognized and regulated as an expression of the individual will of the *pater familias*, to whom the legal system attributed a central importance.

The Roman legal system was in fact built around the figure of the *civis/dominus/pater familias*, who possessed specific rights that were protected. In this context, the law, through the testament, provided him with an instrument to confirm and perpetuate his predominant power in the final moment of death, and so prolong his will beyond it. As has been aptly observed, the natural fact of death was overcome by Roman law 'by means of a legal artifice supported by the force of the legal system, in keeping with the core values of society, which resolved with lucid determination to recognize the subjectivity of the testator's capacity to overcome the seemingly insurmountable boundaries of the end of life.'[287] This gave rise to the 'artifice' of voluntary succession: an artifice, in the sense that the testament replaced natural succession, governed by the ties of kinship, with succession governed by the will of the testator, who was able to dispose of his estate by dividing it between several beneficiaries, not necessarily bound to him by ties of kinship. Nevertheless, the disinheritance of a child was an extreme case, and could only be done for particularly weighty reasons.[288]

A completely different tradition inspired the Germanic peoples settled in the Western Roman Empire, for whom the individual could not dispose

---

287   So G. ROSSI, 'Il testamento nel medioevo fra dottrina giuridica e prassi', in *Margini di libertà: testamenti femminili nel medioevo*, Proceedings of the international conference (Verona, 23-25 October 2008), edited by M.C. ROSSI, Verona: Cierre Edizioni, 2010, pp. 45-70.
288   *Ibid.*, note 10, p. 63.

freely of the assets he inherited, since they formed part of the family patrimony (*Hausgut*). Such assets could not be the objects of donations and, in case of death, automatically returned to the family.[289] A number of scholars have shown that in the early Middle Ages the institution of the testament underwent a regressive phase, or even disappeared.[290] The particular importance that the will possessed in Roman society, as a reflection of a broader cultural vision, meant that in the Middle Ages the testament practically disappeared. This was caused, or at least furthered, by the new sensibility of the age, which tended to devalue the individual will as opposed to the needs of the family and social group, and to give preference to the community over the individual.[291] In this regard, it has been observed that, 'if recourse to the testament was justified as a way to assert the sovereign will of the subject *ultra vitam*, imposing it, in the case of conflicts, on the interests of the family group, within a horizon that allowed the testator to ignore any considerations of a social or economic nature, aimed at optimizing the exploitation of property belonging to the hereditary axis and pursuing the individualistic tendency to the fullest self-affirmation, it will not seem strange that the testament as such should have disappeared in the early centuries of the Middle Ages. In a period

---

289   *Ibid.*, note 10, p. 63. See O. RICHARD, 'Les testaments de la fin du Moyen Âge dans l'espace germanique', in *Bulletin d'information de la Mission Historique Française en Allemagne*, no. 42, 2006, pp. 97 ff.
290   According to S. HOLGER BRUNSCH, 'Genesi, diffusione ed evoluzione dei documenti di ultima volontà nell'alto Medioevo italiano', in F. Bougard, C. La Rocca, R. Le Jan (edited by), *Sauver son âme et se perpétuer. Transmission du patrimoine et mémoire au haut Moyen Âge*, Rome: École française de Rome, 2005, pp. 81-96, the decline of the Roman-classical model began already during the late Roman period and in particular from the third century on. The author recalls that, according to the prevailing opinion, the last testament of the Roman era is to be recognized in the testament of the *patricius* Abbo of 739, in favour of the monastery of Novalesa, though in the Frankish legal area rather than the Italian. The fragmentation of practices and the spread of hybrid forms with contents not easily classified makes it difficult, however, to pinpoint precisely when there was a return to the use of the testament of Roman inspiration. In particular, recourse to various forms of donation (including *donationes causa mortis*) make it advisable to adopt a rather flexible approach, and to include, in a sort of 'enlarged' scope of the testament, documents that would not, strictly speaking, belong to this strand (for example, because they were construed as irrevocable acts, unlike the testament, which, by its nature, is revocable).
291   Since the seventies, the attention of historians has been concentrated on testaments, considered as a vantage point for the current of the *Nouvelle Histoire*, which seeks to investigate the evolution of the religious mentality, especially in the works of Michel Vovelle, Pierre Chaunu and Jacques Chiffoleau.

marked by the pressing and sometimes anguished need to fulfil the basic and primary needs of survival and self-protection of the community, the naturalistic tendencies prevailing in Germanic law – which did not admit the testament and was based on necessary succession, directly regulated by the self-evident force of blood ties, in the name of the immediately normative force of factual situations – clearly appeared more suitable to cope with the difficulty of the times and attuned to the anti-voluntaristic connotation that was affirmed with the new legislation born from the collapse of the Roman word.'[292] This was accompanied by the gradual eclipse of the most complex forms of Roman law, in favour of new forms of social and legal organization. What mattered above all to early medieval man was not the use of his estate and its fate after his death, but the salvation of his soul. In this way, forms of negotiation unknown to Roman law developed, only remotely akin to the testament, and elements unknown to the tradition (for example, the inclusion, in deeds disposing of an estate, of a clause of irrevocability).

The situation created in the early Middle Ages changed in the late Middle Ages. With the emergence of a new world, the model of succession regulated by the legal system restored voluntary succession, and the testament again began to spread. In this context, the Bologna school, established by Irnerius, played a major part in rediscovering and re-elaborating the classical sources of law. The Bolognese doctrine spread elsewhere, giving rise to a lively notarial practice. It is not, at present, quite clear when this began: whether, as some claim, the resumption of the will can already be found in the tenth century or, as other hold, the recovery was later, and it cannot be identified until the eleventh or twelfth century. In this respect, Giulio Vismara's outstanding work, *Storia dei patti successori*, published in 1942 (reprinted in 1986), shows that there were new wills in Italy, excluding the territories of Ravenna and Venice, only from the mid-twelfth century. He confutes previous researches, which tended to backdate the development.[293] Be that as it may, by the mid-twelfth century, we find 'the drafting of testaments increasingly clear in their structure and increasingly close

---

292   G. ROSSI, *Il testamento*, cit., p. 50.
293   See S.H. BRUNSCH, *Genesi*, cit. pp. 81 ff.

GIANNI SCHICCHI

to the Roman form. The medieval testament therefore found its concrete model, in technical-juridical terms, in the classical testament, whose appearance is fully delineated by numerous regulations collected in the *Pandects*, the *Institutes*, and the *Code* of Justinian. As in the ancient world, there again emerged the profile of a unilateral act, *mortis causa*, personal and always revocable, with the function of disposing of an estate, with its minimum content identifiable in a valid and effective *haeredis institutio*.'[294] According to the latest research, the transmission of these new documents was initially concentrated in what are now the regions of Tuscany and Lombardy.[295]

In the late Middle Ages, the testament of Roman origin therefore re-emerged, but in a quite modified form.[296] First – in full harmony with the human sensibility of the Middle Ages – the content of the document was enriched with measures that did not concern the destiny of the estate, but that of the spirit: place of burial, legacies for the soul, pious legacies in favour of the Church and the poor (just as 'poor Buoso' did), and requests for prayers to the advantage of the testator.[297]

Notarial practice reused the ancient Roman schemes, in a space of law that was essentially occupied by practice, and in which we have no (or only sporadic) records of legislative measures. In the Middle Ages, the law did not regulate the nature of the testament, its content, or the structure of the relations between voluntary succession and testamentary succession.[298] It was then mainly notarial practice, first developed in Bologna in the thir-

---

294   G. ROSSI, *Il testamento*, cit., p. 53.

295   *Ibid.*, p. 17, which notes that the highest concentration of documents can be found in cities. For Tuscany, the richest one is Lucca. In the countries forming part of the Holy Roman Empire, the situation is rather complex, but most medieval wills are kept in collections in cities which actually enforced the obligation to register testaments (such as Lübeck, Vienna, Cologne, Brunswick, Lüneburg): see O. RICHARD, *Les testaments*, cit., p. 100.

296   M. LA SOUDIÈRE, 'Les testaments et actes de dernière volonté à la fin du Moyen Age', in *Ethnologie française*, nouvelle séries, T. 5 (1975), pp. 57-80.

297   See, also for recent references, C. BARRALS, C. MARCHAL, A. WAGNER (edited by), *Le testament spirituel, du Moyen-Âge à l'époque moderne. Legs, salut de l'âme, miroir de vertus chrétiennes*, Collection du CRULH, 50, 2013, pp. 7 ff.

298   The law would intervene much later. For example, it was only in 1512 that Maximilian I issued an order aimed at unifying testamentary practices in all countries of the Empire (although, still in 1541, Regensburg followed its own specific discipline): see. O. RICHARD, *Les testaments*, cit., p. 99.

teenth century, that revived the institutions of Roman law, adapting them to the new sensibility, and it is precisely this practice that we find in Puccini extraordinary opera.

4. The story of the comedy by Martin du Gard, *Le testament du Père Leleu* (1914), which, as we have seen, is one of the sources of *Gianni Schicchi*, shares the theme of impersonation and the falsification of the will. The context is naturally different: *Le testament du Père Leleu*, subtitled *farce paysanne*, is set in the countryside, in the Berry region, in the centre of France, in the twentieth century. The original text, states the premise, was written in the dialect of the region, but its difficulty of comprehension led to the French translation. This is probably a useful fiction that enables the author to recommend the adoption of particular rules of pronunciation of the text in order to reflect *sa véritable saveur* (its 'true flavour'). Even the characters are different, being adapted to the setting. The idea of replacing the dead man with a fake testator, in *Le Testament du Père Leleu*, comes from Torine, a servant of *père* Alexandre (and his mistress), who after years of patient waiting and promises, expects to receive a substantial legacy. But *père* Leleu (Alexandre's neighbour) providentially takes the place of the deceased and dictates his will in the presence of the notary.[299]

Dictation of the will occupies a good part of the third act, wending its way through legal formulas, and the actual content of the will. The notary asks the testator for clarifications and explanations, as well as details concerning the assets covered by the will. As in *Gianni Schicchi*, also in *Le testament du Père Leleu* the notary appears particularly careless, not bothering to verify the identity of the testator.

5. In French law, a will drawn up in the presence of a notary is regulated by Art. 971 of the *Code Civil*, under which, 'Le testament par acte public est reçu par deux notaires ou par un notaire assisté de deux témoins.' The rule of the two notaries has been in force since 1950: previously the French Civil Code required it to be signed by two notaries, in the presence of two

---

299   In the stage directions included in the text of the comedy, Martin du Gard states that the two characters, *Père* Leleu and *Père* Alexandre, must be played by the same actor.

witnesses, or by one notary in the presence of four witnesses.[300] This formality was derived, in turn, from the *Ordonnance 1735* (promoted by Louis XV's Henri François Chancellor D'Aguesseau) dealing with testaments,[301] which required the presence of seven (!) witnesses.[302] The number was then reduced to four by the 1804 Civil Code, and more recently two by the law of 8 December 1950.

It seems, in practice, that the public testament is now little used in France. This is due to its notable level of formality, while notaries seem to discourage it for fear of being held liable for irregularities. These factors do not seem to be offset by the greater certainty and security that it offers over alternative forms, and, in particular, the holograph will.[303] Yet in France, it is reported that recently online services have been promoted – amid various controversies – making available specific IT instruments that serve as templates for drafting holograph wills (to be written out, however, by the testator, since a holograph will drawn up by mechanical means would not be valid), so furnishing assistance and advice.[304]

Who knows? Maybe, today, Gianni Schicchi, Buoso Donati and Père Leleu would use a computer and the assistance of a site offering readymade wills on the Web, instead of calling in a notary. As for Puccini, today he might decide to set his *Gianni Schicchi* in a cybercafé, or hold a video conference on Skype. The idea is almost certain to be taken up sooner or later – alas! – by some preposterous stage director, ready to prevail upon the librettist and the musician, as we often see nowadays in opera houses around the World.

---

300   See P.-A. MERLIN, *Répertoire universel et raisonné de jurisprudence*, vol. 33, Brussels: Tarlier, 1828, p. 38.

301   See *Explication de l'Ordonnance du mois d'Août 1735 concernant les testaments*, Avignon: Chez François Girard, 1740.

302   The provision was introduced, in the *Ordonnance* of 1735, with the explicit purpose of recreating a connection with the tradition of Roman law (which required the presence of seven witnesses to an oral testament) but, at the same time, in order to prevent recourse to purely verbal testaments, that is, those not enshrined in a written document. Art. 1 of the *Ordonnance* laid down that 'toutes dispositions testamentaires ou à cause de mort, de quelque nature qu'elles soient, seront faites par écrit. Déclarons nulles toutes celles qui ne seroient faites que verbalement, / defendons d'en admettre la preuve par témoins, même sous prétexte de la modicité de la somme dont on auroit été disposé.'

303   On this topic see PH. MALAURIE, C. BRENNER, *Les successions, les liberalités*, Paris: LGDJ, 2014, p. 267.

304   See, in particular, the website https://testamento.fr/fr/.

Silvana Editoriale

Direction
Dario Cimorelli

Art Director
Giacomo Merli

Editorial Coordinator
Sergio Di Stefano

Copy Editor
Filomena Moscatelli

Production Coordinator
Antonio Micelli

Editorial Assistant
Ondina Granato

Photo Editor
Alessandra Olivari, Silvia Sala

Press Office
Lidia Masolini, press@silvanaeditoriale.it

Silvana Editoriale S.p.A.
via dei Lavoratori, 78
20092 Cinisello Balsamo, Milano
tel. 02 453 951 01
fax 02 453 951 51
www.silvanaeditoriale.it

Reproductions, printing
and binding in Italy
Printed by Modulgrafica Forlivese, Forlì
November 2017